# Eleven Houses

# Eleven Houses

## A Memoir of Childhood

CHRISTOPHER FITZ-SIMON

PENGUIN
IRELAND

PENGUIN IRELAND

Published by the Penguin Group
Penguin Ireland, 25 St Stephen's Green, Dublin 2, Ireland (a division of Penguin Books Ltd)
Penguin Books Ltd, 80 Strand, London WC2R ORL, England
Penguin Group (USA) Inc., 375 Hudson Street, New York, New York 10014, USA
Penguin Group (Australia), 250 Camberwell Road, Camberwell, Victoria 3124, Australia
(a division of Pearson Australia Group Pty Ltd)
Penguin Group (Canada), 90 Eglinton Avenue East, Suite 700, Toronto, Ontario, Canada M4P 2Y3
(a division of Pearson Penguin Canada Inc.)
Penguin Books India Pvt Ltd, 11 Community Centre, Panchsheel Park, New Delhi – 110 017, India
Penguin Group (NZ), 67 Apollo Drive, Rosedale, North Shore 0632, New Zealand
(a division of Pearson New Zealand Ltd)
Penguin Books (South Africa) (Pty) Ltd, 24 Sturdee Avenue, Rosebank, Johannesburg 2196, South Africa

Penguin Books Ltd, Registered Offices: 80 Strand, London WC2R ORL, England

www.penguin.com

First published 2007
1

Copyright © Christopher Fitz-Simon, 2007

The moral right of the author has been asserted

Set in 12/14.75 pt Monotype Bembo
Typeset by Palimpsest Book Production Limited, Grangemouth, Stirlingshire
Printed in England by Clays Ltd, St Ives plc

A CIP catalogue record for this book is available from the British Library

ISBN: 978-1-844-88105-5

www.greenpenguin.co.uk

For
Samuel, Ellen and Eva

# Contents

Eldron, Smithborough, County Monaghan     1

Mount Louise, Scotstown, County Monaghan     26

Whinsfield, Sandyford, County Dublin     44

Annaghmakerrig, Newbliss, County Monaghan     66

Seaview, Murphystown, County Dublin     91

Back to Eldron     109

Anchor Lodge Mews, Newcastle, County Down     128

Maidenhall, Bennettsbridge, County Kilkenny     154

Milltown House, Strabane, County Tyrone     178

Annaghmakerrig Again     195

Aviemore, Hill Street, Monaghan     218

144 Seacliffe Road, Bangor, County Down     241

Mount Callan, Inagh, County Clare     272

*Envoi*     295

Acknowledgements     296

*(All drawings by the author)*

Eldron, Smithborough, County Monaghan

'I'll never be talked into installing electricity in this house!' declared Great-aunt Zane. She was descending the crooked stairs of Eldron Cottage, sideways because of an old injury to her ankle, and clutching a paraffin oil lamp that flared dangerously. 'The electric current would set fire to the thatch. Tell me this and tell me no more: where would we be then?'

She said it was all very well talking about the houses we knew whose darkest recesses were revealed – in many cases to their detriment, she thought – by the snap of a switch, but those houses all had *slate* roofs, and they were in *towns* where there was a fire brigade handy. 'And anyway,' she remarked, with a slight sigh, placing the lamp on the circular table in the porch and turning down the flame, 'Lizzie would never take to the electricity.'

This put an end to all argument about modernization. Lizzie McMahon, my great-aunt's capricious servant, refused to have anything to do with the manual egg-beater Zane had bought for her at Patton's in Monaghan, preferring the ritual of thirty minutes' strenuous whisking with the kitchen fork. It was impossible to imagine that she would bring herself to contemplate the intricate knobs and switches of an electric cooker.

The thatch was of immense concern at Eldron. Great-aunt Zane's brother, Dr John Elliott, from whom she had inherited the house, had believed as much in the traditional sanctity of the thatcher's craft as in the practical properties of a thatched home: warm in winter, cool in summer and never a damp spot on any of the walls. When everyone else in rural Monaghan in the 1930s was replacing their thatch with orange-coloured tiles from the new factory at Kingscourt or – depending upon their financial status – corrugated-iron sheets from the foundries of Belfast, he continued to provide employment after the harvest was in to the few surviving thatchers who lived just across the border at Roslea. He died the year after I was born, having made a number of other changes to the house since coming to live with his two maiden aunts, Eliza and Clemina Elliott, towards the end of the nineteenth century. These were the addition of a very large porch, which came to serve as an extra sitting room – too large, many people said, to suit the proportions of the cottage – and a new bedroom and bathroom on the ground floor. He also installed an additional flush lavatory in one of the outhouses, reached by a laurel-shaded walk where Lizzie could take a stroll without her departure from the kitchen causing embarrassment. She would return with a few sticks of kindling for the range or a couple of Worcester Pearmains from the apple shed and no one the wiser as to the true purpose of her expedition.

Eldron Cottage was situated half a mile from the village of Smithborough and six miles from Monaghan town. There was no electricity in the village either, but there was a telephone in Miss Rooney's post office. You could ring from there during her hours of business, but an emergency at night or on a weekend would have to wait until next day. Neighbours would be called in to help if a cow was having a hard time calving, or a tree had fallen across the by-road in a storm. A house fire would have burned itself out by the time someone cycled helter-skelter into Monaghan and roused the members of the fire brigade from their beds, or beckoned them out from Mass on a Sunday morning.

There were two shops in the village, owned by Mr Kerr and Mr Toal. My aunt favoured Mr Kerr, for to the left of his grocery and animal-foods counter there was a small section devoted to drapery. Mrs Kerr would be called out from the back room if a lady wanted to buy a length of knicker-elastic or a new simmit. Furthermore – though this remained unspoken – the Kerrs were Protestants. In fact, they were somewhat superior Protestants for they were members of the Church of Ireland parish of Drumsnat and therefore did not attend the unassuming Presbyterian church in the centre of the village. On Sundays the Kerrs would be seen driving out to Matins in their smart pony-and-trap while we walked into Smithborough for worship that included lengthy prayers, which the Reverend Andrew Alexander made up as he went along, and much hymn-singing. The Roman Catholic church was at Magherarney, quite a distance out along the Newbliss road. We would meet Mass-goers returning on foot and exchange words of greeting; there were a great many more of them than the Church of Ireland and Presbyterians put together. My aunt observed that they did their business at Mr Toal's.

My great-uncle John was said to have believed in the continuity afforded by trees. 'A house without trees to fix it in the landscape is not a house at all,' he was quoted as saying. He planted several copper beeches and sycamores and

dozens of apple trees against the time, a generation or two
hence, when the older plantings, inherited from the eighteenth or nineteenth century, would topple in the wind. Five
immense old beech trees, seen as you approached the house
from the railway arch, appeared to be growing out of the
thatch; this was because the drumlin rose so steeply above
the roof that the eaves almost touched its lower slopes. If
you looked closely you could see that the hill had been
excavated to allow the house to fit comfortably into it. The
planters of two hundred or so years ago probably never
envisaged their saplings achieving such height or mass, nor
considered what might happen to the house if there was a
great gale.

Other trees, also of extreme age, peopled the level ground.
A huge horse-chestnut had grown so heavy its boughs dipped
to the grass and soared up again, like the banyan tree in a
picture-postcard my father sent from India. In May, and
especially at dusk, the horse-chestnut's chandeliers of blossom
seemed to illuminate the whole countryside. There was a
lime tree, its fronds cascading to the ground concealing a
circular bower, or prison, filled with cool green light. This
was the haunt of bees – perhaps it was for want of imme-
morial elms that they came here, for we had no elm, but if
one were to judge by their contented murmuring they were
satisfied enough. Two immense cypresses guarded the
approach to the house; somebody said that an ancestor had
brought the seeds from Cyprus, but this notion was dispelled
when my aunt, reading in the *Belfast Telegraph* of the German
invasion of Cyprus, pointed out that the spelling was entirely
different.

Almost up against the house, smothering it from most
views, were lilac, syringa and japonica. Virginia creeper grew
in swathes on the walls; every year a family of spotted

flycatchers flew all the way from Morocco to nest in it. A
cutting from a yellow rambling rose had been brought from
the garden of the Manse in Armagh and was known as
'Great-grandmother's Rose'. Rising up the hill to the side
of the house was a rockery, very steeply laid out with a little
flight of rough stone steps half covered in periwinkle and
London pride, leading to an ornamental wooden gate in a
prickly hawthorn hedge; over this gate the cattle gazed
constantly, aware of the succulent herbaceous plants growing
so tantalizingly out of reach below.

Between the house and the rockery, and seeming to stem
from the roots of one of the towering beeches, was a kind
of half-natural, half-artificial altar. (My Monaghan relatives
did not use the word 'altar' in relation to a church, preferring
the less showy 'communion table', but my Dublin relatives
did speak of 'the altar' and of the priest 'giving out on the
altar'.) This was an ivy-shrouded ledge decorated with a
collection of mementoes gathered from around the world.
('Grotto' would also have had the wrong connotation.) All
sorts of curious objects had found their way here: a mug
without a handle with 'A Present from Grasmere' in fancy
lettering; some pink and brown shells the size of bakers'
loaves, which Great-uncle Charlie Elliott had sent from
Queensland – you could hear the surge of the Pacific Ocean
if you put your ear to them; a limestone quern with a hole
for the wooden stick that had turned it; and a flat, semi-
circular stone that in times gone by, before the Beeston range
was installed, had been placed in front of the open hearth
for baking oatcakes. There were also bits of white marble,
flat and polished and covered with beautifully incised letters.
I tried to piece them together like a jigsaw puzzle but nothing
fitted. Then I stood them up against the roots of the tree as
one would stack delft on a dresser, and one day, when my

aunt was forking manure around the Orange lily, I asked her
what they were.

'The words are French,' she said. 'My brother – your great-
uncle Brereton – brought the pieces back from Flanders at
the end of the Great War, long before you were born. They
were part of some famous cathedral, I think.'

'How was it smashed up?'

'Oh, it was the Germans, or perhaps the British. It could
have been either. And the cathedral might have been Arras.
Or Amiens. Somewhere like that. It was completely destroyed.
Bertie found these fragments and brought them home.'

I imagined my great-uncle Brereton, whose photograph
I had seen – a big, smiling man with a moustache and a
smart uniform – picking up the pieces of marble from the
ruined cathedral and putting them in his haversack, thinking
they would look well in Ulster under the beech tree.

I had come to live with my great-aunt Zane – everyone else
called her Jane, but to me she was Zane – at Eldron when
I was two and a half years old. Before that there were only
flashes of people and places. Did I really remember Tompa
the butler in Trichinopoly, or was that because he was later
described to me? Or was Tompa the name of the butler's
*monkey*, who chased the ducks across the compound, beating
their retreating tails with a little stick? And who was the lady
with the dark face and shining teeth who looked over the
edge of my cot and said I'd soon have a new brother or
sister? There were wide sands and warm waves that you could
sit in and then the waves were shockingly cold and my
grandmother (or someone) said that I had got too used to
the beach at Negapatam, and Portstewart would soon harden
me up. I didn't think that was a nice thing at all, but my
mother said it wouldn't be long before we were all back in

India and I'd be able to bathe in the warm sea as often as I
wanted, and I'd see Lily Tiger Tail and Esmeralda again.

'Oh, yes,' I said – but who were *they*?

'Our cats, of course! Don't you remember them?' my
mother asked. 'Lily Tiger Tail had a striped tail and used to
sit on the roof of Daddy's car.'

But we didn't go back to India to see Lily Tiger Tail and
Esmeralda and Daddy. We were in my grandmother's house
in Belfast and a man was playing a barrel-organ outside the
window and she handed me a penny to give to him, but
when she opened the front door I was unable to move, so
she went out and gave him the penny herself. Upstairs there
was a new baby called Nicholas in a cradle that swung to
and fro and had a white canopy over the head end. At night
I heard a long, shuddering sort of noise in the wall. My
grandmother said it was only Elsie drawing water in the
kitchen. Drawing water? Was she scraping her pencil along
the wall to make the long noise? Was she drawing houses
and people and animals? And did she have coloured pencils
like mine? Would I see them in the morning, the whole
kitchen wall covered in coloured drawings?

After that there was nothing for a long time, until the
Monaghan landscape slowly unfolded. I was at Eldron, and
this was Zane, and the other person in the house was Lizzie.
Did it not occur to me to enquire, or even to wonder, why
I was there? What had been all the talk about going back
to India? Why had I been left behind? If anyone had asked
me where my mother was I might not have known, but no
one did ask.

The earliest sound I heard in the morning was Lizzie
brushing out the cinders from the sitting-room grate with
the wing of a goose. Except for lacing my shoes I was able
to dress myself. Then Lizzie was making toast on a wire fork

at the kitchen range, and Zane appeared from the bathroom
in a grey belted overcoat that had once belonged to Great-
uncle Brereton. She disappeared into our bedroom, appearing
once more in a long, coloured dress and smelling of lily-of-
the-valley, which she kept in a little green bottle; and then
Lizzie set the tea and toast on the table and we heard her
going out into the backyard and calling the hens to their
breakfast.

Lizzie McMahon had been born and reared in the one-
bedroom gate-lodge of Brook Vale, about a quarter of a mile
out on the Monaghan road. She had three brothers who
now lived in a two-storey stone house in the village. The
eldest was Davy. He walked to Eldron every day with his
dog Flossie, pushing a bicycle that he was never seen to
mount; he minded the animals and the garden. His brother
Joe had retired from working on the Great Northern Railway.
Charlie was the youngest but looked the eldest; Lizzie said
he was a great help in the house and he loved to mop the
kitchen floor and sweep out the bedrooms. My aunt told
me he had not been 'like other little boys – but *by no means*
an imbecile! – and you must be sure *never* to stare at him'.
All this I learned when we were taking what she called the
'daily constitutional', which her brother John had advised
the time she twisted her ankle on the stairs – it would keep
her ankle supple. We stopped to look at the old gate-lodge:
it had no roof, but it was easy to see that it had once been
a neat little house. Zane said she could not possibly imagine
how the McMahons had all fitted inside, for there had been
seven children altogether.

Lizzie had come to work at Eldron when the previous
housekeeper retired. She slept in the smaller of the two
bedrooms under the thatch, but walked to Smithborough

each evening to cook her brothers' supper and do their washing. My aunt's evening post was delivered to the McMahon home along with the Enniskillen edition of the *Belfast Telegraph*, and these Lizzie brought back before making tea for whoever was in the house. The creaking of the stairs signalled that she was on her way up to bed, a stone hot-water jar under her arm.

She was tall and angular. Her hair was the colour of blanched carrots, her eyes pale blue. She possessed two outfits of clothing: a black dress, which she wore on weekdays with a wrap-around apron, and a blue dress in a shiny material for Sundays. I naughtily named the dresses her 'beetle' and her 'bluebottle', but she resembled neither insect to the slightest degree. It was when dressed as a bluebottle on the Sabbath – the Day of Rest, when her only duties were lighting and stoking the range, cooking the breakfast, dinner and tea, and trimming the lamps – that she was wont to sit in a large wooden armchair and sing a hymn or two. (I think she did not know any other songs.) One of her favourites was 'Shall We Gather at the River?'

> *Yes, we'll gather at the river,*
> *The beautiful, the beautiful river,*
> *Gather with the saints at the river*
> *That flows by the Throne of God . . .*

There was another hymn, which contained the words 'Bright James for His Crown'. I wondered if Bright James was a particularly intelligent saint, or if the brightness was to do with the light of his countenance. When I asked Lizzie, she said, 'No, james are like jewels,' which left me no wiser.

There was one domestic task that Lizzie conceded to my

aunt. This was the making of the green jelly on a Saturday night in readiness for the Sunday dinner. Lizzie considered the melting of the gelatine square, the pouring of the mixture into a copper mould and the turning out of the quivering castle on to a china dish too subtle an activity to take on herself. She explained to visitors that she was 'a plain cook'.

A square black Ford that had belonged to Great-uncle John was kept in the motor-house across the yard. Sometimes Davy McMahon could be persuaded to take it out to drive Zane to wherever it was she wished to go – but with reluctance, for he had the three cows to milk twice a day, and the potatoes to dig, and the grass to be scythed, and the water to be pumped from the well into the tank that supplied the house. Would he be able to spare the time – on Thursday afternoon perhaps? – to drive into Monaghan? He could be getting a fill of petrol for the car at Given's, and be ordering the yellow meal for the calves, and a washer for the kitchen tap, while she was choosing a skein or two of wool from Miss McCaldin on the Diamond and getting the cough bottle for the boy at Mr Black's. 'And the *Bank*,' she concluded, with perceptible emphasis. Davy would think a bit and then agree that this might all be managed; and then Zane would consult with Lizzie as to what groceries should be put on the list – a packet of Cream Puffs because Mr Kerr in the village only stocked Rich Tea and Digestives, and half a pound of prunes and perhaps some dried apricots. And then, of course, she could hardly pass the door of Dr and Mrs Killen's house, Aviemore, without dropping in to see how the babies were getting on. A couple of hours was all she'd need.

When Zane went on these visits to the outside world I was left with Lizzie, who told me I'd have to make myself useful for she had loads and loads of work to do. She swept the carpets with a hard brush and the boards with a soft one; she brought wood in from the coach-house for the fires, which she kept slacked down when there was no one to sit beside them. On Mondays she lit a fire in the old iron stove in the wash-house across the yard and then she went backwards and forwards for buckets of water from the kitchen tap, filling a huge galvanized basin on top of the stove. When this showed signs of coming to the boil she threw a block of carbolic soap into the water, swirling it round with half the handle of an old broom. Then she plunged the garments into the now shadowy waters, fishing each out in turn and rubbing it energetically on the serrated washing-board. This accomplished, she threw the result into a big basin of cold water, which stood expectantly on the floor nearby. By now it was time for dinner, so we went back to the kitchen where, by means of a series of lightning-like visits, she had boiled a pot of potatoes and a knob of bacon, and these we ate while Lizzie considered the afternoon's order for rinsing, squeezing, shaking and hanging out, all the while giving spasmodic glances at the sky and issuing black imprecations as to what she would not do if it came on wet. Rain or no rain, by tea-time the clothes were stretched out in a dancing line suspended over the grass beyond the blackcurrant bushes.

Every second day there was baking. This meant I could stand on a stool at the ark, a great wooden chest that contained bags of everything you needed for making bread and cakes: plain flour, self-raising flour, cornflour, wheatmeal, oatmeal, bread-soda. It had a flat top where the dough was rolled out. If Lizzie was in good humour she would let me cut out the shape of scones with an egg-cup. When there was nothing for me to do, or when Lizzie had decided that

I was being over-helpful, I would talk to the dogs who drowsed in front of the range, Donny, a dumpy black cocker spaniel, and Brian, a red and white setter, who Lizzie said was *lost* for want of shooting since the doctor passed away. She said there had been another big dog, an Irish setter called Red Brian, but he had been killed on the railway and that was a terrible thing.

As well as walks with Zane to Mr Kerr's shop and Miss Rooney's post office and to see the quarry where men with little hammers sat breaking stones to fill the potholes in the roads, we also went to visit people in the neighbourhood who lived within walking distance, like Mrs Hanna at Brook Vale, a house that was thatched like ours though much longer and lower, and to Mrs Dunn's house, Keenogue, on the top of a grassy hill from where you could look back at our hill, though our house was invisible because of all the trees.

To reach Keenogue you had to walk down our avenue, along the by-road for a quarter of a mile and then up Mrs Dunn's very steep lane. Her house had a door in the centre with a window on either side, three windows upstairs, a grey slate roof and two chimney-stacks. It had a sentinel-like look, watching out in every direction over the rushy fields that were bounded by osiers and muddy sheughs. There were clipped yew trees on either side of this house and they also looked like sentinels. Mrs Dunn was very old – so old that Davy said she had saved enough five-pound notes to stuff a mattress. I asked Zane if I could see the mattress and she said certainly not, and if I was even *thinking* of mentioning such a thing she would not take me with her that afternoon when she was calling on Mrs Dunn about a matter of business – and I mustn't mention her age either.

'But what age is she?'

'As near to ninety as makes no difference.'

The matter of business related to Mrs Dunn's red bull who lived in a low-lying field known as the Bottom, surrounded by willow hedges and a dark drain that was neither a sheugh nor a stream. We had often paused on the road to look at this bull, who gazed back at us with his big brown eyes, and when I said I would like to pat him Zane said that would be a very dangerous thing to do because a bull was really a very fierce animal and that was why it wasn't allowed to roam beyond the Bottom.

It was a very hot afternoon. Zane said I must wear my blue coat for the sake of appearance. I kept looking at Mrs Dunn's house up on its hill and thinking it was getting no nearer. A full moon sat in the sky. It was quite easy to see the marks of its face, which Zane said were extinct volcanoes. When I asked why it was there, when it was usually there only at night, she replied that it was always there, though we could not see it. I turned my attention to my new shoes, which were growing greyer and greyer from the dust of the road. Then I heard Zane say, 'Well, here we are!' – but we were not here, we were only at the gate and we still had to climb the lane. There was a heavy scent of meadowsweet. I thought I might be getting a headache and if I did I would surely be sick, probably in Mrs Dunn's house.

At the clipped yew trees my aunt had to decide if she was going to turn left along the path to the front door or go on into the farmyard. I saw some redcurrants in the enclosed garden and a turkey with its neck outstretched, chasing a fly. When I shouted, it stopped chasing the fly and rustled its quills, letting out a loud gobble. I shouted louder to make it gobble again, but Zane told me to leave the poor thing alone. She thought we should take the garden path, for although the back door was always open on a fine day it would be more correct to knock at the front door and wait for it to be opened.

Theresa, Mrs Dunn's maid, answered our knock. After a short parley, she showed my aunt into the front room, from which some muted words of greeting emerged, before taking me down a shiny brown corridor to the kitchen. Here she sat me up on the scrubbed table and told me I was a terrible weight but then I must be getting on for four years, was that right? I said I would be four next week and Lizzie was going to bake a cake but Zane would make the icing because Lizzie didn't know how.

'No more nor myself,' said Theresa. 'You'd need to be very sure of your hand to ice a sweet cake.' Then she asked if I'd like a drink. I was hoping she'd give me orange squash, but she poured milk into a cup and then she cut a slice off a farl and spread butter on it. The milk was slightly turned, and there were currants in the farl that looked like goat's droppings, but I thought that if I ate and drank slowly I'd be all right. Through the back door I could see three ducks and a drake sifting succulent morsels from a dark puddle where Theresa threw out the water from the washing-up basin. The minutes hung heavily in the woodsmoke from the range as Theresa boiled a kettle and took some scones out of the oven. Occasionally I could hear murmuring from the front room. An old clock, with a little window where you could see the pendulum wagging to and fro, struck – or, rather, rasped – the hour: four. Theresa started making tea for Mrs Dunn and my aunt. She confided that Mrs Dunn was ninety-two, could I believe that?, and I said I could because Zane had already told me she was round about ninety. Theresa said that Mr Dunn had died when Mrs Dunn was seventy-three – a year before Theresa was born, wasn't that an amazing thing?

I asked if Mrs Dunn would live to be a hundred and Theresa said she probably would if she was spared, but Theresa wouldn't be around to check because she was getting married and going to live in Ballinode. I said I wanted to see the turkey, and Theresa said that was all right so long as I didn't get my good clothes dirtied in the dunkel or Miss Elliott would have her life. Then she took the tea into the front room.

I let myself down off the table and went out round the side of the house. The turkey was nowhere to be seen, but I ate some bunches of redcurrants and a stick of rhubarb and six Brussels sprouts. Then I heard Theresa calling so I went back to the kitchen door. She told me that Mrs Dunn had rung the bell and I was to go into the parlour.

The two ladies were seated on straight-backed chairs on either side of the chimney-piece, in which stood a white paper fan speckled with soot and a pale plant in a pot. The blind was drawn down over the window, creating a porridge-coloured gloom. Mrs Dunn was very thin, dressed in black and as upright as her chair. I shook, or rather felt, the beige hand she held out to me from a tangle of shawls. There was a smell of camphor and dried ferns.

Mrs Dunn looked at me and remarked that I must be great company for my aunt.

Not knowing how to respond, I said, 'Yes.'

'Yes, *Mrs Dunn*,' my aunt corrected, with an amused smile.

'Yes, Mrs Dunn.'

'That's the good boy. And your papa and mama are out in India, I hear. That's a long way away! And so hot, too. I don't think I'd survive out there at all at all.'

I had some notion that my papa and mama *were* in India, but as it was not a thing to which I gave much attention any more, I replied, 'Yes, Mrs Dunn.'

'Will you be going out to them, or will they be coming back to see you?'

'It isn't decided,' my aunt interposed. 'When his little brother was taken ill in Belfast just after his birth it was felt most suitable that the baby be left with his grandparents and Christopher come to me.'

'Oh, indeed,' said Mrs Dunn. 'I heard something to that effect. I think Mr Alexander told me after church one Sunday.' She turned to me. 'Weren't you out in India before? And your mama didn't bring you back with her?'

'She decided to leave both children at home this time,' said my aunt.

'Well, indeed,' said Mrs Dunn, 'there's a good reason for everything.'

'He was looking quite peaky when he came to me. I think the fresh butter and eggs have done him good. Goodness knows what he was eating out there.'

'All sorts of queer concoctions,' Mrs Dunn agreed, 'and butter and eggs and plenty of fresh air are good for the three Ls: the lights, lungs and liver. If you devote yourself to those three gentlemen, young man, you won't go far wrong.'

'Yes, Mrs Dunn.'

She laughed, and started rummaging in a polished wooden box that stood on the table beside her. I wondered if devotion to the three Ls was responsible for her living to the age of ninety.

'Hold out your hand, now!'

A large coin was pressed into my palm. I thought it must be a penny, but when I snatched a look at it I saw it was a silver half-crown. I thanked Mrs Dunn, in the way I knew my aunt would approve. Mrs Dunn told her that I was a nice, polite young man, and a credit to her in every way. My aunt looked pleased and told me to sit by the window to see if I could make out our house, while she and Mrs Dunn finished their chat. I said I couldn't because the blind was down and Mrs Dunn told me to raise it an inch or two so long as the sun didn't destroy the carpet. All I could see was the beech trees and the chimney of the wash-house, but the field on the hill was visible and there was a figure moving about.

'I can see Davy!'

The conversation droned on. The dredging of the sheugh was mentioned. There was something about the bull. The ladies' voices hovered warily over the word, like birds hesitant about alighting on some delicate bough. My aunt said it was difficult to arrange these things with no man in the house and only one farmhand who was not the easiest to talk to. She said he'd bring over the heifer on Monday.

I looked at my distorted face in the bowl of a copper warming-pan. I felt sick. Probably the sour milk and the goat's currants. I thought that if I really did get sick I could make for the green plant-pot in the fireplace. Presently Mrs Dunn rang a little brass handbell shaped like a lady in an old-fashioned skirt, and Theresa came in. My aunt and I were shown out into the glare of the front garden. I held the half-crown tightly in my fist, glancing at it from time to time to see the silver horse on one side and the harp on the other. When we reached the foot of the lane we disturbed the ducks, who were preening their wings on the grassy verge. I chased them along the ditch, the drake quacking angrily yet also taking flight, until they all landed in the sheugh, making four big dark splashes. At the same minute my stomach rumbled, I opened my mouth and what seemed like all the breakfasts, dinners and teas of the past week came up and swelled the muddy waters.

'Oh, my goodness!' exclaimed my aunt, searching for a handkerchief in her bag. 'Are you ill? Have you got a pain?'

I said I was all right. I knelt on the ground and wiped my face on the moss growing under a tree.

'And you were feeling sick all the time we were in Mrs Dunn's?'

'Yes,' I said, 'but I thought I'd be able to hold it in.'

'That's a good boy. Are you able to walk home, or will I get Davy to come put you on the carrier of his bicycle?'

'I'm far better now. I'm always better after I've been sick.'

My aunt asked if I'd like her to keep my half-crown safe in her handbag.

The half-crown!

We walked up and down the verge where I'd chased the ducks but there was no sign of it. I said we should go up the lane to the redcurrants because that was where we were the last time I took a look at it. Zane was mortified in case Mrs Dunn would see us poking in the grass – she might send Theresa out to ask what we were doing and we'd have to admit that I'd lost her very generous gift, but I said I'd pulled the blind right down to the bottom before we left. We walked shyly up the lane. The turkey was back in the redcurrants and looked at us in an annoyed kind of way, but I didn't shout at it this time in case it would gobble. There was no sign of the half-crown.

Next morning I climbed the path to the orchard to get a better view of Keenogue. I had formed the idea during the night that I should visit Mrs Dunn on my own to tell her how sorry I was that I had lost her half-crown. I would say that I had been holding it very tightly but that the big turkey had flown out of a bush with a very loud and frightening gobble, giving me such a start that the coin had shot from my hand. I would ask her for the loan of her walking-stick so that I could poke about in the ditch where I thought it had fallen. If I was later to report that I had been unsuccessful, I envisaged Mrs Dunn reaching into her box to find another half-crown.

I looked out over the Bottom to calculate how quickly I could reach Keenogue without being missed. I saw two cars drawn up by the yew trees, and then another – more like a van with glass sides – moved slowly up the lane. Two men got out and went into the house. Then another man came out and drove away. With all that activity it was clearly the wrong time to think of visiting Mrs Dunn. I would wait until the afternoon. I climbed one of the apple trees and then I went into the byre, where the marley hen had a nest, and found two eggs. I carried them carefully into the kitchen.

'She was ninety-two,' Davy McMahon was saying to my aunt, adding in a confidential tone, 'And I hear her lungs and that were as good as new.'

'To think I was with her at four o'clock!' said my aunt.

'Yon wee Theresa Gillanders found her aroun' six sittin' up in the chair and not a bother on her,' said Davy. 'Wee Theresa had to run over to Martin's to get one of the girls to go to Miss Rooney's on the bike for to ring for the doctor, but of course it was too late.'

Two days later Lizzie and I sat hidden in the long grass above the orchard to watch the comings and goings at Keenogue. Zane had put on her Sunday coat and the black hat that tilted over one eye, and was driven in the Ford by Davy, who wore the navy blue peaked cap that Lizzie said he had not put on since the time he used to drive the doctor to the dispensary. There were nine cars manoeuvring slowly up and down the steep lane and dozens of people pushing bicycles. The roof of the black van, which Lizzie called the motor-hearse, was covered in little dots of red and yellow and white – flowers, as I could see when the procession moved nearer to us out on to the road. There were about fifty people walking. I saw Davy take off his cap as the hearse passed him and then he got into the Ford and followed the other cars to Smithborough Church.

'There's people here today all the way from Emyvale and Glaslough,' Lizzie said, clearly disappointed that she would not have the enjoyment of meeting these visitors from distant parts in the church hall over the tea and cakes after the service, because it had fallen to her to stay at home with me. I was wondering what would happen to the half-crowns in Mrs Dunn's shiny wooden box, and whether Theresa knew about all the five-pound notes stuffed in the mattress.

The McMahon men were members of the Orange Order and that was the reason, Zane told me, why Lizzie always got in a terrible fuss coming up to the Twelfth of July. The men would go off early in the morning on the excursion train to Enniskillen to walk in the parade, and she was always afraid that Charlie would get lost in the crowd because one time he had failed to return with Davy and Joe. Both of them were 'rather the worse for wear' (which meant they were tired) and said they'd *told* him to meet them at the station, but when he wasn't there they thought he must be already on the train so they got on board and off it went – but there was no Charlie in any of the compartments. Lizzie was quite demented and told Davy to go to the Civic Guards, which he was reluctant to do because it would make him look foolish, so she went herself and they telephoned the Royal Ulster Constabulary, who found Charlie having a great time in a pub near the station where the remaining members of the parade were buying him drink. Because he had no visible means of support he had to spend the night in the cells and next day a constable put him on the train for Smithborough. '"Deported from Northern Ireland", I suppose you'd call it,' Zane said, when she was repeating the story to her friend Mrs Hanna.

On the day following this particular Twelfth, Lizzie was in great good humour because nothing had gone wrong and she bought me two ounces of conversation lozenges in Mr Kerr's. She said that the next big occasion would be the Orange Tea and she was sure Auntie would let me go to it. It was winter by the time the Tea was next mentioned and I'd quite forgotten her promise. Auntie would not be going, because the only ladies were those who made the tea, but Lizzie said I could come along with her, though I'd have to wait while she washed the dishes afterwards. The Orange Hall was at the top of the back lane above Mr Kerr's shop. There was a very big room and in it a huge picture that I knew to be of King William. There was also a kitchen with a range big enough to boil two big black kettles, and a shed out the back. It was quite dark because there were only two Tilley lamps, which hissed and spat and had to be pumped up every few minutes by Lizzie's friend Martha. The men were in their good blue suits, among them Davy, Joe and Charlie McMahon.

Before the tea was served by the ladies, the Reverend Alexander said they would sing 'O God, Our Help in Ages Past', and as they all knew the words there was no need to pass around the hymn-books. Then he welcomed three ministers from neighbouring congregations, who smiled and nodded their heads when their names were mentioned. There were ham sandwiches and rock buns and seed cake, and Lizzie kept putting more on my plate and filling up my cup with tea. Everyone stood at the trestle table, except some very old men with wizenedy faces who sat crouched on chairs. Then Mr

Alexander announced that the Reverend Dunwoody, who had
travelled all the way from Newbliss specially for the occasion,
would give the address, and the minister standing next to him
stepped forward and spoke for a very long time about God
and the King, and everyone looked very interested. I whispered
to Lizzie that I wanted to go to the lavatory and she gave me
a look as if to say, 'Couldn't you hold on a wee bit?' I said I
needed to go *now*, so she tore a piece off a paper bag and
lighted it from a lamp and hooshed me towards the back door.
We crossed the lane to the shed where there was a wooden
seat with a hole in it. 'There you are now!' she said, throwing
the flaming paper down the hole, where it illuminated a pit
full of old dry turds. 'I didn't think you'd make such a show
of me!' she said. Then she left. The turds put me in mind of
the old men in the Hall. I peed into the pit, aiming successfully at the burning paper, which I extinguished with a
satisfying hiss.

I went back by way of the dark kitchen, so as not to draw
attention to myself again, and found I was at the back of
the crowd beside the portrait, which had old ropes and tassels
hanging from it, and I reckoned must be a kind of banner,
perhaps meant to be carried in a procession. I was fiddling
with one of the tassels when it came off in my hand. I knew
that if I told Lizzie what I'd done I'd never hear the end of
it from Davy, and as the Hall was so shadowy and no one
was looking my way I poked the tassel under an old chest.
The Reverend Dunwoody was saying that in spite of the
way things had gone over the past number of years they
would always remain loyal and nothing would ever put a
stop to their singing 'God Save the King' with heart and
mind and voice. Then they sang 'God Save the King', not
all together or with all the right notes, because there was
no organ or piano to get them going.

'Isn't he a very good boy?' said Martha, as she dried the cups with a tea-towel. 'Listening so intently to His Reverence and singing the hymns too!'

Lizzie looked as if she wasn't sure how to reply, and I knew that if I'd owned up to damaging King William's portrait she would have had to admit to her friend, and later to my aunt, that I was not fit to be taken out on a special occasion.

Zane started taking me with her when she went out in the car, Davy McMahon sitting stiff and silent at the steering-wheel with a look on his face that plainly said he had not been placed on this earth to drive *weemen* and *childer* up and down all the roads of the county.

It was then that Smithborough began to shed its carapace as the centre of the world, allowing other worlds to form around it. There was Annaghmakerrig, looking more like a collection of houses than a house that anybody would want to live in; and Aviemore, the tall house in Monaghan town where I met my cousins John and Margaret Killen – they were only babies, but quite soon, it seemed, they were big enough to ride on the carriers of their parents' bicycles and spend Sunday afternoons at Eldron. Their parents were called Marcus and Mat.

'I'm your mother's brother,' Marcus said. 'Do you know that?'

I said I did, but I didn't really. I couldn't remember what my mother looked like.

In another big country house, Ballyleck – not as far as Monaghan in the Ford, yet too far to walk – we met my Killen grandmother and grandfather, who looked for all the world as if they had always lived there, though I knew I'd seen them in some mysterious and distant time at their house in Belfast. They said they liked to move from place to place, having sold (it was explained to me) their home when Grandfather retired from being Master of the Benn Hospital. They were now lodging with the Graham family at Ballyleck for the summer, and in the winter they liked to go back to Alma House on the Esplanade at Portstewart, where they could look out on the Atlantic waves and where, they said, Mrs Dunphy made them very comfortable. My grandfather was a very big man with a white moustache; he always wore a brown suit that seemed a bit large even for him and my grandmother was constantly reminding him to hitch up his trousers when he sat down because he'd get 'knees' in them – but the knees were already there. My grandmother, Zane's sister, was very thin and always very smartly dressed in black, white and shades of grey. She wore *pince-nez* spectacles with purple lenses and a ribbon that was pinned to her blouse; I loved to put the glasses on my nose and see the world looking as if it were in a state of perpetually regal twilight.

A baby lived with them at Ballyleck, my brother Nicholas, whom I had seen very briefly in Belfast and was now called Nicky-Bill. He started coming over to Eldron with them when they could find someone to give them a lift, or when Davy had time to collect them in the Ford; and much later he spent long periods there with Aunt Zane and our grandparents when they were not off on their rounds of other relatives and seaside boarding-houses; and after my mother made her reappearance out of the nowhere that was called India she often stayed with us at Eldron, before making off again to join my father wherever he was in some corner of the distant adult world.

With this widening circle it seemed that these places – Annaghmakerrig, Aviemore, Ballyleck – began to take on a certain reality and to cease to be merely the stuff of Zane's

reminiscences about my grandmother's and my great-uncle
Bertie's and my great-uncle Charlie's and my great-uncle John's
and her own childhood at the Manse in Armagh – I came
to know that city almost as if I lived in it myself. The stories
she told about my mother's and my uncle Marcus's visits to
Eldron when they were small, 'not so very long ago', began
to take on a different character; and when she read out the
letters from my mother and father, postmarked Ootacamund
and Trichinopoly and Madras, that was a completely different
dimension to do with today. There also began to be a clear
difference between such places and the places in the stories
Zane read out of books, which were really *pretend* places –
Tabbytown in *The Cat Who Couldn't Purr* and Egypt in *Baby
Moses and the Bulrushes*.

A letter came from one of the places in India saying that
my parents were 'returning on extended leave', and Zane
said that, after a voyage of several weeks in a liner, they would
come here to fetch me; but weeks were a long time and
merged into months or even years and I did not at all feel
that things were going to change, or even that the night
would come when I would hear no more the drowsy chirping
of the starlings as they rustled in their nests over my head
in the thatch, or that I would wake no longer to the morning
sound of Lizzie sweeping out the hearth with the goose's
wing.

Mount Louise, Scotstown, County Monaghan

When Great-aunt Zane told me that I would be going to live with my parents 'for a bit' at Mount Louise, the information was hardly even of passing interest. I had a tabby kitten called Micky-Puss, a present from a lady in Monaghan. His welfare, and especially his protection from the intolerance of Lizzie, who believed he should live in the yard with the other cats, engaged my attention to a far greater degree than the prospective visit of two people of whose existence I had been kept aware but whose faces I could not picture. I could not really imagine anyone going to live in that solemn-looking house beside the dark lake a couple of miles down the Scotstown road.

Davy McMahon had driven Zane and me to Mount Louise one afternoon because it was just that bit too far to walk. We met Miss McGarry, who owned the house but lived somewhere else not far away. She showed us into every room, scraping open the shutters to let in more light. She said that on a sunny day it was really quite bright and assured us that she had never noticed any sign of damp. Zane agreed that it was a handsome enough house and said she believed that her niece – she meant my mother – would probably remember it from Mr Evatt's time, when she was a little girl. Miss McGarry hoped that when my aunt was writing to her niece she would say that once the windows were opened for a couple of hours the slightly *dank* smell would unquestionably disperse. She gave me a little package tied with a brown ribbon containing three handkerchiefs, saying that a little bird had told her I had just had a birthday. When we were getting into the car Zane whispered to me to thank Miss McGarry for the lovely present.

'Thank you for the lovely present.'

'Oh, aren't you the well brought-up young gentleman!'

Davy, his face a barometer of silent scorn, revved the engine and headed for home.

Davy drove us to Monaghan for Zane to do some shopping and for me to choose a birthday present from my parents. Mr Jenkins sat in a glass compartment just inside the door of his shop with a pair of magnifying lenses attached to his spectacles so that he could see the insides of the watches he was mending. There were clocks of all sizes on one side of the shop and boxes of paper and envelopes and pens and pencils and bottles of ink of all colours imaginable on the other. Mr Jenkins directed us up the wooden stairs. At the top there was a row of dolls lying in boxes of tissue-paper like beds, and a dolls' house with a front that opened. I saw an aeroplane with double wings and a propeller that twirled round when you tweaked it, and a red and green traction engine with real wheels and a roller that was meant for crushing stones on the road, but Zane said they were far too expensive and, anyway, she was sure my father would like me to have something sporty, so in the end I chose a tennis racquet. 'Would he like a wee ball to go with it?' the lady behind the counter asked. Zane said she thought that might lead to broken windows if not broken bones.

When we got home I made a ball with string and scrooged-up paper, which worked quite well, and then Zane remembered that there might be a shuttlecock somewhere in a box that had never been opened. She rummaged in the bottom of an old press, where all kinds of mysterious objects like a Masonic apron and a rubber tube for sucking poison out of a person's stomach had been left at one time or another, and found an oblong carton with *Badminton De Luxe* written on the outside and a picture of two ladies in white dresses holding long-handled racquets hitting something to one another over a high net. The shuttlecock we found inside the carton had a rubber nose and stiff white feathers, and when I hit it with my tennis racquet it sailed up into the air, then floated gently down. Zane said the thing was to hit it again and again and keep it airborne.

Over the following days she kept reminding me that my parents would soon be with us. They would stay first with my grandparents and Nicky-Bill at Ballyleck, and then Nicky-Bill and I would go to live with them at Mount Louise. I thought that Micky-Puss needed a wash so I put him in the birdbath outside the porch door. He miaowed a lot till Zane came out and told me that it was *very* cruel to wash a cat because they hated water. She dried him with a glass-cloth and put him in a paper bag in front of the kitchen range where Lizzie eyed him balefully.

'Cats do enjoy warmth!' said Zane.

'Och, always looking for the comfortable spot, you may be sure,' observed Lizzie.

My mother turned up at Eldron one afternoon in a yellow car with a roof that you could fold back – she said it was

called a Vauxhall Coupé. She was a very tall lady with dark
brown hair and brown eyes. After she and Zane had sat for
a long time talking in the sitting room she came out into
the garden and we played with the shuttlecock, taking it in
turns to hit it into the air and catch it in our hands as it
came down. When it fell into the long grass Micky-Puss
pounced and started trying to pull out its feathers.

'He thinks it's a bird!' my mother said. 'Clever cat!'

I said he was *very* clever, far cleverer than the yard cats,
who always ran away when they saw you. My mother told
me I should call her Mummy and that Daddy was at Whinsfield near Dublin with my other grandparents and would
soon be coming to Ballyleck, and then we'd all go to Mount
Louise and be together again – and it would be such
fun!

One afternoon Zane dressed me in the blue box-pleated
coat that I wore only on Sundays. She combed my hair and
put brilliantine on it because it was always falling forward
into a fringe. She said that my dad would like to see me
looking smart as he was a military man and they were always
very particular. Davy drove us to Ballyleck, where we found
my grandparents sitting under the pillared portico with my
mother, who had Nicky-Bill on her knee.

'And here's your daddy!' my grandmother announced, as
a man came out from the doorway behind them.

'Shake hands with your daddy now,' urged Zane in a low
voice.

There was silence from everyone as I moved towards the
man. He had an ink stain on one of his fingers. We shook
hands and there was a general murmur of approval.

'Welcome home, Daddy,' I said, in the way that Zane had
taught me.

'And I'm very glad to *be* home,' said the man, and then

he turned to Zane and said, 'Oh, Jane, you've looked after him so well!'

Zane smiled and looked away. After that I was allowed to go and find Margaret Graham, whose family owned the house, and the two of us went down the winding path to the Mouse Wood where we hunted for fir-cones and saw a rat caught in a trap. Mrs Graham had laid out a big tea in the dining room with lots of very grand china, which my grandmother said had come with the house, and all the beautiful furniture when the Grahams had bought the place from the Montgomerys. Then Davy, who had sat in the car all this time, drove Zane and me back to Eldron.

Mount Louise was approached by two overgrown avenues that wound and dipped their way through spinney and bog. The back avenue was used only by the farmer who rented Miss McGarry's land. It was a morass in wet weather but, being a short-cut, Davy nosed the Ford between its gateless pillars and then, to his great vexation, was forced to reverse when the front wheels stuck in the mire. For some minutes it looked as if we would have to abandon the car and walk while he went looking for a horse with a rope to drag it back, but once he had spread an old sack on the ground and given angry jabs to the accelerator, the car jumped backwards and we continued our journey ignominiously by means of the front avenue, which was identified by a white wooden gate.

Had it not been for this gate no one would have known that a big house existed beyond all that density of foliage. It stood on a slight eminence looking out towards the lake across two rushy fields scarred by outcrops of sloe and briar. The lake looked like two lakes, but my father said that the division was only reeds and you could row the boat through

them. When we did, the reeds made a swishing sound. The
water was usually black, but at certain times of day and in
certain lights it turned to silver, but never to blue. The fields
grew marshy as they neared the water's edge where there
were flags and bulrushes. In the distance endless low hills
stretched west into Fermanagh. Dense woods came right up
to the house to left and right, but at the back there were
the remains of a kitchen-garden with rows of straggling apple
trees and a glass-house with cracked and broken panes.

The Evatt family had lived at Mount Louise until Mr
Humphrey Evatt died and the rest of the family moved away.
Mr Evatt believed that boys should be able to swim by the
age of eight, so on each son's eighth birthday he took the
boy out in a rowing-boat and tossed him into the water: it
was either swim or drown. This was related to me by my
grandfather, who did not say if he thought Mr Evatt had
done right or wrong – in fact, he told the story with amusement as if it were something he had made up, yet I sensed
that these events had actually happened so I dreaded going
on the lake when my father was taking the boat out fishing.
If you looked into the dark water at the jetty you could just
make out the skeleton of a sunken boat: it was like the corpse
of someone who had drowned and had been forgotten.

There was a rowing-boat tied to a post, and this was the
one used for fishing, although it had water up to the floor-
boards and I was sure that more would leak its way in and
the boat would sink. One time my father took a bucket of
cooked potatoes to throw into the lake to encourage the
pike to swim that way – there would then be a better chance
of catching them. He told me to tip the bucket over the
side, but I held it awkwardly and most of the potatoes ended
in the bottom of the boat. I had to scoop the mess into the
water with my hands, and each time I leaned out the boat

gave a lurch. I was certain it would capsize and I would join the remains of the other boat, and perhaps Mr Evatt's sons, ensnared among the stems of water-lilies.

We had not long moved into Mount Louise when my grandparents and Zane drove over for tea. My parents had engaged a nurserymaid called Mary to look after us, and after she had put us to bed we could hear the talk and laughter of the grown-ups downstairs. When the sounds grew louder we sensed that the visitors had moved into the hall and were about to leave. I kept calling out, 'Zane!' and Nicky-Bill kept calling out, 'Gaga!' – our name for our grandmother – but they did not come up the stairs. Then we heard the banging of car doors and the sound of the Ford moving off and we both dissolved into tears. It was the same every time our grandparents and Zane came to Mount Louise, and so my mother made a joke about it, imitating our cries of 'Zane!' and 'Gaga!'. At length she said we'd really have to get used to the fact that we now lived here, not at Eldron or Ballyleck.

'I want to see Micky-Puss!'

'We can certainly go over to Eldron to see Micky-Puss. You may be sure he's very well looked after.'

I never saw Micky-Puss again.

The hours after we went to bed were quite frightening, even though it was autumn and still bright. Sometimes distant but menacing bangs were heard. In answer to my cries my father came upstairs and said it was only some of the neighbouring farmers out shooting.

'But will they come near?' I asked apprehensively.

He said no, they would be moving further and further away. 'Listen: that one's probably over at Allagesh. And that one's definitely away out beyond Drumgoast Lake.'

I thought he said 'Drum Ghost Lake', and the idea that there should be a place with a name like that was not one bit comforting.

My uncle Marcus came over from Monaghan to shoot snipe and duck with my father and some other men. My aunt Mat and my cousins John and Margaret came too, and when we were having tea outside the front door the men put jam-jars on the sundial and aimed their rifles at them; they were all such good shots that no one missed and soon there was a big pile of broken glass. My father said I could be his gun-dog when he was out shooting on his own. We went by way of the marshy margin of the lake, where the reeds grew tall, and then through a briary coppice. He said that if we were very quiet and kept low among the bushes the birds wouldn't know we were coming. We came to the edge of a deep dyke and he raised his gun, waited, and suddenly there was a loud bang.

'Got 'im!' he said. 'A snipe. Now we'll go and find him.'

We went along the dyke till it got narrower and then jumped across. My heels got stuck in the mud and one of my shoes came off. My father climbed down and picked it up; it was all squelchy inside. He pointed out where he thought the snipe had fallen, but when we got to the place it was not there. Then we heard a kind of squeaking and a rustling noise, and among the clumps of rushes we saw a bird trying to struggle towards the lake. Its wings were trailing and it couldn't walk properly. My father bent down and picked it up. 'Not a good shot, that,' he said.

The snipe looked at us silently.

My father took a long pin from the lapel of his jacket and stuck it into the snipe's head. It fluttered for quite a bit but it did not make any sound, except a sort of hiss, and then its head hung down.

As I was the gun-dog I had to carry the snipe back to the house. At night it came alive again in my hands and fluttered and fluttered till its wings were beating my face, beating and beating, and I couldn't breathe and I couldn't speak or cry because the words got trapped in my throat and all that came out was a hiss, just like the snipe's last breath. I was shaking and shaking and then Mary was saying, 'You've had a nightmare. Go back to sleep again!' I asked her to leave the candle lighting and she did, but the dream kept coming back.

One night Mary was cross and said, 'You must quit these dreams now, waking people up in the middle of the night like that!'

I said I couldn't help it. The bad dreams were just there.

My mother bought me a ticket to a children's party at a church hall in Monaghan. There would be games and lemonade and cakes and perhaps even ice-cream, and the money would go to buy nice things for all those little children who never saw lemonade and cakes and didn't even know that ice-cream existed. I asked what ice-cream was and she said it was frozen cream flavoured with vanilla or strawberry – and did I not remember the ices that came out of the big fridge in Trichy? She said that, come to think of it, I couldn't really be expected to remember the time when I was only two years old, and the reason I never saw ice-cream here or at Eldron was that a fridge needed electricity to make it work and, of course, you only had electricity in towns. I wanted to know what a fridge was and she said I should think of a big white cupboard that was icy-cold inside.

When we arrived at the hall all the other children were already there, laughing and shouting and running round hitting each other with coloured balloons on strings while a lady played the piano in a corner. I could not remember ever having been with more than two or three other children at one time and they were always my brother and cousins, who were less than two years old. I was given a blue balloon but I had no idea who I should hit with it or when to fall on the floor or when to get up again when the music stopped or started.

My mother sat on the bench that ran round the walls. I threw my balloon to her and she threw it back. We did this many times until a lady announced that the next game was Oranges and Lemons, and my mother told me to join the end of the line and hold on to the boy in front of me, but when I did he looked round and said, 'Who are *you*? Go away, I don't know you!' so I wandered about among the revellers before returning to try the balloon-throwing again with my mother. Then the balloon landed on her cigarette and it shrivelled without even a pop.

Another lady opened a door and shouted, 'Tea-time, little people!' All the children rushed into the next room. I followed, and a place was found for me on a bench between two big girls who talked across me all the time. I ate a cherry bun slowly, crumbling it on the cardboard plate in front of me.

'Oh, he's crying,' said one of the girls.

'No, I'm not!' I said.

'He's not crying, he's laughing!' said her friend. Then they both started laughing and they kept on, spluttering into their fizzy lemonade, till the lady came round with bowls of pink and white ice-cream. I mashed mine up slowly and then stirred it so that the pink went into a whirl in the middle of the white and then it all turned into a sort of sludge.

'Do you not like your ice-cream?' said the bigger of the two girls.

'I'm making it last,' I said, and they started to laugh again.

When we were leaving the first lady gave me a present of a little wooden gun.

It was a dark wet night and my mother found it difficult to turn the car into the white gates of Mount Louise so that she had to get out and see where she was, then back the car off the verge. She got quite wet. When we went into the house I could see my father reading a book at the fire in the dining room by the light of the Aladdin lamp.

'He behaved like an absolute *rabbit*,' my mother was saying, as she took off her damp coat. 'Odd, because he loved the children's parties in Trichy.'

My father called me into the dining room. 'What present did you get?'

'It was a gun.' I had it under my coat.

'Yes, but do you know what type of gun?'

'No.'

'Well, if you won't show it to me I won't tell you how it works.'

I handed him the toy.

'It's a revolver. You put your finger there and pull the trigger and the bullet goes out of there, bang!'

But the gun was made of one piece of wood and the trigger didn't move. There was no bang.

Across the gravel from the dining-room windows was a building that Miss McGarry called the Monastery. The ground floor was old stables and byres and a coach-house where our car was kept – Mrs McGarry's, which she never drove, was wedged in at the back. The upper floor was reached by a slippery outside staircase to a door over which was fixed a pair of stag's antlers. My father said we could go up and see what things Miss McGarry had left behind. A long loft with slits for windows ran the whole length of the building but very little light came in through them. There seemed to be a lot of old furniture and trunks as we poked around.

I gave a scream because of what I saw.

'What's wrong?' My father's voice came through the gloom.

A man was hanging from one of the beams. His clothes were flapping in the draught and his boots didn't seem to belong to his legs.

'It's only old Evatt's uniform!' my father cried. 'Nothing to be scared about!' He dragged open the door and leaned a box against it to let in some light. 'Old Evatt was County Sheriff – you can tell by the buttons and the plume in the hat. He must have been a midget – look at the shortness of the jacket and trousers!'

I thought Mr Evatt's uniform looked enormous and menacing, hanging there in the gloom.

The trunk of a huge beech tree had been sawn through where it had fallen across the avenue in a storm a long time ago. Great swathes of lichen covered its boughs, on which I climbed and swung. My grandmother said I'd certainly fall and break my neck, but I had no fear of falling so I clambered about in the branches that were nearly as high as some of the other trees, just to show that she was being silly.

'Gladys, that child will come to a sticky end!'

My mother didn't seem too concerned. She probably sensed that I had a good head for heights.

I came down and stood beside the sawn-off bole of the tree. The rings showing its age had rotted away in places so

that if you started your count at one side you had to move
to another place in the same arc where the traces could be
taken up again. From opposite sides we counted a hundred
and fifty-four and a hundred and sixty. My father said that
proved that the tree was more than a century and a half old
and the others still standing in the surrounding wood were
all probably planted at the same time, before the Act of
Union (whatever that was). He and my grandfather speculated
upon who had planted them and why. Had the Evatts always
lived at Mount Louise? Zane said she remembered a long,
thatched house, longer than Eldron but of only one storey,
and she also recalled the time when the house we were
living in was being built, but she wasn't exactly sure if the
thatched house was on the same site or a little bit to one
side; anyway, it was gone. My grandfather said that once a
thatched dwelling was left unoccupied it would decay very
quickly – he'd noticed that a ruined house beside the road
to Eldron had mouldered away in a couple of years. Zane
said there were now only two thatched houses left in the
neighbourhood – Eldron and another at Elliott's Cross.

My father cut some branches and built a wigwam under
an immense copper beech, one of two that framed the lake
from the windows of the house. We were expecting some
children to come for tea, Julia Butler and friends of hers
from Annaghmakerrig. I showed them the wigwam but it
was too small for us all to squeeze inside. When the time
came for them to go home Julia and I hid in it, and her
parents, Hubert and Peggy, started shouting, 'Julia! Julia!
Where are you?' When we didn't reply we heard Peggy
saying, 'They couldn't have gone to the lake, could they?'
She started to run down the field and then Hubert heard
us laughing and shouted after her, 'They're here! They're
playing Babes in the Wood!' and then Peggy came strolling

back through the falling leaves. As they were about to drive off, Peggy wound down the window of their Morris 10 and said we'd all have to come to their Christmas party at Annaghmakerrig.

It had been raining for days when we set out for Annagh-makerrig, and when we got just beyond Smithborough the floods were up and we had to turn round and try the Clones road. After we crossed the bridge at Annalore there was deep water and my father said he was afraid it would get into the exhaust pipe. He reversed out of the flood and we saw a big boy holding a sack over his head who said he'd show us the way through the lanes at Killycoonagh if we'd give him a lift. Our car had only two seats and, as Nicky-Bill and I were in the space for luggage behind them, the boy had to stand on the running-board and hold on to the door-handle. I thought he might fall off. We splashed our way to Killevan, where he jumped off and we all shouted, 'Thank you!'

When we got to Annaghmakerrig Peggy Butler said she had felt sure we wouldn't come and we ought to have telephoned for news of what the roads were like, but she didn't know that there was no telephone at Mount Louise. My mother had told me that Peggy's mother, Mrs Guthrie, was a friend of Zane and was blind, but Mrs Guthrie knew her house and garden so well she could find her way about without help. This turned out to be true, for my father wanted to borrow a book she was talking about and when she said it was in the study she led the way through the dark hall and past the staircase and then she felt for a candlestick and a box of matches. She had to ask my father to light the candle, but when we were in the study she went straight to the bookcase and said, 'I think that book's about *here*,' putting her hand on one of the shelves, and it was.

There was great activity in the Mount Louise kitchen on

the evening before Christmas. Margaret Storey the cook made heaps of little sandwiches and laid them out on big plates on the dining-room table with lots of glasses for wine. Who was all this food for? For Santa Claus, who would be very hungry when he arrived. When we went up to bed my mother read from a book called *The Night Before Christmas* that had pictures of Santa Claus all dressed in red stepping into a snow-covered chimney-pot and another of him hanging up parcels round a fireplace. At the end of the book he flew away into the sky with four reindeer pulling his sledge. Later I heard a lot of people downstairs, so Santa must have brought more than the reindeer with him.

In the morning all the dirty plates that Santa's friends had used were piled up by the sink in the scullery waiting to be washed. My mother said that Santa would be coming back again at tea-time with presents for all of us because he had had too much to carry last night. Aunt Mat and Uncle Marcus, with John and Margaret, arrived from Monaghan and then my grandparents and Zane came in the Eldron Ford driven by Davy. My mother took me by the hand and we went into the porch. There was a bright red scooter propped against the door: Santa Claus had left it there because he couldn't get it down the chimney. I asked if I could ride it now and we went outside, but the ground was too rough and I couldn't get it going properly so it was decided that we'd take it out on the road next day – but now I must come inside because Santa would be back any minute.

It was beginning to grow dark. Zane was cutting a cake with red and white icing. Nicky-Bill and John and Margaret didn't like it – 'It's the fruit,' said Zane, 'the currants, nasty little black things, not nice at all at all' – but there was a tin with pictures of all kinds of biscuits and when this was opened the same biscuits were inside and they liked those.

Suddenly my mother said, 'Here he is!'

We crowded over to the bay window. Uncle Marcus was trying to push up the sash, which had got stuck.

'It's the damp,' said Zane. 'These windows probably haven't been opened since old Mr Evatt's time.'

Dimly we could see a red figure waiting outside. Marcus heaved and pushed and my grandmother attempted to loosen the frame by sliding the cake-knife all around it. Suddenly the window shot up with a clatter and Santa Claus stepped in. He had a white beard and moustache, just like in the pictures, and his face was red too. His red robe came nearly down to the ground. He was carrying a sack, which he swung on to the carpet, and said, 'Merry Christmas, one and all!'

Nicky-Bill, John and Margaret started to scream.

Santa rummaged in his sack and pulled out a parcel. 'John,' he said, reading the label, 'Happy Christmas from Auntie Mimi.'

Nothing could persuade John to take the parcel. He ran to his mother, roaring and crying.

'It's the red face,' said Zane. 'I could have told you.'

Nicky-Bill wouldn't take the parcel that Santa held out to him either, and took refuge behind our grandmother on the sofa. Margaret continued to wail and Mat took her out to the bathroom.

'Christopher, with best wishes from Aunt Hester,' said Santa, handing me a rolled-up book tied with string.

Hesitantly I took the book. I thought it not very fair that Santa was giving out presents that really came from other people.

When he had taken everything out of the sack and turned it upside-down to make sure there was nothing left, he said to me, 'Now, shake hands with Santa!'

I half held out my hand because Santa Claus looked a bit

frightening. He took it and told me I was very brave.

Then all the grown-ups laughed in that annoying kind of way so you didn't know if they were laughing at you or something else, and you wondered if you had done some stupid thing.

It was always raining at Mount Louise. Often we couldn't go out to play because of the drizzle, and when we went on 'expeditions' in the yellow Vauxhall we had to take raincoats and wellington boots. The longest expedition was to Dartrey, where we were joined by the Eldron and Ballyleck relatives driven by Davy. I wanted to go with Zane and I thought she wanted that too, but my father said that if we swapped places one of them would have to squeeze into the back of our car and that wouldn't be comfortable. Dartrey was a huge mansion rather like Annaghmakerrig, except that it was closer to its lake and had steps and ornamental balustrades leading down to the water. There had been an auction at Dartrey where my mother had bought a four-poster bed that was being stored for her at Ballyleck – 'until the time when we have a house of our own', she said. She had paid five pounds for it.

'It really is a shame all that lovely furniture going for next to nothing,' said my grandmother, 'but the house is so remote no one would dream of coming all the way from Dublin or Belfast. If they had, the prices would have been quite different – I'm sure Gladys would have had to bid up to ten or fifteen pounds for that old bed. I think people were buying pieces just to take pity on them, or on poor Lady Edith, who looks as if she could do with a few shillings. Mat bought a spinet for a pound, and no one at Aviemore knows how to play it!'

We walked through dripping shrubberies to see a monument on an island and then returned to the balustrades where we were supposed to have a picnic, but because of the wet we had to eat our sandwiches in the cars. The voices of women chanting echoed eerily from inside the house. Zane said it was the nuns, who had bought Dartrey when Lady Edith Wyndham fell on evil times and moved into the steward's house. 'Soon all the big houses will be convents for nuns,' she said.

My father's leave from the army came to an end, but my mother was not going away with him this time. He was off to Palestine, the Holy Land that the Reverend Alexander read to us about every Sunday in Smithborough Church – 'And may the Lord add His blessing to this reading of His Holy Word, amen!' he would always finish by declaring. My father told us that he would be seeing Jerusalem and the Sea of Galilee and the Mount of Olives and Golgotha, and while he was away the three of us would spend some time with our Dublin grandparents, at Whinsfield.

## Whinsfield, Sandyford, County Dublin

'It's a *modern* house!' I kept shouting, as we explored Whinsfield, for this was the word my mother had used in describing my Fitz-Simon grandparents' home to Zane.

'*Very* modern. There probably isn't anything else like it in Dublin or, indeed, in the whole of Ireland. Simon's mother designed it herself.'

My mother always called my father 'Simon' because she didn't like his real name, 'Manners', but he was always 'Manners' in the Fitz-Simon family.

'Simon's mother planned the whole house and then got an engineer to do the hard bits. It looks like something you'd expect to see on the Mediterranean – you know, a white cube, Tunisia or somewhere.'

Whinsfield was white outside and inside, with metal windows that opened out like doors, and doors that had their handles placed so high you had to stretch up to turn them. My Fitz-Simon grandmother said she mustn't have been thinking of children when she drew the pictures showing where the door-handles were meant to be, but they were the latest thing.

'Can you reach up? Good, and Nicky-Bill? No? Well, it won't be long before you can. Christopher: you can open the doors for him just to show how tall you've grown! And, yes, you're right, the house is full of light, that's what I wanted – the hall's really a kind of conservatory. And the stairs are cantilevered out from the walls – that means they don't have any visible means of support, like a pair of trousers with no braces! And the bedrooms open on to that balcony: it goes all round so you can look down into the hall or up to the glass roof. Go up now and see for yourselves!'

Nicky-Bill and I raced up the cantilevered stairs looking into the five bedrooms, each of them with a big window and a wash-basin and electric bedside lights that we kept switching on and off.

'H and C running water in every room!' said my grand-mother. 'So different from my poor old Moreen.'

Moreen was her family home, which she'd sold just before I was born because, my mother said, 'It was far too big and was getting quite dilapidated, as well as costing a fortune to heat, and when your grandfather gave up riding there was no need to have a house with all those stables and so many fields – so your grandmother built this house on a corner of the Moreen land and, of course, it *is* much more *conven-ient.*' I knew by the way she said 'convenient' that she didn't like Whinsfield very much, and probably preferred Moreen, which we could see from the Sandyford road – a big old mansion with two ramshackle gate-lodges and curving avenues with weeds growing all over them.

In Whinsfield there were electric fires that you plugged into the wall and the kitchen had an electric stove made of speckled grey enamel called a Moffat, which had come all the way from Germany. It had big white knobs on the front that you turned with a click and at every click the plates on the top got hotter. There was a copper kettle that you plugged in beside it that took only five minutes to boil. It was quite different to Eldron and Mount Louise, where the range had to be lit in the morning and the kettle would not boil for at least an hour.

'It's a *modern* house!' I repeated, every time something new was discovered – like the electric bell that my grandfather pressed under the dining-room table, or the service-hatch at which Eileen Boylan appeared when she heard the bell ring in the kitchen. There was a clipped hedge outside in the shape of joined-up Zs – it was called 'the zigzag hedge' and anyone who came to the house thought it was very modern too.

'Very *angular*,' said my mother.

My grandmother told us she got her ideas from a house near Hampstead that she'd passed several times in a London bus but never had time to stop and look at. She'd also seen pictures of houses that were somewhat similar in a magazine, but the idea for the hall, stairs and landing all in one space with the sunlight coming from the roof was her own, and she'd also thought up the zigzag hedge.

My mother said the garden was wonderful – probably because she hadn't said nice enough things about the house. A rockery sloped up towards the Three Rock Mountain, and an old granite quarry had been made into a pond with lilies floating on the water.

'Oh, yes,' said my grandmother. 'I wanted the plain exterior of the house to make a contrast with all these boulders and whin bushes. We're exactly on the line where the mountain meets the fields, you see. The rockery and the quarry belong to the mountain. The lawn and the vegetable garden beyond the zigzag hedge are the start of the Sandyford plain – you can see how the stream comes dashing down and then levels out. It leaves loads of sand all around when it's in flood – that's how Sandyford got its name.'

I crossed the sandy ford when I went with my grandfather to Mass in St Mary's Church. There was a path called the 'right-of-way' that led from Lamb Doyle's pub down by the old look-out turret and the remains of the Pale wall, descending steeply and stonily through gorse and bracken till it reached the edge of the Whinsfield garden where my grandmother had planted a yew hedge, 'for privacy', she said, 'because that's the short-cut used by the Barnacullia people coming down to early Mass and you can't have people peering in to see what you're having for breakfast, especially on Sundays when there are hordes of them!' She did not go to early Mass, but drove herself in her Ford 8 to Matins at Kilternan at a later time.

When you left the Whinsfield garden by a wooden gate in the yew hedge you could cross the right-of-way and enter the Moreen woods. My grandfather used to go for walks there, even though it did not belong to the family any more. There were all kinds of mushrooms and toadstools in strange colours with speckles and dots – 'very poisonous: don't dare to touch them!' – and puffballs that exploded with a little cloud of dust when you trod on them. At the furthest side of the wood there was a long avenue of trees called the Beech Walk, which led towards the old house. To go along it was like walking in a cathedral built of leaves. Only green light came through, though you could glimpse the ordinary light of day at the furthest end.

Beside the iron gate on to the Sandyford road was the hen-run. My grandmother looked after the hens, giving them a mash of potatoes and yellow meal in the morning and a scattering of oats in the afternoon. They were all Rhode Island Reds, for she believed that this breed combined the best characteristics of laying and table fowl. They had a little aluminium fountain where they could drink, stooping to sip the water, then raising their heads and opening and closing their beaks in a way that helped them to swallow. In the evening we went into the hen-house and collected the eggs from the laying boxes in a wicker basket; sometimes a hen would still be sitting in her box and you had to put your hand stealthily under her from behind or she would give you a sharp peck. At the end of the week my grandmother cleaned the eggs with butter-paper and put them into containers of six or a dozen, which she sold to her customers in the neighbourhood. In a smaller pen were two dozen enormous turkeys, which she used to drive across the road to Mr Aiken's field so that they could pick up stray seeds of corn left in the stubble after threshing. 'It helps to fatten them up,' she said. I knew that if you screeched at the turkeys they would all join in a chorus of answering gobbles. 'Ah, the poor old turkeys, don't be annoying them,' said my grandmother, 'they haven't much time to enjoy themselves, with Christmas never far off.'

Nicky-Bill couldn't say 'Granny' properly. When he was asked her name he always said, 'Guy,' and soon we were all calling her that. She didn't seem pleased when my grandfather remarked, 'Well, you are a guy!' because he'd been telling us about someone called Guy Fawkes who had tried to blow up the Houses of Parliament in London and he thought she was always trying to blow up things too. My grandmother said that Nicky-Bill hadn't pronounced the word like 'Guy', but softer and more drawn-out, like 'Gaay', and she didn't mind being called that. Everyone in Sandyford called my grandfather 'Mister', so we called him that too. My grandmother called him Dan. His real name was Daniel James McGillicuddy O'Connell Fitz-Simon and there were several pictures of my great-great-great-grandfather Daniel O'Connell in the house and a little statue of him, named 'The Liberator', standing on a black and gold Chinese cabinet in the hall.

Mister went for a walk every day with Roy, the cocker spaniel. He wore brown tweed plus-fours and a Norfolk jacket and carried a blackthorn stick covered with knobs and spikes that he'd cut from a hedge and given to an old man called Mooney to sandpaper and varnish. He did not need it to lean on it like my other grandfather – 'It's just for show!' he said, giving it a twirl, then shouting, ''Tis me auld shillelagh!' Sometimes we went up the mountain as far as Ticknock where you could see the smoke of Dublin beyond the Ballinteer woods, with the square tower of Taney church rising up out of them. Other times we went along the leafy road to the gates of Leopardstown racecourse; there were horses in the grounds of the big houses round about and Mister would stop to admire them and to tell me which he thought would be worth putting your money on and which hadn't a snowball's chance in hell.

There was a grassy lane off the road up to Lamb Doyle's that ended at another mountain stream where stepping-stones crossed a shallow pool. Three cottages stood at the end beside the pool, two of them in ruins and one where Mary Mulligan the washerwoman lived. Mister said that Gaay had once owned these cottages, which were called the Slate Cabins, and she used to rent one of them at a shilling a year to her friend Con, Countess Markiewicz, who came out from Dublin at weekends with other arty people to do sketching. He said that Con was a very good painter, exhibiting in some of the best galleries. 'She wasn't a bad marksman either, to give her her due,' he observed, as an afterthought. 'Many's the time she'd stop at Moreen to tell us she'd be "in residence" at the cottage for a few days, and if anyone was to come looking for her we were to judge if they were friends and if so give them directions – but if they looked as if they had something else in mind we were to say she definitely wasn't there and we had the key to prove it. "There it is, sitting on the hall table!" we'd say, and off they'd go, but of course she had another key. These people were detectives or plain-clothes policemen. They thought Con was stirring up feelings against the government – and I can tell you this for nothing: they were dead right!'

'Why did the policemen want to get her?'

'She was training young boys, not much older than yourself, to fight so as to get the British out of Ireland – and she succeeded in that too, after a time, with the help of others.'

We looked at the roofless cottage where Countess Markiewicz used to meet her friends. There was not a slate left, and most of the beams had fallen down inside.

'One afternoon I was out for a walk with your dad,' said Mister. 'He was fourteen or fifteen at the time, home for the holidays from school in England, so he didn't know what was going on here. We were standing on the Pale wall turret looking out over the woods when he noticed three cars edging their way up the lane. "Why are they stopping at Con's cottage?" your dad asked me. There was certainly a lot of activity – men taking boxes out of the cars and bringing them inside, and then they started unloading rifles. I said: "You didn't see that!"'

'But you and my dad *had* seen it.'

'Yes, but at that time we kept our eyes shut. We didn't want the police coming and arresting Con. She was in a house of ours. What's more, I was a Justice of the Peace under the British Crown, and I'd certainly have been given the boot from that position pretty quick if it became known that I was harbouring a rebel!'

My grandmother also spoke of the Rebel Countess. 'Ah, poor Con. She went a bit cracky in the end. I think she killed herself trying to get food for the poor people in the city and better houses for them. The slums were terrible! You should have seen her funeral – there were thousands on the streets, people you wouldn't normally see out because they kept to the tenements. In those days – and it's only twenty years ago! – the slum people never ventured into Grafton Street. They were afraid of being hunted.'

'They knew their place,' said my grandfather, with a smile, 'not like now, when every jackeen thinks he owns the place!'

'*You* wouldn't have hunted them,' said my grandmother. 'You'd have opened the gates of the Castle to them if it was easier! Well, anyway, I'll never forget the day Con arrived in a lather of sweat at Moreen after riding all the way from Rathgar on her bicycle. "The English police have sent over a warrant for me and the only place I'll be safe is London where I'm not known!" So I harnessed the pony-trap and drove her down to the Mail Boat at Kingstown. I was sure she'd be arrested at the pier, and I thought they'd probably arrest me for being with her, but she travelled steerage without a maid and only a little bundle of clothes so the local police – who were probably only watching the first-class gangway – missed her.'

Gaay said that when my father was about the same age as me he hated being kissed by Countess Markiewicz because she had a moustache – 'But I told him what can't be cured must be endured and he'd have to endure the bristles for the sake of good manners! And that goes for everything else.'

Mary Mulligan lived beside the pool next to Con Markiewicz's cottage. She washed our clothes and bed-linen and did the same for most of the people living round about. The Swastika Laundry van came out from Dublin as far as Sandyford once a week but Gaay said they charged an arm and a leg for a shirt or a pair of combinations and, anyway, they didn't do the job half as well as Mary Mulligan, and if the local people stopped giving her their washing she'd have nothing to live on as she wouldn't qualify for the old-age pension for a year or two, even if she was able to prove her age – and that was a bit of a conundrum. She charged a penny for a pillowslip and tuppence for a shirt because there was more ironing in it.

Mary Mulligan came to Whinsfield on a Monday to collect the washing in a big basket. Eileen Boylan gave her a cup of tea and a slice of brack in the kitchen and she sat there for a while, stroking Whiskers the black and white cat and wondering if there would be good drying weather tomorrow. She was very thin and had a pale face with a purple carbuncle on her chin. She seemed to delay a bit as if she was enjoying the talk or else putting off carrying the basket up the Slate Cabins lane. Once I saw her sitting in the ditch at Lamb's Cross with the basket beside her, but it was far too heavy for me to lift so I didn't offer to help. She washed the clothes in the stream, then hung them out to dry on a long line that stretched from a thorn tree to a hook on the cottage wall.

If you crossed the stepping-stones at Mary Mulligan's you'd find yourself in a furzy field, and if you pushed your way through the bushes you'd come out behind the Carnegie

Library, where Gaay helped Nurse Conlisk with the Baby Club. Once a month the mothers of Sandyford would bring their babies to be weighed on a scales and Nurse would give them medicine for coughs or diarrhoea or whatever they had wrong with them. 'It's all to do with malnutrition,' Gaay told my mother. 'They can't afford good food. And what can you say to a woman whose child has rickets when her husband has no work?' There was always a lot of bawling and screeching from the babies but the mothers didn't seem to mind and they chatted away among themselves while sitting on the bench waiting for their turn.

Nurse Conlisk travelled all over the parish on a rugged black bicycle. It was tough going for her, Gaay said, because the parish stretched up to Glencullen, which was mountainous, and the roads not much better than lanes. Sick people didn't have to pay her because the Jubilee Nursing Association, of which Gaay was honorary secretary, provided her with a cottage and Gaay went from door to door of the better-off homes collecting money so that there would be no fear of Miss Aylward, the Jubilee organizer, posting Nurse to somewhere else because of the local subscriptions falling short of what was needed.

Gaay never went out without a hat, even if it was to do a bit of gardening or to clean out the hen-house. She had dozens of them, on the tops of wardrobes and in boxes under her bed. If the front-door bell rang and she thought someone was dropping in for a cup of tea she always ran upstairs for a hat while Eileen answered the door. She had a large number of dresses, too, hanging higgledy-piggledy in a little room she called her glory-hole where there was a sewing-machine and a tailor's dummy called Mary-Ann. Most of her clothes were lilac or mauve or mint green – she never wore blue, red or yellow – but she always put on a black dress in the evening. Her hair was a bright orange colour, and when she was getting ready to go out to a meeting or a concert she thrust a metal curling tongs between the bars of the electric heater till it turned red and then she crimped her hair with a sizzling sound and a smell like frying soap. My mother saw her putting the tongs in the heater and mentioned that she could easily get a shock, but she dismissed this as 'an old wives' tale' and said there was too much mystique about electricity altogether. It was one of the wonders of the modern world and really much simpler than it was cracked up to be.

When anyone came to tea or we met people on the road there was talk about the threat of war. The names Hitler and Mussolini were spoken everywhere. Gaay said that people she knew in the Gate Theatre – the actress Betty Chancellor and the violinist Bay Jellett – had gone off on a tour of eastern Europe. 'Everyone told them they were mad! Mrs Jellett is in a fit of nerves – oh, a fit! – and last week what did Mr Mussolini do only go and invade Albania – the very day the Gate people were due to arrive! – but no, it turned out they weren't going to Albania after all, it was some other place with a peculiar name, because Mrs Jellett got a card from Bay the next day to say the cherry blossom was a sight to behold and there was no sign of a war breaking out at all.'

Letters arrived for my mother and grandmother from Palestine. The Whinsfield neighbours were saying wasn't it well my father was posted so far away because Mr Hitler only set his sights on places nearer to Germany – and wasn't it well too that we were here in Ireland because the same Mr Hitler would never bother his head about us, so poor and so remote as we were?

My Killen grandparents, who had no home of their own since selling their house in Belfast, took a seaside bungalow called Arc-en-Ciel at Greystones for the summer of 1939, and we joined them there. Gaay drove us to Greystones in her Ford 8. At White's Cross she banged into a black Hillman, severely denting the mudguard. The accident would have been much worse had not my mother seized the handbrake and pulled it hard with a rasping sound just before we hit the Hillman. The driver jumped out and angrily pointed to the damage. 'Agh, only a *scratch!*' Gaay exclaimed, and then she drove off, complaining to my mother that it was very *dangerous* to pull on the handbrake without warning. When we reached Greystones she invited my other grandparents to tea at Whinsfield, but they never had a chance to accept because they had no car and it would have taken them a whole day to get to Sandyford by train and bus.

Arc-en-Ciel was modern too, with electric light and a Moffat cooker, but not as modern as Whinsfield. It was pebbledashed in colourful little stones that you could pick off the wall, and there was a wooden balcony opening off the sitting room that my mother said was a bit like the veranda in Trichy. The garden was enclosed by high hedges of flowering escallonia – the only hedges that would grow at all in the sea wind, Gaay said. The crushed leaves gave off a bitter smell if you tried to crawl your way between the stems, but the foliage was so thick it was impossible to get through to the field alongside the house where there was a hut in which a band used to practise on Sunday evenings. Sometimes the band would come out and march along the road, playing 'Donall Abú' and 'Buachallaí Loch Gharmain'. They were young soldiers of the Irish Army. My Killen grandmother said that scrawny youths like them wouldn't have much chance against Mr Hitler if he decided to invade Ireland at Greystones beach.

In Greystones I went to Miss Hanna's school on Church

Road with my neighbour, Ruth Reid. There were five other children and we sat round a table covered with a green cloth. We wrote out our numbers and the alphabet in coloured crayons and built houses with dominoes. Miss Hanna had an incubator in her scullery and, if spoken to nicely, she would lift off the cloth that kept out the draught and let us see the yellow chickens clustering comfortably round their red lamp, cheeping in a contented kind of way. Sometimes she would put her hand in and pick one out for us to touch, but she never let any of us hold one because they were such delicate little things it would be all too easy to squash them by mistake. At half past twelve my mother came with Nicky-Bill in a pushcart and we walked home, or sometimes Mrs Reid sat me on the saddle of her bicycle while she walked and Ruth pedalled along on her tricycle. We passed Mrs Beckett's pink-tiled house that Mrs Reid called 'the house of seven gables' on the corner of Portland Road, and if Mrs Beckett was in her garden she often asked us in to see her birds.

We knew Peggy Beckett because she was the aunt of a sculptor called Hilary Heron who lived near Whinsfield. Gaay told my other granny that the Becketts and Herons were an artistic bunch. She considered this strange because they came from wealthy business families who played rugby and tennis as if their survival depended on it and all the talk was of the Yacht Club and the Motor Show. She wondered how the artistic strain had managed to clamber out from under all that Philistinism. 'At the time when I was secretary of the United Arts Club in Dublin, people like Mr and Mrs Yeats and Mr George Russell would have laughed at the very *idea* of a Beckett or a Heron producing a work of art – it would be like expecting a concerto to be written by a Cosgrave or a de Valera!' My Killen grandmother said she supposed it took all sorts, but she agreed that politicians tended to be a trifle uncouth.

Peggy Beckett wore long, filmy dresses of petunia or mauve or lilac; gossamer scarves wafted from her neck, clinging to the fabric of her dress as she moved. Her fingernails were painted in the same colours. The best thing was her aviary. She had parakeets and canaries that swooped about in a netted enclosure in the garden. When I got tired of playing with my bricks on the veranda at Arc-en-Ciel, or pulling the huge snails off the cauliflower leaves in the garden – they would cling on till you pulled harder and then come away with a satisfying plop – I would ask whatever adult was present if I could go to see Mrs Beckett, and I'd be told yes, but not to stay too long or I wouldn't be welcome again; but it was the birds I wanted to see. Mrs Beckett had a grown-up son called John who was constantly playing the piano – from three or four houses away in St Vincent's Road you could hear the trills as his hands raced up and down the keys, mingling with the twittering of the birds in the summer air. Sometimes his cousin Sam would be there and they'd play duets, but more often Sam kept to himself, especially if there were visitors, sitting in a corner of the garden in a deck-chair, peering through his dark-rimmed glasses at a book, or scribbling words on a scrap of paper.

At the end of the summer my mother and I returned to Whinsfield while Nicky-Bill went with our other grandparents to stay with Zane at Eldron. There was a school in the Carnegie Library in Dundrum run by a lady called Miss Carroll, who had a face like a permanently annoyed pug. I was taken to meet her and she agreed that I should be enrolled as a pupil. Each class sat around a table in a big hall. I would be in the lowest class, nearest to the door, and if I *worked very hard* I would be moved to the next table to join Mervyn Hayes. Professor Hayes had three children, Robert, Joan and Mervyn; they lived near Whinsfield on the Gullet road and the professor – who could speak five languages – drove his children to school in the morning, stopping at Whinsfield to take me on board. Everyone had to bring a sandwich and some milk in a bottle; mine was a Worcester sauce bottle with a little glass stopper that fascinated a classmate called Dorothy – she called it 'Mr Man' and made him walk over all the sandwiches and books and pencil-cases. I did not think this was the right thing to do but I did not say so because she and her friend Glenn said they were the Rulers of the Table and the rest of us had to do what they commanded. One day they said they were Hitler. With some misgiving I brought myself to tell them that *two* people could not be Hitler, to which Dorothy replied that they both *were* Hitler and if I didn't like it they'd tell Miss Carroll that I'd wet the floor of the cloakroom one day because I hadn't been able to get to the lavatory in time. So they were Hitler.

When I told this to Mister and Gaay they agreed that two people could not *possibly* be Hitler – Dorothy and Glenn must be very silly to think so, and I should take no notice of them.

'And what kind of a name is that?' Mister asked. 'Glenn? You might as well call your unfortunate child Valley or Mountain. Take no notice of a child with a name like that. He can't be any good, nor the people he comes from!'

All the same, I did not relish having to sit opposite them in class, and I would keep looking out of the window when it was coming up to one o'clock, hoping to see the maroon Ford that was my getaway car, with my grandmother at the wheel.

On Fridays we were visited in school by an elderly clergyman who called the fire – in front of which he stood to address the whole assembly – the 'farr'. We learned prayers and listened to his droning voice telling us about the 'muracles' performed by Our Lord: He turned water into wine and also walked on water. I thought I might try this on the pond at Whinsfield but only succeeded in getting my gymshoes and socks wet, and when I blessed the water in the glass jug on the dining-room table it remained as clear as when Eileen had drawn it from the kitchen tap. One Friday this clergyman told us to learn the verse of a hymn for next week. When the time came everyone seemed to have forgotten his instruction. 'Have none of you taken the trouble to larn a single vairse?' he enquired, visibly wounded. I had learned a hymn at Smithborough Presbyterian Church ages and ages ago so I put up my hand and said, 'Yes!' He told me to recite it.

> *Do no sinful action,*
> *Speak no angry word;*
> *Ye belong to Jesus,*
> *Children of the Lord.*

I made some hesitations and mistakes so that Dorothy and Glenn would not call me a swot.

> *There's a wicked spirit,*
> *Watching round you still,*
> *And he tries to tempt you*
> *To all harm and ill . . .*

It seemed from the bored faces of the other pupils that I was going on too long so I said that was all I'd had time to learn, and sat down. The clergyman said, 'Amen!' and told the others they should follow my good example. Dorothy and Glenn did not call me a swot: they called me a goody-goody, which was much worse.

My grandmother was cutting Michaelmas daisies for the altar at Kilternan Church when Mister called out that war had been declared. She and I came in through the french windows. The wireless was on the piano and Mister was standing beside it. He told us that Britain was at war with Germany – 'and only twenty years after the last war! Wouldn't you think they'd have learned a lesson from that?' My grandmother said it might not affect us, because Mr de Valera wouldn't want to join the British but certainly wouldn't go in with Germany either. 'And what about Manners? Gladys will have to be told.'

When my mother came in from taking Roy for a walk she said she'd known all along that this was coming, but that didn't make it any better. Mister said that Hitler had only invaded Poland, and what everyone was saying was probably true, that being so far away in Palestine, Manners was in the safest possible place. My mother went upstairs, 'to write letters'.

There were announcements on the wireless telling everyone never to show a light at night – 'It's only a precaution,' Mister said. The street-lamps in Sandyford stopped coming on and my grandmother said it was really quite like the old times before the days of electricity. She went into Dublin and bought yards of black material, which she made into curtains on her sewing-machine, and I helped her to thread them on to rings and hang them on bamboo rods. Every night when it began to grow dark my job was to go into all the rooms to pull the black curtains across to make sure that not a chink of light would get out; we never turned on the hall light because Hitler's warplanes might see it through the glass roof. Men came to the school and painted all the windows of the hall and passages a very dark green, which was supposed to be better than black, and the Carnegie librarian arranged for big frames covered in black paper to be made, and these were clipped into place over the classroom windows at what Miss Carroll called 'lighting-up time'.

One morning my grandmother said she had heard an aeroplane in the night, so she switched off her bedside lamp and peeped out through a chink in the curtains. At the same moment she noticed that Mrs Huggard on the Gullet road had turned on her light, the better to observe the plane, she supposed. No plane was seen, but when my grandmother was delivering a half-dozen eggs to Mrs Huggard next day she took it upon herself to mention that if you wanted to see what was in the sky at night you should turn *off* your lights and it was really quite dangerous to leave them on, for these Nazis would drop their bombs wherever they saw even a glimmer – 'and we don't want Sandyford to become a bomb-site, do we?' It was clear from the silence that followed that Mrs Huggard was not a bit pleased with the advice.

My other evening ritual was to press the handle of the soda-water siphon that stood beside Mister's bottle of whiskey and fill a brass measure with fizzy water, which I poured into his glass. Then I filled a measure of soda-water for myself, drinking it quickly before the bubbles went away. Sometimes, 'for a treat', I was allowed to stay up for dinner. My grandmother always had a bottle of Guinness's stout; she said it was what kept her going. My mother hated even the smell of stout, but sometimes she had a glass of sherry. No one at

Eldron ever had these kind of drinks – the only alternative
to tea was cocoa.

After the coal supplies from England stopped, because of
the war, Gaay arranged with a man in a lorry to deliver turf
from our banks on Glencullen mountain, which he'd dump
in a shed next to Flavin's pub in Sandyford. There was a big
boy called Alan Geraghty whom she used to consult about
which families were in most need of fuel, because she didn't
like the idea of going round the cottages herself – 'in case
I took on the appearance of Lady Bountiful, which I certainly
am not for I've hardly any more money to scrape together
in my purse than the people who are known as "the poor"'.
She said it was just fortunate that we still owned some land,
and even if it was poor land it did produce 'that most valuable commodity, the sod of turf'. She gave out these sods to
the people of the village, who came once a week with bags
and wheelbarrows and even old prams to collect as much as
they could carry.

My mother posted letters to Palestine in the green letterbox
at Sandyford Corner, often remarking that they might never
get there because of the upset to shipping in the Mediterranean.
We looked for Palestine on the map and she explained that
Mussolini's ships might intercept the British ones and the
letters would be thrown away if the ships were captured – or
the ships might even be sunk. I pictured all the letters floating
on the sea. She had snapshots of me and my father in India,
which she often showed me, but there were none from
Mount Louise so I could not really imagine what my father
was like now, though I didn't tell her that. My grandmother
said that the Reverend Peters in Kilternan Church had said
prayers for soldiers, seamen and airmen and for all those who
travelled by land, air or water, and Mister was quite surprised

when Father Gaffney announced at Mass in St Mary's that the prayers of the faithful were offered for all those engaged in the conflict in foreign parts.

Father Gaffney was a large, red-faced man who was noted for what my grandfather called his 'blood and thunder' sermons. He wore magnificent vestments that had been embroidered by the ladies of the parish and when, to the jangling of the altar-boy's bell, he raised the monstrance containing the host, it was quite an awesome moment. He always seemed to be angry about something. Everyone had to be very attentive during his sermon. Once he stopped and said, 'There's a child down there screeching: would its mother take it out immediately?' and a lady who looked really frightened scuttled out by the back door carrying a blubbing baby. We sat under a window with a picture of Jesus talking to some children. He had a blue halo round his head with a red cross on it. In a panel at the foot of the window a priest was giving first communion to some other children – he looked much milder than Father Gaffney, which was probably why the children didn't look frightened. All around the church were carved and painted Stations of the Cross, which told the story of the scourging of Jesus and the Crucifixion – much more absorbing than the feeble pictures in the window.

In the church porch there were shelves with books, post-cards and calendars beside the font where I'd been baptized. That had been in June 1934, Mister said. He bought me a little book called *The Penny Catechism*, which had pictures in it rather like the ones in the window. 'We had a priest called Father Lambe then, quite different from Father Gaffney. In fact, his name was like his nature. Your dad and mam were here and your mam's friend Miss Wadsworth was your godmother, and your dad's brother Tib was your godfather.

Then we all went back to Whinsfield where your grandmother had tea waiting for us. Your uncle Tib is now
studying to be a monk at Mount St Mary's in Milltown, did
you know?'

I learned some of the catechism. 'Who made the world?
– God made the world. Can God do all things? – God can
do all things, for He is almighty. Where is God? – God is
everywhere. If God is everywhere, why do we not see Him?
– We do not see God because He is a spirit.' We did not
see Santa Claus coming down the chimmney at Eldron, so
he must be a spirit too, I thought. Perhaps it is God who
comes down the chimney and not Santa Claus at all; but
God looked very different from the Santa Claus who had
stepped through the window at Mount Louise – for one
thing He did not wear a red costume, and for another He
was always swirling about in clouds and you never saw more
of Him than his face and beard and sometimes His arms if
He was wielding a compass or bolts of lightning. I thought
Jesus had a rather stupid face in *The Penny Catechism* but I
didn't say so.

The two Miss Overends, Naomi and Tottie, who lived at
Airfield House in Dundrum, organized classes in 'First Aid
for the Injured', which my mother and grandmother and a
large number of neighbours attended. They brought home
a little black book printed by the St John's Ambulance Brigade
with pictures showing how to make splints and tie them on
to wounded people's legs and arms, and how to cut slings
out of cloth if there were no bandages handy, and how to
lift people on to stretchers without hurting them. My grandmother said that Hilary Heron, who was used to rolling great
lumps of wood around her studio and chiselling big slabs of
marble, would hardly get first prize for her gentle treatment
of the maimed, for in spite of her slim figure and elegant

posture she had muscles like a man – 'and she'd do better than me lifting a corpse any day'.

When one of Mr Hitler's planes dropped its bombs on Ballybough on the north side of Dublin none of the ladies who were being trained by the Misses Overend were called upon to help; in fact, they did not even hear of the incident, in which twenty people were killed, until they read the papers next day. The fire brigade and the army had dealt with the emergency most effectively, the paper said. Mister thought that the efforts of the Misses Overend, though no doubt most public-spirited, were perhaps not exactly what was needed. He said the air raid was probably Mr Hitler's revenge on Mr de Valera for keeping Ireland out of the war. Gaay thought the bombing of Ballybough could have been a mistake – the pilot might have lost his way.

'How could he lose his way?' said Mister. 'Do you think he wouldn't have proper instruments of navigation up there in that yoke?'

'He might have been confused and thought he was over Liverpool – or Belfast.'

'Liverpool or Belfast me backside!' said Mister. 'Those cities are well blacked-out. Dublin's only half blacked-out because, as usual, the people here are half-baked and don't do what they're told. You may be sure there'll be more of this.' He turned to my mother. 'It's what I said: Manners is much safer out there in Palestine. The real danger zone is Dublin!'

## Annaghmakerrig, Newbliss, County Monaghan

'What a pity Annaghmakerrig is such an ugly house!' my mother said, as Davy McMahon eased the Eldron Ford around the semi-circular curve of the front avenue – which I later came to know as the Half Moon – disclosing in turn three sides of the massive building as well as the great lake, a mile long and a quarter-mile wide, over which the house kept watch.

Coming from Whinsfield, we had spent some weeks at Eldron, where Nicky-Bill was still living with Zane and our Killen grandparents, while my mother made plans with Peggy Butler for us to live at Annaghmakerrig and share a governess 'for the duration of the war' – those words were always said when no one seemed quite sure about how long something was going to last. We were to be 'paying guests', though Peggy often used the word 'lodgers' in the kind of voice I knew was meant to be a joke. My mother said that the twenty-five shillings Peggy charged for her and the twelve-and-sixpence for me was really quite reasonable, but she didn't yet know if that included laundry.

I had been to Annaghmakerrig several times from Eldron. We were related to Peggy's mother, Mrs Guthrie, 'through the Fosters and Mooreheads', my mother said. 'We're connections, you see, not relations, but there were always lots of comings and goings between the two houses, so we know the Guthries much better than we know many of our cousins – and here we are.'

I thought the house looked like some kind of palace in a picture-book – something that had been placed on the top of a hill by an unseen hand and might just as easily be snatched away again. The front door was definitely palatial, immensely tall with iron loops instead of handles, and I remembered my first visit to a Christmas party when I'd thought that as this portal slowly scrunched open it might reveal either a dwarf or a giant, depending upon whether a servant or the owner was coming out to greet us. On this occasion it was scrunched open by the bustling parlourmaid, Chrissie Morgan, who said she was delighted to see us, and went to look for Mrs Guthrie because Mrs Butler had gone out along the Oak Walk with the children to gather kindling for the fire – 'and they have the wee Chinese dog along with them, oh, a real terror he is!'

Mrs Guthrie went up the stairs ahead of us to show us the Blue Room. She said everyone called her 'Mrs G' and we were to do the same. I remembered that she was blind and that she knew the house and garden so well that she sensed where everything was; she could make out shapes and could see the white blob of her Scottish terrier, Betsy, who always walked in front of her. In our room there was a high bed with a white canopy covered with blue dots and a small bed beside it. Near the door was a marble washstand with a jug of water, a basin, a soap-dish, a toothbrush-holder and a slop-pail, all with a pattern of roses, and a po to match in a little cupboard by the bed. On the top of a mahogany wardrobe a porcelain cat gazed out of the windows towards the Oak Walk. I said I had never seen a yellow cat with a blue face before, and Mrs G agreed that it was certainly rather odd. She told my mother that her son Tony thought the cat looked like the actress Diana Wynyard.

'Tony's producing plays all the time now for the Old Vic theatre,' she said. She turned to me. 'That's in London.' She said he had decided to do *Hamlet* with a very young actor called Guinness – 'such a nice young man, no relation of the Dublin brewing family' – and had brought him to Annaghmakerrig to rehearse some of the scenes in the big End Room so as to give him confidence before meeting the more experienced players. She'd had a letter from Tony saying that young Alec had turned out to be much, much better than Larry Olivier in the part, but the audiences weren't coming in to see him. Mrs G said they must be very stupid – real stick-in-the-mud people for not wanting to see the play in modern dress. 'Tony likes to do things differently – to give the people an opportunity of witnessing something unexpected.'

Over the chimney-piece there was a notice carved in old-fashioned writing: 'From the old house at ...' Mrs G seemed surprised that I could read it and I said I could read everything except the next word. '"Philadelphia",' she said. 'Some of my Moorehead ancestors went to America and when Annaghmakerrig was being enlarged in the 1860s one of them brought over this chimney-piece from the house where they'd settled in Pennsylvania.'

Mrs G said she would leave us to do our unpacking, and then we should explore outside. I asked my mother why Mrs G was so annoyed about the play.

'Mrs G hates to hear about things going wrong for Tony.

She's always very cross when there are criticisms of him in the papers. *Hamlet* is a very old play, written by a man called Shakespeare when ladies wore wide dresses with jewelled ruffs and men wore puffy breeches and cloaks – like Queen Elizabeth and Sir Walter Ralegh in the picture-book.' She added that she would certainly be in two minds about buying tickets for *Hamlet* if it was done in modern dress and not in clothes to match the time when it was supposed to have taken place.

At the back of the house there was a courtyard with a circular pond, and then the buildings stretched on towards the farmyard, with people living in what seemed to be separate houses. All the doors and window-frames were painted red. My mother said that when she was a child the woodwork had been dark green, which made the house look very gloomy indeed – it was Peggy Butler who had convinced her mother that bright red against the grey limestone would be much livelier, especially in winter. The farmyard had an inner yard, with a big byre for about twenty cows, and a calf-house with calves in it, and a cart-shed where, as well as an orange and blue farm cart, there was a hay-buggy, a spring-cart, a pony-trap and a side-car. 'I haven't seen one of those old side-cars for years!' my mother said. 'I don't imagine they still use it. They were also known as "Irish jaunting cars" – you used to see them illustrated in old stories.' A belfry sat on the roof of one of the buildings. 'All big farms had a bell that used to be rung to bring the men from the fields in to their dinner – but I don't imagine that's used any more either.'

We walked round to the front of the house from where you could see the lake, brimming in its trough of wooded hills. I'd noticed hundreds of little Christmas trees growing on the slopes as we approached Annaghmakerrig; my mother said that this was Hubert Butler's idea, the beginning of a forestation plan, and if we came back in thirty years' time we'd find a huge forest of conifers, which would be felled by degrees and new trees planted – much more money-making than trying to grow oats or barley on the wet Monaghan soil. The reason Hubert was away a lot at present was that he was helping people to escape from the Nazis, who were the nastiest kind of people you could possibly imagine.

Then we saw Peggy and Julia coming from the Oak Walk with a lady who turned out to be Julia's nurse, Florrie Morgan, and a boy of about Nicky-Bill's age called Joe Hone. They had a tiny dog with its tail growing in a curl over its back. The dog's name was Pin Win; he was a Pekinese and had come from Hubert's home in Kilkenny as a present for Julia. I didn't know what I should say to all these people so I didn't say anything.

We had our meals in the Servants' Hall, which Hubert and Peggy had just finished painting in buttercup yellow and had decided to rename the Breakfast Room. There were pottery bowls with swirly patterns that might or might not be meant to be flowers, which Peggy said she had chosen on a stall in Dubrovnik. Sometimes she wore a blouse all covered in embroidery, which was what Croatian peasants wore. Julia had been to those places, but she couldn't remember them, like I couldn't remember India. In the kitchen there was a huge iron range that was constantly being stoked with wood and turf by the cook, Ellie Scollins, who was also constantly to be seen stirring cauldrons of mutton stew and large pots of tapioca pudding. On Sundays we joined Mrs G, with her companion and housekeeper Miss Worby, for lunch in the dining room: this was because Ellie and Chrissie had alternate

Sundays off and Miss Worby said you couldn't reasonably expect one person to manage two dining rooms at the same time, even though my mother and Peggy helped. Peggy was in charge of the catering for our half of the house and Miss Worby for the main house, but Miss Worby was the one who decided all the important things, and it was she who supervised the weekly shopping list for Carnew's grocery in Cootehill, and she who ordered each day's vegetables from the kitchen-garden.

Miss Worby said that anyone who called Mrs Guthrie 'Mrs G' must, as a matter of course, call her 'Bunty', a kind of pet name given to her because, my mother supposed, she was 'of somewhat small stature'. She had been a nurse at the hospital in Tunbridge Wells that Dr Guthrie had founded, and when he died and Mrs G was going blind she had been engaged to come to Annaghmakerrig as a lady's companion. Her hair was of a sandy colour – 'Very Anglo-Saxon,' said my mother – and she dressed in merging shades of fawn, beige, buff, oatmeal, *café-au-lait* and biscuit. If she had lain down by the seaside she might easily have been taken for a dune. She helped Mrs G with her typewriting and read out the letters and the news in the *Irish Times* every morning after her conference with the cook, then both ladies took up their knitting-needles to make thick pullovers and stockings for the soldiers and sailors who were fighting in the war.

After Bunty had written the day's menu on a slate, Ellie opened the window in the back corridor and blew a whistle. Presently the gardener, John McGahey, would appear and be told if it was cabbages or turnips today and to be sure to fill up the big basket with spuds, for there were eighteen mouths to feed and it would be worse when the new lot that Primrose Morgan was talking about would be coming and that would make it '*Twenty-one* – can you beat that for a crowd to cook for?' said Ellie, casting her eyes dolefully up to heaven.

Next to the kitchen there was a scullery and next to it the still-room (always locked) where Bunty kept the bottled gooseberries, plums and greengages that were labelled and stored for winter. There were smaller jars of raspberry, strawberry, blackcurrant and blackberry jam, as well as crocks of eggs preserved in isinglass. A covered passage called Bob's Entry – because that was where Bob Burns presided over the turf and logs and the oil for the lamps – led past sundry storerooms to the outside world that continued with the terrace of houses that contained the dairy, the laundry, the ironing room and then the Daley family's house, which you approached through an arch called Daley's Entry. The Daley girls, as I quickly discovered, lived here with their parents – Eddie, the farm steward, and Mammy Daley, whose real name was Annie and who looked after the dairy. Beyond this was further evidence of Bob's domain: Bob's Motorhouse in which sat Mrs G's green Austin – beautifully polished by Bob, using a tin of Simoniz that smelled of sweet new leather – and Hubert and Peggy's grey Morris, which no one bothered to polish at all. There was also a stone trough known as Bob's Tank in which rainwater was collected for washing the Austin, and it was colonized by a family of frogs. 'Poor things!' exclaimed Bunty. 'Doomed to spend their whole lives in Bob's Tank!' We released some of their number from time to time, though there always seemed to be others coming along whatever the time of year. Bob said they had their own way of getting in and out.

Bob Burns had come from Newbliss village as chauffeur, then married the housemaid, Mary Morgan, sister of Chrissie, Florrie and Primrose. The Morgan girls lived in a house seven miles away at Clontivrim, right on the border. The front door opened into County Monaghan and the back bedroom window into Fermanagh. Sometimes Free State Customs inspectors would come to check if there were any 'contraband goods' in the house, but they never looked into the bedroom because they knew it was situated in Northern Ireland and was therefore outside the scope of their investigation. If anyone in the North, or in England, wanted to send a parcel to Annaghmakerrig but did not want it to be opened and inspected by the Customs they would address it in care of Mrs Morgan but at her Northern Ireland address, and the Royal Mail postman would deliver it, presumably through the bedroom window. Then a message would be sent to Annaghmakerrig and whoever was next passing that way would pick it up – via the front door.

It was through the Morgan family that Jennifer Cullen and her baby sister Pamela joined the household of paying guests. Jennifer and Pamela's parents were in the Sudan, and Primrose Morgan was helping to look after them at their granny's house in Belfast. Primrose spoke of the arrangements at Annaghmakerrig as reported by her sisters and so the granny, who was becoming nervous about the German air raids, came by train to speak to Peggy.

'She was quite snooty about the *disloyal* Free State,' said Peggy to my mother, as she waved goodbye to her visitor in the taxi for Newbliss station, 'but evidently she thinks we're *respectable* enough for her grandchildren to mix with and the promise of a *trained* governess seems to have impressed her.' And so it was that Julia and I were joined by Jennifer, who was six, like me, but had no difficulty in settling in among strangers. I began to think no one had noticed that I found these new people intimidating, but Jennifer was not intimidated at all. 'I think she's going to be a bit of a bossy-boots,' said Peggy.

After some weeks Nicky-Bill, who had now become plain Nicky, arrived from Eldron and he and Joe Hone immediately became friends. Joe, my mother told me, was living with the Butlers because his mother (like the old woman who lived in a shoe) could not look after all of her children herself. I envied Nicky and Joe, for they did not have to take lessons with Miss Roberts, who arrived one evening in the Newbliss taxi, complaining of the discomfort of the train from Dublin, the differences between Dublin and Paris (to Dublin's marked disadvantage), the absence of cafés, observed as she passed through Newbliss, and the weather.

Hubert Butler said that Miss Roberts had lived in Paris until the outbreak of war and was taking refuge with us in County Monaghan. Refuge, I supposed, from something she didn't like, and my mother explained that Hubert was working very quietly with 'the Quakers' to help people on the continent who were in difficulties. Fairly soon it became clear that she didn't like us either. Every morning Julia, Jennifer and I had to be seated at a small table in Peggy and Hubert's sitting room at a minute before ten o'clock. We had to have our exercise books open where we had left off the previous day; our pencils must be arranged parallel to our books, rubbers and pencil-sharpeners must be in a neat formation before us. Rubbers – Miss Roberts called them 'erasers' – were viewed with disdain because she believed they encouraged incorrect writing; one should always be correct the first time and, in any case, they left an unpleasing *smudge*.

At ten o'clock Miss Roberts entered, usually carrying a shawl because, as she said, she found the room grew somewhat chilly when Florrie Morgan neglected to put more wood on the fire, which was almost always. Florrie whispered that Miss Roberts could throw a log on the fire herself if she'd rouse herself up from her chair; she also said that Miss Roberts dyed her hair, because she had seen a dark bottle with a label in a foreign language on the washstand in the White Room. I looked at Miss Roberts's hair, which was a kind of chestnut colour, but it was impossible to know if it was dyed or not, and from the secretive sort of way Florrie had disclosed this information to her sister Primrose during an afternoon walk to Miss Reilly's post office at Doohat, I knew better than to ask.

'*Bonjour, mes élèves!*' declared Miss Roberts, announcing her entrance at ten o'clock.

'*Bonjour, Mademoiselle!*' we replied in chorus.

'*Comment allez-vous ce matin?*'

'*Très bien, merci, Mademoiselle. Et vous?*'

Miss Roberts replied in English that she was in reasonably good health, thank you, considering the Circumstances, whatever these might have been. She liked using long words that took us some time to understand. When we did Physical Jerks she said, 'Commence!' when she meant 'Begin'. My mother told me this was probably because the French for 'Begin' was '*Commencez.*' (My mother recalled that, when she was at school in Switzerland, she had started to dream in French after about six months, which showed how another language could take over the way you thought; Miss Roberts was probably still thinking – and dreaming – in French.)

We soon found that Miss Roberts did not enjoy country walks. Things seemed to go wrong when she was in charge of our trudges to the post office or to Mrs Hall's shop or to old Susan Atty McKenna's with a can of milk. At the White Gate Lodge Mary Burns's flock of hens roamed freely, scratching and pecking in the mossy sheughs. The Pekinese dog, Pin Win, took delight in running among them, and one afternoon a skittery white Leghorn took fright and made for the supposed safety of the rhododendrons, cackling in a most provocative way. This was too much for Pin Win, who pursued her mercilessly. There was a lot of barking and cackling, and then Pin Win emerged from the bushes with the hen in his mouth. We were all quite upset – 'The *poor* hen! *Naughty Pinny!*' – but none more so than Miss Roberts, who demanded to know who was the owner of *cette poule malheureuse*? We made a little procession to the door of the Lodge where, all talking together, we explained the fate of the hen to Mrs Burns, who surveyed the scene with a thunderous look on her face. She said nothing, but bent to pick up the hen, which Pin Win had placed neatly on her doorstep as if it were the altar in a Chinese temple. Mrs Burns was perhaps considering that the corpse might be saved for soup, but Pin Win clearly had second thoughts about his offering to the spirits of his ancestors and snatched it back from her, disappearing forthwith into the innermost confines of a thicket.

A donkey called Sugar Spice had been borrowed from a neighbour. It was thought that its presence might make our afternoon outings more diverting. Sugar Spice, however, displayed no inclination to walk further than Daley's Entry. Miss Roberts prodded him with her cane, while standing back as far as she could in case of an accident. Florrie Morgan said what the ass needed was a good skelp with a sally-rod, but there were no sallys growing nearby. Miss Roberts then pulled on the halter while the rest of us shouted, 'Shoo!' from behind, and in about an hour we had succeeded in travelling a quarter-mile along the Doohat avenue, after which the expedition was abandoned, the day's letters remained unposted, and Miss Roberts declared that her shoes were beyond salvation.

'I don't think the donkey likes you, Miss Roberts,' said Jennifer, to which Miss Roberts muttered something about *cette bête affreuse* and withdrew to wipe her shoes with a chamois cloth. Florrie said that no one in their right mind would go out in shoes the like of *those*, with their high heels and their fancy laces. Some weeks later, when Julia failed to recite her multiplication tables correctly, even after writing them out in her jotter, Miss Roberts sent her out into the corridor, where my mother discovered her in tears. For the next few days Miss Roberts was unusually tight-lipped and her punishments dwindled from learning long, boring poems to standing for five minutes in the corner. We sensed that something had been said, and this was confirmed by the talk in the kitchen where the Morgan girls always knew what was going on in the front part of the house, which we rarely visited – 'But all the same,' said Chrissie, 'she played bridge last night in the drawing room so they can't be out with her entirely.'

It had evidently been agreed that Miss Roberts need not go for walks, because henceforth she remained in her room 'studying literature' in the afternoons, but when Peggy asked her to undress Julia as Florrie had gone over to Clontivrim to see Mammy Morgan, she announced in front of us all that she was 'not engaged as a nurserymaid'. Next day Peggy cycled to Clones to arrange with Mrs Baldwin Murphy for us to join the dancing class she organized there, reporting to my mother on her return that Mrs Murphy's husband, a solicitor, had told her it was very dangerous to dismiss a person when there was no written agreement. The words 'breach of promise' were used. Peggy and my mother looked perplexed, and next morning there were no lessons because Miss Roberts was in bed with '*la grippe*'.

'Do put on your best halo and go up to the White Room

to ask if *poor* Miss Roberts would like some more Farola pudding,' Peggy said to me. So alarmed was I at the idea of seeing Miss Roberts in bed – she might be wearing a nightcap like the wolf who ate Red Riding Hood's grandmother – that I stood for what I considered to be a plausible length of time outside her door, then came downstairs to say, 'She doesn't.' A few days later we were told that Miss Roberts was much better and had left for Dublin as she was not really a *country* person, and we would shortly be joined by Lilias Mitchell, who was much younger, and whose brother Frank, the archaeologist, we had met some months previously when he had come to dig for the remains of the Monaghan mammoth in the bog.

Lilias Mitchell had finished her art studies in Dublin and was wondering if she should be a sculptor or a weaver. She rolled back the carpet in the White Room and spent the afternoons knocking splinters off a big flat piece of wood with a hammer and chisel. She said it was 'St Francis and the Birds', but I couldn't see anything until one day she drew her finger along the surface – she called it a *bas-relief* – and suddenly I saw what it was and wondered how I could possibly have failed to make out the emerging shapes. Lilias said we should all do pictures of our favourite saints in crayon or watercolour, so I used my new paintbox to make a picture of St Patrick with his sheep on Slemish Mountain. Hubert said we looked like apprentice artists in a Renaissance studio – in Florence, perhaps – and Annaghmakerrig should be divided into a number of rooms, each one containing a person illuminating a manuscript or embroidering a tapestry, and we should make our own pigments and spin our own wool.

Every Wednesday at half past twelve we went down to

the big drawing room with Lilias to hear Miss Anne Driver in *Music and Movement* on the BBC – 'Now, children, here is your uncle Humphrey, and he's going to sing a lovely song all about an Esquimeau child on Baffin Island dreaming of the melting snow and the coming of spring' – and after we had listened to Uncle Humphrey, Miss Driver would tell us to 'Spread out!' as the piano went tinkle-tinkle-tinkle. When we weren't imagining we were pixies in a wood, we were lupins in a herbaceous border. At exactly one o'clock my mother and Peggy would come in with Mrs G and Bunty to hear the news on the wireless, and we had to leave the room very quietly because there were important things they had to know about the War.

All the talk in the Daleys' house was of Mr Hitler's invasion. Tank traps – cement pillars like gateposts connected with a lot of barbed wire – appeared on the street at Newbliss. Eddie Daley said that any German soldier in a tank would have no difficulty in leaving the road, driving into a person's garden and back out on to the road again – and then where would we be? Bob Burns had heard that the invasion would come across the border from Fermanagh and the tanks would be British and it would be up to them to stop the Germans getting here in the first place. Whichever way it would be, they agreed that the Irish Army had made fools of themselves by building such totie wee tank traps there on the street.

Uncle Marcus and Aunt Mat Killen came to tea and said that the safest place to be was the west coast of Ireland because that was the furthest location from which an invasion could possibly take place, whether German or British. The news was all about the Battle of Britain and how hundreds of young pilots were distinguishing themselves shooting down Mr Hitler's planes before they could even get near the cliffs of Dover – but then, my uncle said, you couldn't possibly estimate how long they could keep this up. Peggy knew an artist called Mrs Barnet who had a cottage in Connemara – as far away as you could possibly get – and it was through her that a large house was found by the beach on Ballyconneely Bay. It was decided that we should all join up and go and stay there, at least till the outcome of the Battle of Britain was clearer.

The Butlers, with Florrie, and the Killens, with their maid Kathleen, went on ahead because they had cars. They were to be joined by the Perrys – Betty Perry was a schoolfriend of my mother who now lived in Offaly with her husband Phil, a miller, their daughter Sarah and Sarah's baby brother David – and, of course, the Perrys could not go anywhere without Nanny Perry. Primrose Morgan was left behind at Annaghmakerrig to look after Pamela – the fact was they couldn't be fitted into the Morris, even though Hubert decided to stay behind too because of his work, so Peggy set off with Florrie and Julia, Jennifer and Joe wedged among the bundles of sheets and blankets and the baskets of cabbages and apples in the back.

There were fewer trains than there used to be 'because of the war', and my mother found that in order to travel the 150 miles to Connemara we would have to stay a night in Galway. Bob left us to Cavan station, where we got a slow train to Mullingar. Then we changed into an even slower one.

When we arrived in Galway the Killens were already at the Imperial Hotel, and Nicky and I had great fun with John and Margaret, running up and down the corridors and shouting, '*Boo!*' at the man who was called the Boots, until Mat came upstairs and asked had we no sense at all, tormenting an unfortunate fellow like that? Next day a rickety red bus took three hours to deliver us to Clifden, where Mat was waiting in their Vauxhall. She told us that the Butlers and Perrys had already arrived in Ballyconneely and were deciding who should have which room; it appeared that there was no place for Nanny Perry to sleep and this was causing some *friction*. Mat wasn't sure if Florrie could crush in with Julia, Jennifer and Joe, but fortunately she had found a bed for Kathleen in the room she had quickly picked for John and Margaret. She said that as we didn't have either a nursemaid or a cook she had put our name on a little green room off the lounge-hall where there were two beds, and Nicky would sleep in a cot.

The Lodge, Ballyconneely, was a big bungalow with two bedrooms in the attic and two extensions with several rooms that had been added at the time when it had been a guest-house. Somehow everyone was fitted in, though when we arrived Nanny Perry was muttering darkly that a room under the eaves, which you had to reach by a ladder from the scullery, wasn't what she was used to and Florrie agreed conspiratorially that it was not a bit like Annaghmakerrig (it was not) and wasn't it a terrible long way to go to empty the chamber-pot? Oh, a *trek*, that's what it was, Nanny Perry declared, and carrying that article in your hand through the lounge-hall to empty it would be the death of her, with everyone casting their eyes on her as she passed.

The house was surrounded by pines, bent by the Atlantic wind, and palm-trees that stood up as straight as if they had never left Africa. Across a field full of kingcups and bordered by fuchsias was the crescent of white sand that was Ballyconneely Bay. The sea had all the colours I liked best in my paintbox: blue and green and turquoise and aquamarine. Every morning as early as possible we made for the strand, nine children and whatever mother or nursemaid was 'on duty', as Nanny Perry liked to say. The only two men in the house, Phil Perry and my uncle Marcus, vanished with fishing rods and were not seen till the evening, when they returned with the boot of the car jumping with sea-trout and salmon. Boys with no shoes came to the door with a string of mush-rooms for a penny and lobsters for a shilling. 'It would be wonderful,' Peggy remarked, 'with all these *fruits-de-mer*, if you could find somewhere that actually sold a crust of *bread*' – and she was right, for there was nothing to be bought in the Ballyconneely shop but packet peas and bunches of dried onions, so there had to be frequent expeditions to Clifden for bread and butter, enough for seventeen people. My aunt Mat explained that the country people made their own bread and churned their own butter so there was no need for the shop to sell them. 'Such admirable self-sufficiency does have its drawbacks,' said Peggy.

Now, 'with the war on', you couldn't get oranges or bananas in any shop. When the supply of Annaghmakerrig apples ran out, Peggy reported that Mrs Barnet had told her the local people boiled *carraigín* moss, a kind of white seaweed, to make a delicious pudding, so Mrs Barnet was invited to show us the best pools. The *carraigín* was put in seawater on the range to boil. A kind of syrup resulted, which was then mixed with milk, and when this had cooled it turned into a pale grey jelly – 'Doubtless crammed with vitamin C,' Nanny Perry surmised. Vitamin C or no, it was the worst thing I had ever tasted – in fact, the sensation of slime running down my throat was worse than the taste. After one spoonful Jennifer was sick into her bowl (so she didn't have to eat any more) and Julia sat looking at hers for hours with tears in her eyes, until Florrie relented and said she could leave it. Sarah spent a lot of time in the lavatory and when her mother opened the door to ask if it was 'action or polly?',

Sarah replied that it was neither but she was definitely thinking of getting sick.

The food was of far greater concern than the course of the war. Nicky and I had often whinged about the fatty mutton stew at Annaghmakerrig, but Peggy invariably replied that it was 'very wholesome', and when further reluctance to eat it was shown she said we must 'eat up and be thankful!'. My mother had assured us that the cooking at Ballyconneely would be organized by 'Mat, Betty and me', but in the whole time we were there I never saw my mother in the kitchen, so it was clearly Mat and Betty who were in charge. One evening when we returned from a picnic at Manin Bay Mat started sniffing. '*What* is that dreadful smell?' she enquired of nobody in particular, and certainly there was quite a stink coming from somewhere. Mat's nose led her to the kitchen, where a huge saucepan was boiling over. 'It's that brew of Betty's!' she exclaimed, and seizing the offending pot she ran outside and emptied the contents into the ditch.

There was also a kind of undeclared war between the older and younger children. Julia, Jennifer, Sarah and I enjoyed and probably flouted the privileges of seniority. Uncle Marcus called Nicky, Joe, John and Margaret 'the underground movement' and encouraged them, I suspected, to wreck our superior plans. I wondered if he knew of the plot against knitting – an activity that Jennifer took very seriously. Encouraged by Bunty at Annaghmakerrig, she had brought a skein of dark blue wool with her and was in the process of creating a muffler that would, in time, protect the neck of a member of the Royal Navy against the rigours of the North Atlantic. When, inexplicably, her knitting could not be found, there was pandemonium. Florrie looked into every drawer and cupboard in the house, to no avail. A search party was formed, and the bushes and shrubs in the garden were combed with rakes and forks. Then Marcus happened to notice something on the roof of the bedroom extension. Jennifer immediately identified it as the half-knitted missing muffler; someone must have thrown it out of an upstairs window. We all stood speechless as Phil Perry climbed a step-ladder and descended triumphantly to have the knitting snatched by Jennifer, who set herself to counting the stitches and the needles and anything else that could be counted. There was tittering among the smaller boys.

We had no wireless, so the talk of the war around the grown-ups' dinner-table amounted to wondering about what might be going on. The *Irish Independent* was bought from time to time, but Marcus said it was so heavily censored that there was as much information about the war on the front pages as there was in the *Curley Wee and Gussie Goose* cartoon. We noticed a young man leaving his bicycle in the bracken at Doon Hill every morning, and there he sat all day looking out to sea. The postman told us he was employed to watch for German submarines and if he saw one he was to cycle to the Garda barracks in Ballyconneely where the sergeant would telephone the military in Galway sixty miles away and it was expected that by the end of the day an armoured car would be sent out. If it looked as though the invasion was on its way, one of the officers would go into Ballyconneely and ring for reinforcements.

We often looked for submarines, hoping to see a periscope on the horizon so that we would be the first to tell the man with the bicycle, in case he hadn't noticed it himself, but all we ever saw were hookers with their brown sails making for Roundstone harbour, or currachs that went out fishing from the little harbour at Bunowen, and the men who rowed them never seemed in the slightest bit afraid that they might be an easy target for a torpedo that would smash their frail.

canvas-covered craft to smithereens in an instant. 'They're not a bit bothered,' said Mat. 'In fact, they don't even know how to swim. They think it unlucky to learn. They believe that if the sea wants you it will get you in the end.'

In September we returned to Annaghmakerrig, no invasion having materialized. My uncle Marcus said that Mr Hitler, if he'd had any imagination at all, should definitely have landed at Ballyconneely and taken the whole world by surprise. My mother, Nicky and I travelled via Whinsfield, to break the journey and see our Fitz-Simon grandparents. There were very few cars in Dublin because of the shortage of petrol, and the taxis had big balloons on their roofs filled with coal gas.

This was the first of many returns to Annaghmakerrig, where we stayed sometimes for as long as a year, sometimes only for a week or two. It was now 1941, and that winter and the one after it were said to be the coldest ever known. The lake froze. Only a few very old people, like Susan Atty McKenna, who lived in a kind of witch's house on the edge of the pinewood, and Robert Potts, who was Mammy Daley's uncle, could remember that happening before. We watched the swans flying in, their great yellow feet sending up a spray of snow as they slid to rest on the unexpectedly hard surface. Word came that Mickey-Joe McGoldrick had ridden his bicycle for half a mile up the lake with no sign of the ice cracking. Then Bunty and her dog Topsy walked right across the deepest part of the lake from the boathouse to Kilmore, and that was the signal for us to clatter out on to the ice. Peggy found an old pair of skates and my mother swirled gracefully up and down in the way she had learned long ago in Switzerland, while we carried little chairs down from the house and arranged them like carriages in a train with

Peggy and Florrie pulling us along the ice on a rope. In the sunset, the snow-covered lake turned orange and the swans flew up in a great V, circling the country and looking down for a place where they could find water, the orange glow colouring their feathers.

Then we all got sick. Peggy said it couldn't be diphtheria because we'd been immunized on the day all the children in the neighbourhood came to the Annaghmakerrig pantry for Dr Costello to give injections – 'Diphtheria is deadly!' the man on the wireless was always saying, and there were notices in the post office saying the same thing – so it must be influenza, and Bunty said it was most important to keep warm because influenza could turn into pneumonia. Joe was the sickest, and Bunty stayed up all night with him for about a week. Peggy sent a telegram to Mrs Hone, and when she arrived from Dublin his temperature was 104°. Then Pamela got very ill, and Primrose Morgan was crying because Mrs Cullen would think she wasn't looking after her properly. Mrs Cullen was in Africa so Pamela's aunt Joan was sent for from Belfast. She was known to be in the Auxiliary Training Service and Primrose told Peggy to warn her on the telephone that she'd be stopped at the border if she came in British Army uniform. Peggy said she was sure she wouldn't do anything so foolish, but Primrose was really hoping she wouldn't come at all. 'Miss Worby's on the verge of collapse!' I heard Peggy telling Dr Costello, as they came up the corridor to the Blue Room, where Nicky and I were in bed and I was very sick – mainly because of the disgusting whipped-egg-and-milk drink that was meant to make me better. Dr Costello said we were so lucky that Miss Worby was a qualified nurse. He looked down our throats and made us say, 'Aah!' and then his toe kicked the po that was peeping out from under the bed and it went 'ting' and we tried not to laugh.

'This is my *hospital!*' Bunty Worby announced, bustling around the rooms, which she called her wards, imagining herself back in Tunbridge Wells. Jennifer said we must have caught the influenza from horrid Miss Roberts, but Bunty said that wasn't possible because it was months since Miss Roberts had left and, anyway, hers hadn't been the 'serious' variety; in fact, Bunty doubted that that lady had had anything wrong with her at all. Ours must have been serious because my mother was talking about taking us to Eldron to get better. Then the new cook, who had only been in the house for a few days after Ellie Scollins left – 'in a proper fury,' Bunty said, to which my mother replied, 'And who would blame her?' – got measles and had to be removed to Clones Fever Hospital in an ambulance. My mother said we'd *all* get measles now because Annaghmakerrig was a *hive* of infection, and she wrote to Zane, who wrote back to say that we should come to Eldron at once and take the New-bliss taxi in spite of the expense because there was no petrol for the Ford. Peggy didn't look at all pleased when we left, all bundled up in blankets.

At Eldron everything was calm. Swathes of snowdrops were spreading like a green and white sea under the horse-chestnut boughs and Zane said she'd give a new penny to whoever found the first crocus. Uncle Marcus came out from Monaghan and prescribed something for sore eyes, which he said we were sure to get with the measles; but the measles never came and one day Peggy came over from Annagh-makerrig on the train and she and my mother went for a walk 'to talk things over'. Zane said it was very hard on my mother because the news from Cairo, where they thought my father was now stationed, wasn't good at all at all. He was supposed to be coming home again for long leave, but that mightn't happen. I felt I ought to be more concerned,

but the fact was I had hardly given my father a minute's
thought since the day at Whinsfield ages ago when I'd told
one of my grandmother's friends that he lived in India and
was black, an error my mother corrected with a laugh that
was meant to show she wasn't annoyed or disappointed,
though I knew she was.

When we returned to Annaghmakerrig a few weeks later,
we found that everyone was better again and no one had
died. Julia, Jennifer and I started going to a dancing-class in
the Pringle Hall in Clones. A lady called Miss Dobbin came
on the train from Dublin every Wednesday and played the
piano while we marched up and down and skipped with
ropes, and after a time we started to learn real dancing, which
meant polkas and gavottes. I kept stumbling over my feet,
and when I noticed the clergyman's daughter, Dorothy
Williamson, looking at me pityingly I knew I must be the
worst dancer in the world. 'But I'm good at marching and
skipping!' I said to my mother, who kept telling me to listen
to the rhythm of the music. 'You have to be good at dancing.
If you aren't, it will stand against you when you're grown-
up.'

Mrs Black tugged the bell-rope at Aghabog Church and a
tinny sound filtered from the little belfry into the frosty
air. I sat under the window where Jesus was shown against
a purple night sky holding a lantern and knocking on a
bolted door. 'I am the light of the world!' was written on
a scroll underneath. In front of me was a brass plaque with
an inscription that said it had been erected in memory of
Sir William Tyrone Power and Dame Martha Power. I
remembered that she had been a Miss Martha Moorehead
of Annaghmakerrig and some kind of connection of my
Elliott relations at Eldron. Sir William's father had been a

famous actor called Tyrone Power, whose portrait was in the Annaghmakerrig dining room. The Reverend Crawford read the passage from St Luke's Gospel that ended with the words 'And all at once the sky was filled with angels singing "Glory to God in the highest, and on earth peace and goodwill towards men!"' The harmonium wheezed and its pedals squeaked as we sang:

> *The Shepherds had an Angel,*
> *The Wise Men had a star,*
> *But what have I, a little child*
> *To guide me home from far,*
> *As glad stars sing together,*
> *And singing angels are?*

On Christmas Eve Mrs G gave a party for the mothers and children of all the people who worked on the farm and in the garden and the forest – the Daleys, the McGormans, the McGoldricks, the Maguires, who had moved into the Doohat gate-lodge to replace the McGaheys, and people from further away whom we did not even know. All the children sat round the oblong table where there were currant scones, cream buns, chocolate éclairs, jelly cake, sponge cake, marble cake and a big Christmas cake, with a frilly paper band in red and green. Bunty and the new cook, Susan Murray, had been making preparations over weeks of stirring and kneading and baking. Mrs G sat at the round table in the window with the mothers of our guests and nibbled shortbread, while our mothers and Lilias, and Chrissie, Florrie and Primrose Morgan handed round the tea.

Then there was the Christmas tree – so tall that Brian McGoldrick had had to cut off the topmost boughs to fit it into the study. It shone with a hundred candles and the floor round its tub was piled with parcels of pullovers and gloves and scarves, which Mrs G and Bunty had spent the whole year knitting when they weren't knitting for the soldiers and sailors. Then we all went into the drawing room to play Oranges and Lemons (though there were no real oranges and lemons this year) and The Farmer Wants a Wife, and Mrs McGoldrick got pulled across the line by wee Benny Maguire and everyone cheered. Then it was time for the guests to go home, their flash-lamps flickering as they moved through the dark fir trees and the snow.

When they had gone, Lilias played the piano for carols and she said that next Christmas our fathers might be home. The night was very clear when we went out on the front steps looking across the white lawn with the black pines fringing the silver lake, and then the moon came up on Mullaghmore and over beyond McGoldricks' the star of Bethlehem shone out.

I was now seven Christmases of age.

Seaview, Murphystown, County Dublin

In June 1941 my mother took Nicky and myself to Bundoran on Donegal Bay for a fortnight. We stayed in Mrs Walmsley's guesthouse, where we were joined by our Killen grandparents. My grandmother remarked that although we were situated immediately above the pier where fishing-boats unloaded their catch every morning, Mrs Walmsley's menu did not extend further than boiled mutton with mashed potatoes and packet peas. She mentioned, in the course of a conversation that also touched upon the surprising absence of a residents' sitting room, that some *fish* would be nice *for a change*, and Mrs Walmsley said she'd think about it.

'Thinking is all she'll do,' said my grandmother, and she was right.

We were also joined by a single lady, whom my grandparents addressed as 'M' – it meant Emily. M was the daughter of the late Dean Haire-Forster and she lived in a house called Killycoonagh, which was exactly half-way between Eldron and Annaghmakerrig. She spent much of her time in a rock pool swathed in seaweed, gargling by means of a little glass

cup that she dipped into the water from time to time, swilling
the brine round her mouth and then expelling it with great
force. We hoped that if we met her on the front step of the
guesthouse she would suddenly spout water at us like a whale,
but she never did. Other residents at Mrs Walmsley's were a
Methodist minister called Mr Morris and his wife. They were
on holiday from Belfast and he was taking the Sunday service
in Bundoran for the local minister, who was away. We went
to his service but the congregation was sparse, there were
no stained-glass pictures of saints and we didn't know any
of the hymns. At Sunday Dinner afterwards Mrs Walmsley
tripped when carrying a tray into the dining room and the
mutton and mashed potatoes went on the floor, but the
minister deftly caught the dish of peas.

'Mrs Walmsley dropped the tray!' I shouted gleefully, and
was immediately shushed by mother and grandparents.

'And Mr Morris caught the peas!' replied the shocked Mrs
Walmsley, reliving the drama of the moment before elaborate
cleaning-up with cloths and basins of soapy water took place.
After a considerable time in which nobody asked what the
alternative dinner would be we were served with slices of
tinned bully-beef and a quarter tomato each.

'She could have fried up a whole shoal of herrings in half
the time,' said my grandmother.

Aeroplanes were constantly passing low over Bundoran
and we soon recognized the elegant Catalina and the
chunkier Sunderland flying-boats, as well as the Lancaster
bombers. My grandfather said it was generally known that
Mr de Valera had made a secret pact with Mr Churchill to
allow the British planes based on Lough Erne to cross the
three-mile neck of Donegal, saving them the long journey
round the north of Malin Head on their mission to guard
the Atlantic Fleet.

The Reverend Morris ventured the thought that Mr de Valera and Mr Churchill were not on speaking terms, on account of the Free State's neutrality.

'They're speaking very clearly on this topic,' said my grandfather.

'Destroying the Nazi fleet would be part of the bargain,' remarked M.

'There'd be money changing hands,' said Mr Morris, in a sneering way. 'It's well known that the Free State's bankrupt.'

'It would be money well spent, ridding the seas of those dreadful submarines,' retorted my grandmother.

My mother decided it was time she took us for a walk. She said she did not like all this talk about ships being bombed and we should put it out of our heads. At the end of a lane near the Marathon Hotel there was a notice saying that a house called Dingli Cush was for sale so we went up the lane to have a look. From the top of the incline you could see a range of mountains with flat tops and cliff-like sides.

'That's Ben Bulben,' my mother said, of the furthest mountain. 'The poet Yeats used to write about it, but he's dead now.'

We reached an old two-storeyed farmhouse and as we were about to peer through the windows a woman came out. 'Are you house-hunting?' she asked.

My mother replied that in a sort of a way she was.

'Well, come in and look,' the lady replied.

The inside was whitewashed and the doors and window-frames were painted in bright blue. The lady said she thought hand-woven tweed was the most suitable material for curtains and covers in a house of this kind, and we'd probably noticed that she'd chosen colours from the bog – purple and mauve for heather and *báinín* for bog-cotton. She said she was lucky that there was always a good supply of turf for the fire since you weren't allowed to use electricity for heating any more and the bog was only half a mile away. It was an ideal location, really, with the sea only a short walk on one side and the view of the mountains on the other.

My mother agreed that the view was perfectly heavenly. She said she hadn't actually come to Bundoran with house-hunting in mind but she was open to any suggestions, however remote. The lady said the railway was very handy, with Belfast only four hours away and Dublin five. 'And how is it you're looking for a house in the middle of the war, do you mind me asking?' she said.

'My husband's coming home. He's on the high seas this very minute.'

'And good luck to him, so,' said the lady. 'He'll need it, with all these submarines around.'

'He may not know we've sold Whinsfield,' my distraught Fitz-Simon grandmother surmised, 'so we'd better be at the Mail Boat pier in plenty of time in case he takes a taxi and goes there and gets a shock. But, then, it's very hard to know what time the Mail Boat's going to arrive with all these warnings about torpedoes.'

It was only when we were on the train from Bundoran to Dublin that my mother mentioned we weren't going to Whinsfield but to Seaview, a much smaller house that my grandparents had moved into.

'But Whinsfield's lovely!'

'I expect it was too expensive to keep up.'

'I want to go to Whinsfield!'

'We can go for a walk and look at it. Old people like to be cosier, and I believe Seaview is a cosy little place. Whinsfield was rather . . . cold.'

Seaview was only about a mile from Whinsfield. It was very small indeed, and there was no view of the sea because the ground-floor windows looked straight into a high wall that separated the house from the Kilgobbin road, and from upstairs if you looked in the direction of where you thought the sea might be the view was blocked by the trees surrounding Boss Croker's mansion, Glencairn. There was a small garden at the back, which merged into a flat, rocky landscape sprouting clumps of whin.

Mister explained that Seaview was attached to a larger house and might once have been its servants' quarters, and he showed us the outline of a door on the sitting-room wall, which had probably been the way through. A fashionable dentist known as 'the butcher Yates' lived there. Mister didn't seem to like the butcher Yates and was always making remarks about him; my mother said it was probably because Mr Yates was the landlord and expected my grandfather to be prompt with the rent. There were two rooms downstairs and two bedrooms upstairs, all of them crammed with furniture I recognized from Whinsfield. At the back there was an extension containing the kitchen and scullery and a tiny room for Bridie Donoghue, the new maid.

Gaay showed us how she had carved enough space for a bathroom out of one of the bedrooms. She was going to sleep on a divan in the sitting room and the three of us were to have her bedroom until Manners arrived, at which time our parents would go and lodge with Mrs Popham at Kilgobbin, just down the road. (My grandmother could not get out of the habit of calling my father 'Manners' when everyone now spoke of him as 'Simon'.)

We were quite near Mount Eagle, where Hilary Heron lived with her mother, Molly. Hilary's sculptures, surrounded by the chippings of whatever material she was using – chestnut, marble or granite – stood around the garden. She looked in at Seaview one morning because my grandmother had been telling her about my drawings of houses, promoting me as either a future architect or a candidate for the National College of Art. Hilary said that many applicants for the college, who were ten years older than me, couldn't draw half as well. This was a source of endless satisfaction to my grandmother, who mentioned Hilary's opinion to the ladies of the Jubilee Nursing Association, which she was still running, though I wondered if Hilary wasn't just being polite.

Hilary told us she'd been paid a wad of money to have her portrait drawn for an advertising agency: her fizzog – she meant her face – would appear in a series of advertisements for Pond's Cold Cream, 'which I wouldn't use in a fit,' she said, 'either on my face or anywhere else.' We looked for the Pond's advertisement, headed 'Charm in Irish Life', in the *Irish Times* every Saturday: there was Miss Diana O'Gorman Quin, who was described as being well known on the hunting field, and the actress Miss Marie Conmée, whose talent was matched only by her beauty, but Hilary was never there. After weeks of watching I saw her name, with the words 'the noted young sculptress' underneath, but the picture could have been of anybody. When my grandmother mentioned that she thought the portrait didn't do her justice, Hilary said that the old critter who drew it was not only cross-eyed but also in an advanced stage of alcoholic dementia, but she'd taken the loot and put it in the post office towards a skite to Paris when the war would be over.

Hilary's mother's unusual approach to decoration at Mount Eagle was a source of continuing amusement at Seaview. She hung curtains on the walls instead of the windows and her study was covered in the scraps of cloth provided by shops as patterns. My grandmother, out visiting one afternoon, found Molly bent over at the top of a step-ladder sticking newspaper cuttings to the ceiling. Her son Barney, who, due to the shortage of leather, had introduced his wooden clogs to the Dublin shoe-shops, was now starting a business in prefabricated timber houses, which he said would be much cheaper than ordinary homes and should last just as long provided they were properly maintained – 'Look at Scandinavia,' he said. 'All you need is a site and a cement base.' Gaay said she found his designs quite attractive, but Mister felt this was just another of the Herons' arty ideas and it would never catch on. 'Wood rots,' he said knowledgeably.

I soon noticed that the Whinsfield grand piano was missing. Gaay explained that she'd had to sell it, but the dining-table with the rope-like legs that Ellen Fitz-Simon had brought by sea from her father's house at Derrynane more than a hundred years before was 'in storage' along with the huge gloomy portrait of Ellen that had hung in Mister's study. The daily routine at Seaview, however, was exactly the same as at Whinsfield. Whiskers the cat did not seem in the slightest bit affected by the change. The Rhode Island Red hens had also moved, apparently without demur. They wandered in the unsheltered garden, their feathers blown backwards by the wind every time they turned to peck at some alluring speck in the dung-heap.

My grandmother took her customary glass of Guinness in the evening and Mister still drank a whole bottle of Jameson's whiskey. He was always the first up in the morning, except for Bridie who had to light the stove. Freshly shaved and smelling of Cusson's soap, he ate a large fried breakfast and then went out for a walk, as if to inspect the property, though here at Murphystown there was little to see but the row of granite-faced council cottages opposite and two new bungalows that were roofed in greenish tiles of a kind I'd never seen before. Down the Kilgobbin road there was a house with a stone plaque over the door that said 'Content in a Cottage and Envy to No One'. Mister said that if the original occupants had gone to all that trouble to chisel such a declaration on a slab of granite they must have been feeling very envious indeed.

A telegram from London signed 'Simon' announced that my father would be arriving on the Mail Boat the following evening. I said he must know that we'd moved from Whinsfield to Seaview because of how he'd addressed the telegram; but, no, my grandmother said, he had sent the telegram to her telephone number, which was still the same, nine-six-two-oh-seven.

It was now three months since my mother had heard the good news that he would not be joining what the wireless was calling the offensive in the Western Desert, 'offensive' meaning a big battle boldly begun. He would be granted home leave because he had been in Palestine and the Western Desert for so long, but how he was to get home he hadn't been able to say. When postcards arrived with pictures of South Africa my mother knew he wasn't sailing through the Mediterranean, which was a comfort because everyone knew it was awash with enemy submarines. We found the Union of South Africa in the atlas; it was a neutral country like the Irish Free State so letters could go freely from one to the other if a ship travelling the right way could be found. After the postcards there was nothing for weeks, until just before we went to Bundoran a cable arrived at Eldron mentioning Kingstown as the probable port of his return to Ireland around the end of June – Kingstown being what he called Dun Laoghaire.

Joe Mellon's taxi brought my mother, my grandmother,

Nicky and myself to Dun Laoghaire harbour. It was a grey evening. A small crowd was waiting where the Mail Boat was supposed to dock, but there was no news of when it might arrive. My grandmother was vexed by the absence of information, telling the man at the gates that surely an *estimate* of the time of arrival would hardly compromise the outcome of the war, but he simply said, 'They never tell us,' and advised us to take a walk on the pier to pass the time. A few people were out with their dogs and we went to the very end – exactly a mile, my grandmother said.

Quite suddenly we saw a little smudge of smoke on the horizon, but it took a very long time to get any nearer. When it was about a mile out from the lighthouse it stopped. Then it appeared to go backwards; and then it zigzagged slowly towards the harbour mouth.

'Avoiding the mines,' said my grandmother.

'There couldn't possibly be *mines* so close to port! How would the Germans plant *mines* without being seen?' my mother exclaimed.

'It isn't the Germans, it's the Irish Navy. They planted the mines to discourage unwelcome visitors. Well, that's what I was told.'

When the ship had docked we were allowed into the shed where there was an exit from the Customs hall. The passengers came out in ones and twos. They were mainly Irish workers from the munitions factories in Britain returning home for holidays, Gaay thought. Nobody resembling my father emerged.

Nicky said that if he was lifted up he might be able to see through the wire mesh on top of the partition that separated us from the Customs hall. My mother hoisted him as high as she could and he said there were still a lot of people having their suitcases opened. He called, 'Daddy!' but said that no one looked up. My mother told him to shout, 'Simon!', which he did, but there was no response, nor was there when he shouted, 'Manners!' When my mother got tired of holding him and let him down to the floor he said he thought there was a man who might be Daddy and then, looking towards the doors, he said, 'That's him!'

And it was.

A crate of oranges was delivered to Seaview by a man with a horse and cart. My father said it had been more trouble transporting the oranges, and the few other presents he'd been allowed to bring us, the five miles from Dun Laoghaire to Murphystown than the thousands of miles from the Cape. Among the presents there were a flexible stick called a *jambok*, which he said the people of South Africa used as whips for their horses, and a thing like a log of wood called biltong, which was antelope meat dried in the sun and which the Boers ate when they had to cross the veld on long journeys. It had no smell, and when I tried it with my tongue there was no taste. 'When it's cooked,' my father said, 'it becomes quite soft, like the tenderest lamb'; but after Bridie had boiled it for hours on the turf range it still had no taste or smell, though it was certainly soft, like a fibrous porridge. I thought that if you boiled the *jambok* for as long it would taste the same.

When it had been decided that my father and others who had been serving in the Middle East would not be joining General Montgomery but would be allowed home leave, he had not known that the journey would take three months. They had set off from Port Said down the Suez Canal into the Red Sea, bound for Jeddah and Aden, all this being familiar from his voyages to India and Burma in the past. Then they went along the east coast of Africa, some ships of the convoy leaving them and others joining. Their longest stay was in Cape Town, where my father had climbed Table Mountain, which he said had the most beautiful view in the world. He was thinking that the route was the same as that which anyone returning from the Far East before the Suez Canal was opened would have taken – but the next thing they did was to swerve away across the South Atlantic and thence into the North Atlantic by way of Jamaica and Bermuda till one morning they came out on deck to see the towers of Manhattan on the skyline. Here they stayed for several days, as idle as a painted ship upon a painted ocean, as it were, with New York only half a dozen miles off, but they never docked and on another morning they woke again to see nothing but the waves. Sometimes the other ships of the convoy were visible but more often theirs seemed to be alone. This went on for two weeks, until suddenly they saw the Needles and Cowes and they were in Southampton Water.

We stayed on at Seaview for a short time when my father went to England to learn about his next posting. He had not told us what he thought of Seaview and I sensed that he didn't want to be asked. We went for a walk with him past Whinsfield, where there was now a family called Sweetman living. I said I'd like to go inside and see what it looked like now, and he said, 'Better not disturb them.' Then we walked up the right-of-way and into Moreen woods. I was surprised that I couldn't find the Beech Walk and when I asked where it was he replied, 'All gone!' Someone had cut down the ancient trees.

When he was leaving for London he said we should all treat ourselves to the Laurel and Hardy picture advertised at the new Dundrum Odeon for the following week – he had seen it in Cape Town and had found it really very funny. Gaay was pleased that there should now be a cinema nearer than the city centre and she said we should give the Dundrum Odeon our support. The number forty-four bus that passed Seaview also stopped outside the cinema, and because of this convenience we went to the last showing, a thing we had never done on our few visits to the pictures in town. I did not find the film more than mildly funny, and when Stan tumbled off a mule into a shallow stream for the fourth time I thought we must surely be near the end of this tiresome picture and, sure enough, the words 'The End' immediately appeared on the screen backed by the 'Dance of the Cuckoos', which was Laurel and Hardy's signature tune. When we came out my mother remarked, 'That wasn't really your sort of film, was it?' and I said, 'No,' but I told her I was glad to have been taken and not left at home. It was dark and we stood at the bus stop for a long time before Gaay asked a passer-by if she knew when the next forty-four bus would come. 'Oh,' said the woman, 'the last bus passed some time ago.'

I had often walked more than three miles — such as to Aghabog Church and back from Annaghmakerrig — and so had Nicky, so the three miles to Murphystown did not seem much of a challenge, but my grandmother did not relish the idea and my mother felt that, because of the lateness of the hour, we should not have to try. She thought we should go to Joe Mellon's house in Main Street and ask him to take out his taxi, but then they found that between them they didn't have the five shillings he would charge for our fare. A discussion followed as to whether there was money in the drawer in Gaay's desk at Seaview, but she rather thought not, and then she said she could hardly ask Joe Mellon for credit because she hadn't paid his last account, so in the end we started up the Sandyford road, past all the big houses whose occupants she knew but from whom she did not feel she could solicit a lift and, anyway, she said, they wouldn't have the petrol. Ardglass (the Crookshanks), Dun Emer (Miss Gleeson), Homestead (the Collens), Belawley (the Shaw-Smiths), Clonard (the Dargans) and then Moreen, the house in which she had grown up and which was the only one whose owner she didn't know, a Mr Myerscough who bred horses. By the time we reached Sandyford Corner my mother was carrying Nicky. 'I *wish* you still lived at Whinsfield!' I said, when we saw the dark silhouette of trees against the night sky that hid the familiar white cube from view.

Our theatregoing was more successful than our trip to the cinema, partly because we went to the two-thirty matinées but more especially because of the excitement in the audience before the show even began. We already knew the story of *Hansel and Gretel*, which only filled three pages in our illustrated book of Grimm's *Fairy Tales*, and so I was afraid the pantomime at the Gaiety Theatre would be very short, but when we sat down and read the programme and saw the list of the Eleven Sparkling Scenes and the names of the Italian jugglers and all the children in Miss Lily Comerford's Troupe of Irish Dancers we knew there'd be a lot more than was in the story. One of the sparkling scenes was called 'The Path Through the Woods'. It was painted on a cloth that descended several times, and I soon grasped the idea that this was so that the bigger scenes could be changed behind it while the Babes were led safely through the forest by their Feathered Friends, or the Gaiety Girls did a high-kicking routine ('Prancers,' said my grandmother), or the Irish Dancers gave a display of jigs, reels and hornpipes, their hands held straight down by their sides, 'And not a smile on one of their faces the whole time they were on,' remarked my grandmother, when the interval came and we bought Lucan Cream Ices in little cardboard pots from a lady in a frilly blouse.

There was a warmth and breadth about the Gaiety, with its three balconies and dainty gilded boxes and its pit filled with musicians in evening dress even though it was the afternoon. The leader of the orchestra was my grandmother's friend Miss Jellett, who gave us a friendly wave and stepped up to the brass rail as we were going out for the interval. She said that Mr O'Dea and Mr O'Donovan, who ran the company, were going to do a weekly variety programme called *Irish Half-hour*, which the BBC was putting on because there were so many Irish people working in England and in the Forces, but the troupe would have to travel to Wales on the Mail Boat every Sunday because the governors of the BBC in Belfast wouldn't allow a programme from the South to be performed in their studios.

'Bigots, that's what they are up there,' my grandmother agreed.

'It would make you ashamed of being a Protestant!' said Miss Jellett. 'Ah, well, we all have to earn our living somehow!' She cast her eyes up to the ceiling and my grandmother laughed.

There were plenty of tunes that we knew, including 'My Dreams Are Getting Better All the Time', and Miss Ursula Doyle, who was supposed to be only twelve but looked quite old – fifteen, perhaps – sang 'Have You Ever Been Lonely?' accompanied by a chorus of elves who looked remarkably like the Lily Comerford Dancers disguised in tight-fitting green costumes made to look like leaves. Jimmy O'Dea was the star of the show. He was Jimmy the Plumber and was also Mr Stalin in a scene with Mr Churchill and Mr de

Valera where they sang to the tune of 'Three Lovely Lassies of Bannion', but instead of 'Bannion' they put in 'Moscow', 'London' and 'Dublin' and everyone laughed. My mother said it was 'a clever parody' and it was very easy to recognize who they were meant to be because pictures of Stalin, Churchill and Dev were always in the papers. Just before the end Mr O'Dea came out dressed as Mrs Mulligan and sang:

> *You may travel from Clare to the County Kildare*
> *From Francis Street back to Macroom,*
> *But where would you see a fine lady like me?*
> *Biddy Mulligan, the Pride of the Coombe, me boys!*
> *Biddy Mulligan, the Pride of the Coombe!*

and at the very end, when the Babes had been brought home by the kindly Forester and their parents hadn't died after all and the wicked Baron had been exiled to Siberia – Mr O'Dea said 'to Belfast' by mistake and then changed it to Siberia – the words of the song 'Every Little Piggy Has a Curly Tail', which had been repeated throughout the pantomime, were lowered on a screen and we all joined in; and when we'd sung it once another screen came down with the words written in Irish and everyone in the audience seemed to be able to read them except us. This made me feel quite foolish and I thought of the Daley girls at Annaghmakerrig and how they were learning Irish at Crapagh School and I thought I must try and find some way of doing so myself.

There was an old house called Kilgobbin that had been derelict for years, just down the road from Seaview, and Gaay said they were asking a very reasonable price for it. After some time, and a lot of letters passing to and from my father in England, my mother told us that she was going to buy it and have it put into proper order and my grandparents could rent it from her if they wished. There was a hint in the conversations she had with my father when he came back on leave in the summer that we might live there, too, at some future time, but the future was always very far away and, anyway, was much less interesting than the immediate prospect of renovating an old house.

My parents lodged again with Mrs Popham, just two minutes' walk from the first property they ever owned, Kilgobbin House, while Nicky and I stayed on at Seaview. Every day we met at Kilgobbin where the building work was starting. Mister said he was appointing Gaay as Clerk of Works, but she had already collected a gang of men in the locality – a carpenter (because all the floors had rotted away), a plumber (because there was no water, not even in the outside WC), an electrician (because the house had been vacated long before the supply had been connected elsewhere in the district) and a plasterer, who was to resurface all the walls before she had them painted. There was much discussion over a selection of colour-cards as to which should be chosen for each room. 'You may be sure your grandmother will have her own bedroom done in some shade of *lilac*,' my grandfather observed, and he was proved right. He visited the building site only once during the renovation because he couldn't bear the smell of raw plasterboard and fresh paint made him feel sick.

Kilgobbin was referred to by the plumber, Mr Tuohy, as 'a Queen Anne house', but my mother said he was 'a bit mixed up in his dates for it was built almost a hundred years after that hideous lady died'. Mr Tuohy had two very long front teeth that came out over his lower lip, and when he laughed you could see that where there weren't gaps his back teeth were completely black. My father referred to him as 'Toothy'. My mother must have thought that was his real name because I was shocked to hear her calling him 'Mr Toothy' when they were talking about the kitchen drains. I expected him to be annoyed, but he didn't seem to notice, or perhaps he was deaf. After that she always emphasized the name 'Mr *Tuohy*' when she was talking to him, to make me laugh. The kitchen was dark and the whole back of the house had a ramshackle look. Mr Tuohy confirmed that that was generally the way with period houses: 'Queen Anne front and Mary-Ann behind!' Henceforth Kilgobbin was definitely Queen Anne and nothing else. Gaay had two big windows inserted in the kitchen so that the sun came in at most times of the day. She had all the window-frames and shutters, which she said were 'original', scraped and painted white and the banisters of the curving staircase painted white as well. It looked very smart and it was amazing to think that two months before it had been little more than a ruin.

My grandfather had done some reading and learned that the house was one of several in what had once been the village of Kilgobbin, situated where the old Dublin-to-Wicklow road crossed the Carrickmines stream. Mrs Popham's house had been an inn, which was thought to be very appropriate since my parents were lodging there, and we found the marks of the two sets of gate piers where coaches had driven in and out. We also came across some ruined cottages in a lane and next to them the remains of a Norman castle, now a picturesque eye-catcher in the grounds of a smart Victorian villa. Our house had a long, walled garden reaching as far as the stream. While work in the house was continuing my grandmother employed two men to lay paths and erect a rustic fence for roses and dig the long-neglected soil of the kitchen-garden, which in a surprisingly short time was providing potatoes and cabbages and the following summer strawberries, raspberries and big yellow vegetable marrows.

We were not on hand when the move from Seaview to Kilgobbin was accomplished. Wherever we happened to be staying – Seaview or Annaghmakerrig or Eldron – my father kept insisting that I ought to be going to 'a proper school'; the fact was that at this time neither I nor Nicky was going to any school at all. I had a friend called Neil O'Donnell Brown, who was also seven and lived at Park Cottage, a few hundred yards up the road from Kilgobbin. When the day came for him to return to his boarding-school he was dressed in grey flannel shorts and a maroon blazer with a black and maroon tie and he wore a cap in the same maroon with CP, for 'Castle Park', embroidered on it in gold; he also had a rugby ball and a very smart leather suitcase. As he stepped into the car in which his parents were taking him back to school – his father was a doctor so they had plenty of petrol as well as plenty of everything else – he hardly felt it necessary to wave goodbye, for I had clearly receded in his estimation into the realm of insignificant people merely encountered during the holidays. I thought he was stepping into another world, one from which I was by nature excluded, and into which I had no wish to follow.

## Back to Eldron

My father had to return to military duties in the north of England, visiting us only when he had a few days' leave due to him, when he would travel by boat from Heysham to Belfast and then come to Dublin on the train. It looked quite a roundabout way on the map but he said it was much more reliable than any of the boats that went to Dublin or Dun Laoghaire. Some time in the autumn of 1941 my mother decided to go back to England with him, and so she took us on the train to Eldron to live with Zane, staying a few days with us until we were 'settled in', as she said – though Eldron was so familiar I didn't need to settle in at all.

Once again Eldron became the centre of our universe, its pastoral lure surrounding us and insulating us from the outside world. Yet there was a daily reminder that other places did still exist, and this was the train.

The Great Northern Railway from Belfast to Cavan passed through the Eldron fields with four trains a day in each direction. Our day was divided into nine unequal segments by the flurry of smoke and the rattle of metal wheels beyond

the orchard. Zane said that in the days before Big Ben on
the wireless if you didn't exactly set the clock by the trains
at least you were reminded of the time of day. Lizzie had an
ear for the comings and goings: 'If yon's the five-past-nine
it must be early – unless it's a special excursion to Bundoran
... Glory be to goodness that must be the *Flyer* and we've
still to gather the eggs ...'

The *Flyer* was the nearest I knew to the picture in my
*Wonder Book of Why and What* of 'a crack express' on some
main line over in England, though in fact it was nothing
near. For no reason that anyone could explain the *Flyer*
stopped at Smithborough, though it disdained other rural
stations such as Tynan and Redhills, and that gave us a sense
of superiority. Unlike the other trains with their black
engines, the *Flyer's* was painted a vivid blue with a red stripe.
This, with the polished wood of the carriages and the succession of brass door-handles, left it in a class of its own. In
winter the flash of its brightly lit, upholstered and peopled
interiors, seen through the bare fronds of the Bramleys,
presented a vision from the *Arabian Nights*. Who were these
privileged beings riding so opulently through the night air?
At what far-flung platforms would they disembark? Surely
not through a gush of acrid steam on to damp gravel clutching
a bag of groceries from Patton's and the weekly edition of
the *Northern Standard*.

If the noble bearing of the *Flyer* caused wonderment, the
same could not be said for the midday train, which dawdled
from Cavan to Portadown, where it gave up the ghost in a
plume of smoke and sparks and you had to change to another
train to reach Belfast. Great-aunt Zane said that it was marked
in the timetable as a 'slow' train. She said it wandered through
the afternoon, pausing at halts and crossings, admiring itself in
the little lakes of Breffni. Ballyhaise, Redhills, Clones, Smith-

borough, Monaghan, Glaslough, Tynan, Killylea, Armagh, Rich Hill – it even stopped at Retreat Halt for the people who wanted to visit the Home for Distressed Protestants. She told me that one time when my grandparents had come from Belfast for the weekend they had hardly sat down to their midday dinner when a telegram was delivered requesting my grandfather to return immediately because a patient in his hospital needed an urgent operation. There was no time for him to walk to the station for they could see that the train was already signalled. He took up his Gladstone bag and umbrella and went down through the orchard just as the train was coming out from under the stone arch. He held up his umbrella for all the world as if he were hailing a taxi in the City of London, and the train stopped for him.

This had happened long before I had come to count Eldron as my home – probably even before I was born.

Lizzie clearly thought ill of my mother for courting danger 'across the water'. In a moment of unguarded emotion she exclaimed that Mrs Fitz-Simon had no right to be there, 'with the bombs falling all around her'. Zane was mortified for she only countenanced positive references to the war, like the bravery of the Battle of Britain pilots, and she failed to keep her voice down when berating Lizzie for this slip. 'Don't ever let me hear you say the word "bomb" again in front of the boys!' she said fiercely, not knowing that the boys were crouching in the closed-in space that concealed the crooked staircase from the rest of the house. The reprimand made its mark because for the rest of the day Lizzie 'wasn't speaking', and when it came to six o'clock she put down the brown teapot with such a bang I thought it would break in two. Zane pretended not to notice and went on buttering a slice of toast in a way that said she had more important things on her mind.

As Nicky and I became older, Lizzie claimed that we grew cheekier. Sometimes, following some unconscious slight, she would become aloof and refuse to answer questions. One day we accused her of being a German spy and I said that the biscuit tin with the picture of the Princesses Elizabeth and Margaret Rose, which she kept on the dresser, was a clever way of drawing the police off her trail. (It did not occur to us that as we lived four miles inside the Free State the police would have little interest in the Royal Family, or in Nazi espionage for that matter.) One evening a Lancaster bomber flew low over the haggard – lost, we supposed – and following the line of the railway back into Northern Ireland. We told Lizzie it was Mr Churchill coming to drop bombs on her for being an enemy agent. She retorted that it was well known she was as loyal as any member of the Orange Lodge and Mr Churchill should have more sense. 'And, anyway,' she said, 'I don't believe you!'

My mother wrote us letters from a village called Yatton near Bristol, where the grocer was called Mr Pink and the postman had a wooden leg that he kept in a sling hung from the handlebars of his bicycle. She was staying in a big country house that had been taken over by the army. Her letters to us were enclosed with longer letters to Zane, which she read to herself with a serious look on her face. Then my mother moved to Bonny Rigg in Scotland because my father had been posted to a military camp south of Edinburgh and this was the nearest place that could be found for her to stay. She thought that her Elliott forebears might have come from around Bonny Rigg, but Zane said they were more from the border country, a bit nearer to the Cheviot Hills. We got out the atlas, which showed Bonny Rigg but not Stobbs Castle, which Zane said had been the Elliotts' ancestral home before some of them came over to Ulster in the seventeenth century. After this the letters had bits of them cut out with scissors by the censor and a stamp on the envelope, which read, 'Opened by Examiner', and a number. When a picture-postcard arrived with the name of the location cut out Zane said it was perfectly ridiculous because everyone knew it to be Edinburgh Castle – here was the Mound and the National Gallery of Scotland and this was the memorial to Sir Walter Scott – and if such a picture got into the hands of the Nazis they'd be pretty stupid not to recognize the famous view.

Zane had a childhood friend called Miss Hogan who had gone on to become headmistress of Armagh Girls' High School. When we were rowdy or disobedient she would threaten a visit from this formidable lady, for Miss Hogan knew all kinds of punishments and would soon make us sorry for our naughtiness. There was therefore something of a *frisson* in the air when Zane announced that Miss Hogan would be coming to stay, for she was retiring from teaching and would be spending some time at Eldron while making up her mind about where to move to next – she had a bachelor brother living at Bexhill over in England and she might move in with him. I asked if she would be bringing her school cane, and Zane said she certainly would – she kept it in an embroidered sheath with the word 'Beware!' sewn on the outside.

It was decided that we would all meet her at Smithbor-ough station. Zane and Lizzie spent some days rearranging the furniture in the Far Room, which had been Great-uncle John's consulting room and was used occasionally as a spare bedroom when the permutations of sharing the other bedrooms became too complex. What was sufficient for our grandparents or my mother was clearly not so for the head-mistress, for a shiny gold counterpane and matching eiderdown were taken from a closet, shaken out and spread for a whole day in the orchard to absorb the aroma of grass, and wet tea-leaves were thrown on the carpet, to which Lizzie later gave a merciless going-over with the twig. Zane cut some tiger lilies and put them in a lustre jug on the washstand and Lizzie remarked that, with all the perfume wafting round the room in the draught, you certainly wouldn't notice the musty smell coming out of the wardrobe. A fire was lit on the morning of Miss Hogan's arrival – the first time I had seen a fire in that room – but the chimney smoked so relentlessly that the fire had to be put out and the charred logs replaced with a little pot of ferns.

I expected a large and formidable person in horn-rimmed spectacles, if not wearing a tasselled mortarboard (like Dr Euphemia Birthistle in a book of stories that had once belonged to my mother called *Marigold's New Chums*) at least carrying one under her arm. As no such figure climbed down from the railway carriage, I turned to Zane in great relief and said that Miss Hogan mustn't be coming after all, but at that moment Zane sprang forward with a kind of cry I had not heard before and I gathered was intended to simulate joy. She seized a dumpy woman and kissed her on the cheek.

As a headmistress, Miss Hogan's appearance was a disappointment. She was small and round and grey instead of being tall, stately and in either purple or black, colours signifying authority. Her grey hair was done into a round bun on the back of her round grey head; the lenses of her spectacles were completely round; she wore a grey wool overcoat, grey stockings, grey shoes with a tightly buttoned strap and a round grey hat like a mixing-bowl. Having greeted Zane she followed the porter to the guard's van to supervise the unloading of her luggage – all of which was grey except for a navy blue hatbox, which I supposed she might have borrowed from somebody else. Then she stood before my brother and myself.

'Are you good boys?' she enquired.

There seemed to be no satisfactory answer to this, so we stood silently looking at her.

'They're good when they're asleep,' said Zane.

'Well, time will tell,' Miss Hogan observed mysteriously.

We had only half a mile to walk and Zane said that between us we should be able to manage the smaller bags and portmanteaux and the rest should be left for Reuben Howe to bring on his farm cart next morning. It must have been clear to those who witnessed the baggage-train of four passing along the village street that our visitor was expecting to stay for some time.

Miss Hogan was horrified to learn that we were not attending the national school in the village. When Zane told her that our mother believed it would be too complicated to enrol us when we'd be moving on at short notice, she replied that that was really not a very good reason. She thought Zane should approach the teacher, Mrs Welch, who was a member of our congregation and therefore might be expected to take a sympathetic interest. Zane felt that the details of our education were not a matter for her but there must have been further discussion, followed by correspondence with Scotland, for within a very few days Zane announced that Miss Hogan had kindly offered to give us lessons every morning and our mother had written to say that she was very grateful and hoped we would listen carefully to everything she said.

When Lizzie had cleared the breakfast, Miss Hogan went off to clean her teeth, returning half an hour later with some exercise books and pencils. She sat us down at the dining-room table. She told us that she believed in the supremacy of the Three Rs – reading, writing and arithmetic. She soon expressed surprise that I could read so fluently and that I could write 'a legible hand', but when it came to what I had decided to call Rithmetic she quickly came to the conclusion that I knew less than Nicky, who was two and a half years younger, and she said so. I could add figures with the help of my fingers and subtract in the same way; I could multiply and divide if given time, and I could manage long multiplication if given even more time – but long division had a way of eluding me, though Nicky found it no trouble. As for the 'problems', which Miss Hogan set from a little book called *The Young Person's Calculator*, they seemed insoluble. 'If two thousand cabbages can be grown on one acre, how many cabbages can be grown on two roods?' There was even a picture of a lot of cabbages growing in a field, which was supposed to be a help. I said I *hated* cabbage: it was my very *worst* vegetable. Miss Hogan responded that this was beside the point. 'If two ounces of bull's eyes cost fivepence, what do three ounces cost?' A big glass jar of bull's eyes was shown, with a lady scooping them into a paper bag. I said it was silly to call black and white sweets bull's eyes because bull's eyes were brown, as could be seen any day in Mrs Dunn's Bottom where the bull was still grazing even though Mrs Dunn was dead, but Miss Hogan said she feared I was introducing irrelevancies because I was too *lazy* to address the problem. 'You must *concentrate*!' she said, and she kept saying this throughout her visit.

For all Zane's desire to avoid overt or alarming references to the war, she was curiously unaware that little boys, apparently absorbed with wooden building blocks or cutting out paper patterns in the next room, might be noting and absorbing the most private of adult conversations. This became clear when she shared the contents of my mother's letters with Miss Hogan – how the big house at Yatton had been torn apart by the soldiers, the mahogany banisters used for firewood, and how there was nothing my father and the other officers could do to stop them; how at night when my mother had been on the roof helping the air-raid warden she had witnessed the city of Bristol – ten miles away! – in flames; how her journey by troop-train from Bristol to Edinburgh had taken sixteen hours; and how there had been an air-raid warning at Crewe at two in the morning and all the lights in the trains were put out. She had joined the Women's Voluntary Service and was now engaged in what sounded like very menial duties, such as collecting old tin cans to be made into bullets. Miss Hogan said it was commendable to engage in war work but surely there were certain things that were unsuitable for a lady to do and certain places where a lady should not be seen. Especially, she ventured, a woman with two children. What would become of them *if* – and then there was a strange silence.

Miss Hogan liked to go for very long walks. Because Zane claimed that her cranky ankle would not stand more than a couple of miles, and as Nicky was only five and not expected to walk much further than the village, I became her outdoor companion. We walked to Drumsnat and looked at the church with its square tower on top of the little hill. Miss Hogan said that Drumsnat meant 'the snowy ridge', probably because in those far-off times when it had been named the country was much colder than it was now. She said there had been a very famous synod of the medieval Church at Drumsnat – a synod was a meeting where all kinds of important things were discussed. Such as what? I enquired. Well, all kinds of important things to do with the medieval Church, Miss Hogan replied. We walked to Skeagh Bridge where the road crossed a broad stream flanked by bulrushes. Miss Hogan said she did not know what 'Skeagh' meant, if it meant anything, but the rushes reminded her of the Ancient Greek story of King Midas, who was so intent in his desire to become rich that the gods punished him by giving him a donkey's ears and ever afterwards the wind among the reeds whispered, 'MidashasassesearsMidashasassesears,' over and over again. I asked what had happened to the donkey who had supplied the ears and she said that that didn't come into the myth, but as a matter of fact there was also an Ancient Irish myth in which a wicked king called Labhraí Loinsigh was given a pair of horse's ears. All the myths of the Ancient World were related, she said. She told me that 'lexicon' was the word for the earliest known dictionary and that it had been written in Greek. I decided Miss Hogan's name was Miss Lexicon, but I never called her that to her face.

At Seloo we passed a pigsty beside a cottage. This put Miss Hogan in mind of a Chinese story, which had to do with the invention of roast pork for dinner. The sty in which the Ancient Chinese pigs were kept was set on fire by a naughty boy who liked whirling lighted sticks around his head. A spark caught the wooden beams of the sty and the poor pigs were burned to death. Bravely attempting to pull them to safety, the boy's fists sank into something soft. Licking his fingers, he realized that he was tasting roast pork for the first time. His parents were amazed by the discovery and from that day forth the people of the Szechwan province kept pigs for meat.

'Why,' I asked, 'did they keep pigs at all up to then if it wasn't for meat? Was it as pets?'

Miss Lexicon seemed startled. Perhaps no one had asked her that question before.

There was a level crossing on the lane near Billory Lough, which reminded Miss Hogan that if you laid two pins on the railway line the wheels of the train would weld them together into the shape of a sword. We were not allowed to cross the line at the bottom of our orchard in case a train came along unexpectedly, but I would not have to cross it: I would lay down the pins and then step back very quickly. When nobody was around I took the biggest pins I could find from Zane's workbasket and went down to the railway. I placed the pins carefully. While we were having lunch I heard the Belfast train go by but when I examined the result there was nothing to be seen. At the next opportunity I had of speaking to Miss Hogan on her own I told her that her idea did not work and she said I must have put the pins down the wrong way. She told me I should bear in mind the maxim of the famous Ancient Scottish king Robert the Bruce:

*If at first you don't succeed,*
*Then try, try, try again.*

I took two more pins and placed them on the line and after the next train had gone by I found, not a gleaming sword, but two squashed pins.

Surmising that the train might crush a stone I put a small chunk of granite (from the Mourne Mountains, Miss Hogan had told me, when we were discussing the geological construction of the railway system) on to the line. Then I climbed to the top of the cutting and waited among the dog-daisies and meadowsweet to witness the anticipated pulverization of igneous rock. When the train was heard approaching I was overtaken by misgivings: perhaps my scientific experiment might derail it? Hundreds of people travelling from Belfast to Cavan would die and I would be blamed and sent to jail, or, if the judge considered me to be too young, to the house of juvenile correction at Bundoran that Lizzie was always threatening me with. I started down the incline but the train was already round the bend and before I could snatch the stone away it had thundered by, unimpeded and mercifully still complete, leaving a little deposit of sparkling sand on one of the sleepers.

I told Miss Hogan that the train was no good at making swords but it could crush granite boulders. She gave me a look that said she knew I was Up To Something, though she couldn't quite make out what. She had come to stay with us in September and it was now nearly Christmas. I asked Zane when she would be going. Zane gave me another kind of look but replied that Miss Hogan was still waiting for an invitation from her brother, whom she had not seen for a very long time. I asked how long Zane had known Miss Hogan and she replied that that would be telling but they had got to know each other when Miss Hogan was starting out as a teacher in Armagh, for Zane gave piano lessons at the High School when the regular music mistress was sick. They had both belonged to the Ladies' Literary and Dramatic Society in the city and they had appeared in Shakespeare's *As You Like It*, Zane playing Rosalind to Miss Hogan's Orlando.

I asked Miss Hogan about her brother in the hope that she would let slip the information about when she was going to leave. She told me his name was Captain Hogan and that he lived in a most delightful part of the south of England. She was sure that he would welcome a woman's hand in the house, for bachelors, she confided, were never any good at housekeeping, even though those who had been in the army were trained to keep their barracks nice and clean. She understood he had a permanent manservant who had also been in the army, a person called Routledge, and there was still some question of how the bedrooms should now be arranged. Captain Hogan had been in India and had once shot a panther just as it was about to pounce on the colonel's wife and everyone had been very proud of his bravery and daring – the incident had been reported in the paper and she would show me the cutting if she could find it in her luggage.

On one of our subsequent walks Miss Hogan remarked that she could see my great-aunt must find it difficult to live in such a remote part of the country without a companion-able spirit. She knew she had taken my great-uncle John's death very much to heart. He, Miss Hogan continued, had obviously been the epitome of the dedicated country doctor, going out on horseback at all times and in all weathers to attend to the sick poor of the neighbourhood. I said that he had had a car, the same one as we had now even though it wasn't used because of the petrol rationing, and she replied that of course I was too young to remember the days before the internal combustion engine had become so ubiquitous. She said that for all its isolation she felt very much at home at Eldron. The cottage was as pretty as a picture – it must look its best at apple-blossom time.

I told Zane that Miss Hogan was looking forward to apple-blossom time. That evening I heard Miss Hogan saying that she would like to contribute to the expenses of the household – 'I do insist, Janey,' she said. 'I don't take your kindness for granted, you know!' Zane told her that it was *she* who was far too generous even to *think* of such a thing and, anyway, there was no necessity since her visit was so short. 'The boys' grandparents will be coming for Christmas, and their mother too, if she can tear herself away from Scotland. In fact, I think she's considering staying on here throughout the spring. She has a conscience about leaving the boys.'

'Oh, but you're so *good* to them!' cried Miss Hogan. 'You're so *kind* to all waifs and strays!'

Reuben Howe called for Miss Hogan's baggage in his cart and we all walked behind to the station to wave her goodbye. As the Belfast train was drawing in she shook hands, and Zane said she hoped she'd come again for a holiday once she had 'settled down in her new abode'. Miss Hogan advised me to persevere with my interests in mythology and geology and she told Nicky he'd be sure to succeed as a mathematician. Reuben Howe put all her belongings in the guard's van; she climbed into the second-class carriage and Mr Walsh blew his whistle, which was followed by a whoop from the engine, as the train dragged itself under the stone arch and out across the bog.

I asked Zane how long it would take Miss Hogan to get to Bexhill and would she be travelling all night on the steamer to England?

'She isn't going to Bexhill. She answered an advertisement in the paper, and as a result she's taking a very nice furnished room in Strabane.'

There was another old lady who was a friend of my aunt but as she lived nearby her visits were more frequent and generally took place in the afternoon. This was Mrs Crawford, the widow of Colonel Crawford of Hollywood House. She was also quite small, but angular where Miss Hogan was round. She always came dressed in swathes of tweed in an unimaginable number of shades of brown. She wore a great deal of beige face-powder that had a way of transferring itself in a light dust to her garments and made her smell like the interior of Mr Black's pharmacy in Monaghan. She drove herself in a tiny Austin 7, which was so old the glass in all its windows was cracked in webs of spreading sunray patterns and the nearside mudguard was tied on with florist's wire. You could hear the rattle of her approach a mile off down the Scotstown road.

When Zane had to lay up the Ford due to the shortage of petrol, Mrs Crawford managed to keep her car going for several months. Davy McMahon, in spite of his humiliation at having to drive women and children on frivolous assignments, yet sorely missing the occasional important event such as a funeral or an auction at which he could wear his chauffeur's cap, intimated to Lizzie that Mrs Crawford must be getting her petrol by means that one would not expect of a lady in her position. She had been seen, Davy said, taking a turn into Northern Ireland on an unapproved road, a mass of old rugs on the back seat barely hiding two large bedroom jugs and a copper kettle. She was known to be friendly with the Archdeacon of Clogher and as the clergy, like the doctors, were allowed a ration of petrol every month, it was likely that she was unfairly connected to his supply. Wherever she got her petrol, Davy found it vexing to see her driving out to tea-parties when people with better reasons for being on the road had to walk or take to their bicycles.

Mrs Crawford drove furiously in bottom gear at five miles per hour along the lanes and byways. She preferred the middle to the left of the road, but as it was a rare thing to meet another vehicle she rarely had an accident. Her perennial problem was reversing. On arrival at Eldron she would pump the rubber bulb of the klaxon horn, creating a sound like a distressed baby elephant. When my aunt appeared she would shout, over the revving engine, 'I'm going to BACK now!' The car would immediately spring forward in a series of frog-like leaps and bury its nose in the laurels. Then, without further warning, it would career backwards. Once she bent her back bumper on the corner of the porch, severing the ropy stem of my aunt's wistaria. 'Am I near the wall?' she shouted.

Her speech upon emerging from the quivering machine was delivered without punctuation in a sort of low moan, which gainsaid her perky bird-like appearance. 'Oh Janey my darling how are you I've brought you a little pot of lemon curd that I made last night with what may well be the last lemons we'll see for years I found them in a little shop in Roslea and only a few of them were bad I ran over a sheep at Mount Louise but I don't think it minded you know because it didn't say baa or anything I had to leave Noug at home because his ears are very smelly Janey what on earth has happened to your wistaria?' Noug was her ancient black and white cocker spaniel.

Hollywood was described by my mother as 'a square Georgian block'. It had a dark basement from which a tunnel fifty yards long led to the farm buildings. My mother said that in the olden days when the people in the big house were looking out of their great windows they didn't like to see the comings and goings of the servants so the tunnel had been built and covered with earth in which trees were planted. In the 1940s this grove also concealed the chassis of several sports cars. They were the abandoned playthings of Edward and Ronnie Crawford, whom my mother had known when they were all young. They were now serving as members of HM Forces in undisclosed locations overseas – Benghazi was mentioned vaguely by Mrs Crawford, and the East China Seas. My brother and I, with our cousins John and Margaret Killen, would occupy these rusting Rovers and Rileys and MGs, ignoring the nettles and ragwort that grew up through their floors as we drove wildly on our imaginary journeys, scorching round the country roads in emulation of Edward and Ronnie Crawford a decade or so before.

As if the decayed motors outside the house were not enough, corrosion and putrefaction were profusely evident indoors. My mother said the Hollywood drawing room had not been decorated for as long as she could remember and that was going back to the reign of King Edward VII. 'The Crawfords, like most of the landed gentry, have no money now,' she said. Stained fawn-coloured blinds excluded the light from the upper sashes of the windows. Swagged curtains were held back by unravelling crimson hawsers, so heavy they appeared to be pulling the entire construction towards the floor. Mrs Crawford declared that she never drew the curtains in the evenings because she was sure the whole thing – rods and rings and all – would come tumbling down, enveloping her in yards of damp yellow brocade. 'Wouldn't that be funny?' she said – and she was right because the thought of this tiny woman trying to burrow out from under such a load of heavy material, like a mouse from a heap of straw, would definitely be quite comical. What if Mrs Crawford never managed to get out? Would Edward and Ronnie's Aunt Daisy find her sister's mummified remains months later?

At the top of the main staircase was a ramshackle bathroom, installed by Colonel Crawford in response to years of hinting by visiting relatives from more up-to-the-minute and hygienic spots such as Eastbourne. The bathroom was separated from one of the bedrooms by a matchboard partition, which certainly concealed the occupant from view even if it did not prevent the escape of sounds or smells. On a high bracket stood an iron cistern, which only worked when you tugged repeatedly on a chain that made a loud clanking noise, eventually inducing about a cupful of water to descend in an unsatisfactory trickle. Mrs Crawford was frequently to be seen mounting the stairs with an enamel jug of water 'to prime the cistern'. The bedroom from which the bathroom had been extracted contained only one piece of furniture, a rocking-chair upholstered in amber velvet that would turn over completely if you rocked very hard. I was delighted when my mother said it belonged to her, one of several pieces that friends and relatives were kindly storing until such time as we had a house of our own.

Away down in the cavernous kitchen three grey and white cats sat blinking at the embers of the range. Mrs Crawford's sister was said to inhabit this region, but we never saw her on our explorations for, as Zane said, Aunt Daisy did not appreciate company, usually leaving the house when visitors were expected. She spent much of her time in the kitchen-garden, where the cultivation of asparagus and artichokes was her chief concern. Once when Davy was driving us up the Hollywood avenue he broke his usual silence with the laconic observation, 'So Miss Fiddis won't be at the party.'

'Why ever not, Davy?' replied my great-aunt, determined to uphold the social orthodoxy of the tea-going classes, yet knowing perfectly well that Aunt Daisy would never be seen dead where there were other people to be met.

Davy stared straight ahead as he negotiated the potholes and replied, 'I see her carting dung.'

There was a terrible silence in the back of the car because he had used such a rude word. (If he *had* to say it, Zane remarked when recounting the incident to my mother, couldn't he at least have said *manure?*)

My mother – as Zane had intimated to Miss Hogan – did return from Scotland for Christmas. She brought the news that my father had been asked about his priorities for his next posting and had immediately said, 'Northern Ireland!' The news had then come through that he would very soon be joining the South Staffordshire Regiment at Newcastle in County Down, and she was going to spend a day or two there to find somewhere for us to live and, if possible, a school. Newcastle was the Seaside, and there would be all kinds of things to do, especially in summer, such as visits to Maggy's Leap and Bloody Bridge, places she knew well from her childhood holidays. It would be goodbye to Eldron again, with fresh and exciting possibilities in view. Zane could join us there for a holiday, if she liked. She said she would, if Lizzie didn't object to being left on her own.

## Anchor Lodge Mews, Newcastle, County Down

At Tynan station we changed from our third-class carriage, with its gravy-coloured moquette benches, into second class. My mother explained that as we had now entered Northern Ireland we could use army vouchers that got us free second-class travel wherever we wanted to go. Second-class carriages had grey buttoned upholstery and there were pictures of the two cathedrals of Armagh – which in a few minutes we could see from the window – and photographs of Donegall Place and High Street in Belfast, with trams and pony-traps dashing about and people in old-fashioned clothes. My mother said it wasn't a bit like that now but the railway company hadn't been making any money for years and probably couldn't afford to replace them. Anyway, with the war on, photography was forbidden in public places. We would change trains at Belfast, she said, to the Newcastle line and altogether the journey would take us about four hours. Daddy would be waiting at Newcastle station and we'd all walk to Mrs Griffin's guesthouse, called Anchor Lodge, right on the Promenade facing the sea.

My mother's foray to Newcastle had almost proved unsuccessful, for other officers' wives were there before her and
there wasn't a decent place left, while all the smaller houses
in the streets by the chapel had been requisitioned for families
evacuated from Belfast because of the German bombing.
Looking out of her bedroom window at the guesthouse she
noticed what looked like a gardener's cottage. Mrs Griffin
said it was known as the Mews and belonged to her sister,
Mrs McGowan, who was thinking of moving to her late
husband's people down the coast at Annalong because the
noisy, unruly sort of people who were around Newcastle
were getting on her nerves. 'Could *I* have it?' my mother
asked. Mrs Griffin said she would have a word with her sister
when the moment was right, which must have been immediately, for Mrs McGowan was only too delighted to vacate
her home for whatever rent was suitable. It was only after
Mrs McGowan had gone to her relatives that my mother
did a proper inspection and found there was no bathroom,
not even a wash-basin, and the WC was in a little brick
structure surprisingly close to the front door.

At Portadown a train full of soldiers was occupying the
northbound platform and we had to wait for what seemed
like hours in sight of the station while men in khaki uniforms
pitched haversacks and what I thought might be bombs into
the guard's van. Then they stood around drinking mugs of
tea. We could see a silver cluster of barrage balloons floating
on the horizon – my mother said they were protecting some
important military depot, perhaps a munitions factory. She
thought that enemy aircraft were probably meant to get
caught in the wires that tethered the balloons to the ground.
We discussed the possibility of this: surely an enemy pilot
would see the balloons and therefore steer away from them,
then bomb the factory from higher up in the sky? Didn't

the balloons indicate that this was a place that *should* be bombed and wasn't that rather stupid?

When we reached Belfast we found that we had missed the only connection to Newcastle. My mother had to decide what to do – perhaps go for the night to her cousin Sis Stephenson in Marlborough Park, but she probably had a full house, or to Professor Brice Mayers who was a bachelor and had plenty of spare rooms, but he mightn't take well to an unannounced visit. She said that, really, the obvious thing was to go to the County Down Railway terminus at Queen's Quay and take a train from there, but she seemed reluctant to do so. She asked at the information office if trains were actually running from Queen's Quay – 'you know, on account of the blitz,' she said, in an undertone – and was assured that they were.

'It's not a very pretty sight, I hear,' my mother said, as we boarded the cross-town tram, which snaked its way through almost empty streets that were not at all like the photographs we had seen in our second-class carriage. Most of the shops had their windows boarded up and those that did not had strips of paper stuck across the glass to stop them splintering in an explosion. We turned into High Street and that was what my mother must have meant when she said it would not be very pretty – but it was really quite exciting. You could see into the buildings in the way you could look into a dolls' house. It seemed as if their fronts had just been opened up to the street so that everything inside became visible. There were living rooms over the shops with their furniture just sitting there, quite neat and normal, and bedrooms on the higher floors with the beds made up as if someone was about to get into them for the night. Further along the street the destruction was much more what you'd expect after bombs had been dropped on them by Dorniers and Heinkels – I had pictures of these planes in the book about the Battle of Britain that Aunt Hester had sent me from England. There were vast piles of rubble and twisted metal and broken beams and buckled gas cookers and smashed wash-basins and torn curtains and shredded mattresses.

'That's where the Merrythought was,' my mother said. 'The teashop where I worked after I left school. The name! *Merry*thought! Just imagine!'

'And what was over there?'

'Oh, I think that must have been Arnott's department store.'

It took a long time to get to Newcastle. We had eaten the jam sandwiches that Lizzie had wrapped in butter-paper with the words 'Town of Monaghan Co-operative Creamery' on it and there were only four squares of Fry's chocolate cream left. I wanted to pee but there was no corridor on the train, and when we stopped at Downpatrick – we knew it was Downpatrick because we could see the cathedral even though the name sign had been taken down to confuse the Germans – I was afraid there wouldn't be time to make a dash to the gents' and back so I held it in. I thought I might pee out of the window, but on surveying this possibility I saw a man looking out from the next compartment and he would have got a splash on the face with the breeze the train was making.

At Newcastle station we couldn't get out of the carriage because the door was stuck, so we banged on the window till a passer-by let us out. I rushed into the lavatory and when I came out expecting to see my father he wasn't there – 'He couldn't have known when we were coming since we didn't turn up on the Great Northern' – so there was nothing for it but to carry our cases down Main Street. 'We can take a rest every hundred yards,' said my mother, making it sound like an adventure. To our left was the largest building I had ever seen, all gables and turrets in pinkish brick, its dozens of windows criss-crossed with paper strips: the Slieve Donard Hotel. My mother said it was now the army headquarters. There were soldiers everywhere, standing outside shops, laughing and chatting in groups.

'Why are soldiers always drinking tea?'

'Soldiers *love* tea. And the local people love giving it to them. And there isn't very much else for them to do.'

Ahead of us, framed by the tall terraces of seaside houses, was Slieve Donard itself, the highest mountain I had ever seen – or could remember seeing, my mother said, for there were far higher mountains in the Nilgiris where we used to go in the summer to get away from the heat of the plain at Trichinopoly, but I didn't remember that so I decided to count Slieve Donard as my highest, and there it was in front of us, with its surrounding smaller mountains and then the foothills and the forests and the grassy cliffs descending to the strand. The tide was out, and the entire beach was planted with posts as high as telegraph poles. What were they there for?

'To stop enemy aeroplanes from landing. A flat beach like this would be just right for them. So, of course, they can't land, and we'll be quite safe.'

Anchor Lodge was opposite the bandstand where Main Street became one-sided, with terraces of guesthouses facing across the road to the strip of grass and shrubs that separated it from the sea. Next door was the Royal Temperance Hotel and next to that a stumpy little church with a notice saying, 'Wesleyan Congregation'. The word 'Newcastle' had been blacked out but it was quite easy to read the letters as they were slightly raised – any Nazi spies who got that far and wanted to know the name of the town would have had no difficulty. I thought it might have been wrong to plant the beach with poles for I rather liked the idea of seeing the Luftwaffe planes with the black cross painted on their sides and the swastika on the tail swooping down and taking a shot at the church and another at the Royal Temperance Hotel and then landing on the beach where all the soldiers would be hiding in the bandstand waiting for them and would shoot the Nazis as they climbed out of their planes, and then the tide would come in and the planes would be washed away and serve them right.

'Well, here you are at last. We thought you were lost!' said Mrs Griffin, opening the front door and hooshing us in with a wave of her arm. She had speckled grey hair and wore a wrap-around overall. Behind her stood a lady who said nothing and who was introduced as her daughter Mildred. 'Your husband was here in the early morning, Mrs Fitz-Simon – he said he was going out on manoeuvres and wouldn't be at the station but I took a ramble up there myself for the three o'clock train and not a sign of you! You must be starving – would an omelette be in order?'

My mother replied that it certainly would, though she had expected to cook a meal in our new home. Mrs Griffin gave us the key of the Mews and told us to be back in twenty minutes. We went out through the back door and across the yard to a house with grey plaster flaking off the walls. The ground floor had a door, a window and a garage. Upstairs there were two windows, so there must be a bedroom over the garage. There was a narrow hall with a bedroom opening off it, and behind that a room, with a table and four chairs and a sofa, where Mrs Griffin had lit a coal fire in a grate

surrounded by toffee-coloured tiles. A window looked out
on the back garden where there were no flowers but rows
and rows of vegetables, fruit bushes and apple trees with their
leaves just beginning to come out.

'This is going to be our sitting room and dining room all
in one,' said my mother. The kitchen was off it and must
have been built later for it stuck out into the garden and
there was a glass door through which we could see a kind
of park bench.

'We're allowed to sit in the garden, but the vegetables are
for Mrs Griffin's visitors.' I harboured a passing thought of
not having to eat cabbage or turnip ever again but hope was
dispelled when my mother said she'd be buying fresh vegetables every day at Thornton's, just along the street. I had
never been in a house where vegetables had to be bought,
so there might be a choice of something different from
cabbage and turnip.

A very narrow staircase with a twist you could see in the
ceiling of the living room led to three bedrooms. Everywhere
the floors were covered in shiny brown linoleum. I had a
tiny room that just fitted a bed and wardrobe. Nicky had a
bed in the larger room, which was to be our parents', and
the third was the spare room for whatever relations were
coming to stay – as it turned out, there would be plenty of
those. And the lavatory? In the yard – my mother pointed
it out. 'At least there's a flush and you must come back in
and wash your hands at the kitchen sink.' And baths? My
mother thought she'd be able to scrounge one from Mrs
Griffin from time to time when the guesthouse wasn't too
busy, but we would mostly have to make do with a galvanized
tub on the kitchen floor. It sounded quite intriguing. 'And,
of course, there's the sea!'

We ate our omelettes in Mrs Griffin's kitchen. They were

fluffy, like the soufflé Ellie at Annaghmakerrig had once made but which turned into a kind of damp leather the minute Peggy put a spoon into it. 'Oh, they're very light, these omelettes,' said Mrs Griffin, when I told her the ones I'd eaten in other houses were more like scrambled egg. 'It's the dried eggs we get in these packets that gives them the rise, a powder. I don't know if there's any eggs in them at all. They say they're made of potatoes and some kind of flavouring, but how would you know?' I told her I thought they were far nicer than real egg and Mrs Griffin said that was lucky because I'd have to get used to the dried stuff when only one real egg a week was allowed in the ration book. She supposed this would all be new to us, coming from the Free State, which was known in Northern Ireland as the Land of Plenty.

The manoeuvres must have ended after we'd gone to bed. My father was down to breakfast before us and was stirring porridge over one of the three paraffin-burners that made up the kitchen stove. He was wearing his uniform and showed us the crown on the shoulder-strap that meant he was a major – when he was a captain there had been three stars and before that one star for a second lieutenant and two for a first so that anyone would know the rank of the officer they were talking to. Next would be a crown and a star for lieutenant colonel. My mother decided to go and see the school that we were supposed to be starting in the following week and to register our arrival at the Food Office. She also had to look for a housemaid – a daily maid, because there was no servant's bedroom at Anchor Lodge Mews.

My father took us for a walk to see the camp at Donard Park where officers were not obliged to stay when they had a wife and family with a house nearby. I was disappointed

not to see tents – the soldiers lived in low buildings with
curved roofs called Nissen huts, all painted in swirls of brown
and green camouflage to confuse the enemy aircraft. Nearby,
on the tennis courts, were ranged dozens of armoured cars,
but much more exciting were rows of tanks with caterpillar
wheels and little guns peeping out of their turrets. 'No, those
aren't tanks,' my father corrected. 'Tanks are much bigger.
These are Bren-gun carriers.' Whatever they were called,
they were most impressive.

As we continued along the Promenade a platoon of soldiers
came marching by. My father stood on the edge of the pavement facing the by. 'Eyes right!' commanded the lieutenant,
who was leading them. All the heads instantly turned towards
my father, who saluted grandly as they passed. 'Eyes front!'
called the lieutenant, and the heads turned to look forward
again – you could swear you heard them click into place. If
the Bren-gun carriers had been impressive, this performance
was even more so. I spent many an otherwise idle moment
being the soldiers clicking their necks to the right and
simultaneously being my father saluting in acknowledgement.
Click. Turn. Salute. Click.

When we returned to the Mews my mother was opening
a tin of Spam she had bought at the grocer's after she'd
collected our ration books. 'Spam isn't on points,' she said,
meaning you could buy as much as you liked. It was made
of a mixture of minced pork and 'whatever else you care to
imagine'. She wasn't used to cooking, and as the Spam was
delicious we ate a great deal of it that summer. She had also
collected our gas masks, which we had to carry with us in
little cardboard boxes – there was a rule that you must never
go out of the house without them because there might be
an air raid while you were away from home. If so, the siren
would sound and we must put on our gas masks and go

under the stairs or into an air-raid shelter if there was one nearby. Our teacher would tell us.

My mother had also been to the Civilians' Employment Bureau in what (when she was a little girl, visiting Newcastle on school picnics) had been the Ocean View Hotel, and they had given her the names of young women who, for one reason or another, weren't doing war work and were willing to be classed as domestics. She had an appointment to interview one that evening. As for the school, she had been to see that too. It was in a suburban house on Shimna Road only ten minutes' walk from the back garden door and was run by a Miss Logan – 'Very pleasant, very respectable,' she said, with a glance at my father, who looked satisfied. She said she had peeped into one of the two classrooms and 'all the children were as happy as bees.' I couldn't imagine anyone being entirely happy at school, and as for bees being *happy*, surely with all their buzzing they were mostly angry. But I kept such notions to myself.

The spring term was already half-way through so we were latecomers at Miss Logan's. On our way to school on our first Monday morning we caught up with a boy of my own age who was carrying a leather satchel. My mother asked him his name: 'John Hinchcliffe, spelt with an e,' he said. He was chatty and told us that his parents were abroad and he was staying with his aunt and grandmother. My mother decided to leave it to John Hinchcliffe to accompany us into the school. He told Miss Logan who we were and showed us where to hang our coats in the cloakroom, which was across a lawn at the back. I did not feel at all awkward as I had done when I went to Miss Carroll's school in Dundrum, nor did I notice any critical looks from the other children.

Miss Logan taught the younger pupils in what would have been the drawing room, which had french windows opening into the garden. As the weather was usually fine we ate our 'lunches' out of doors at the eleven o'clock break; 'dinner' was what you had when you went home at one o'clock; 'tea' was your evening meal. The other teacher, Miss McBennett, taught 'the big girls' in what would have been the dining room. There were no big boys – in fact, it turned out that the biggest boys were myself and John Hinchcliffe and David Lanyon, whose father was also in the army but had never heard of my father, which I thought strange because my father was a major. We sat at little tables on little chairs and did copy-book writing and sums and drawing. Lessons here, it soon emerged, were not at all difficult. We had homework but it only took a few minutes and we spent the rest of the day on the strand. After my Killen grandparents arrived we went on long walks by the Shimna river up to Tullybrannigan with its fields of flowering cherry. From this height you could see as far as Murlough Strand and Ballykinlar Camp where tiny aeroplanes – Mosquitos and Spitfires – were constantly taking off and landing. On Thursdays, we had to bring a penny to put in the little collection-box shaped like a house, for Dr Barnardo to give to the poor children who did not have as nice a school to go to.

When my mother was busy with something else our new housemaid Maureen accompanied us to school. Maureen came in the morning to set out the breakfast and sweep the floors and do the laundry, after which she went home. She lived in Valentia Street beside the Church of the Assumption. My mother asked her if she could make coffee and she said, 'Only bottled coffee,' so we had Irel, which looked like gravy browning – you poured a drop into a cup and added boiling water. It tasted quite nice but not a bit like coffee. Maureen used to bring us to school the long way round, across the bridge and up Main Street, where she liked to pause and talk to the soldiers. Sometimes she let us go on alone, telling us to mind ourselves crossing Shimna Road while she had things to say to 'the Tommies'. Whatever Tommy it happened to be would give us a friendly, perhaps conspiratorial, wink. It seemed to be understood that these encounters were not to be mentioned at home.

My mother rejoined the Women's Voluntary Service 'to help with the War Effort'. She still had her little silver badge from Edinburgh with WVS in red letters and a crown, which she had to wear on her lapel while on duty. Some of the women had heather-coloured uniforms but my mother said they were mostly local residents and she didn't expect to be in Newcastle long enough to make a uniform worth while because you had to pay for it yourself. On Monday evenings she went to give out books at the Forces' Library, and on Saturday afternoons there was camouflage-making in St John's Hall. Huge nets were hung from the roof beams and all the ladies had piles of old clothes off which they tore long strips to weave in and out of the nets – the longer the strips the better, explained Dolly Moran, Canon Moran's daughter, who was in charge and wore the official heather coat and skirt. She complained loudly when people donated old clothes in red or orange or white, which were far too eye-catching. 'Anyone in an enemy plane looking down on camouflaging in bright colours like that would immediately know that something was up!' said Miss Moran. She said that brown and green and grey were best, being nearest to nature – a building, or a row of tanks, covered in netting in these colours would blend beautifully into the countryside and nobody would be any the wiser! I asked my father what would happen to the nets when Miss Moran and her friends had finished with them and he said that they'd be sent as

far away as the Western Desert where General Montgomery
would make good use of them.

I made only one visit to the camouflage factory, because
my grandmother felt it was not a suitable occupation for
a young man of seven – you could get diseases from the
old clothes because you wouldn't know where they had
come from. My Killen grandparents, who had stayed for a
week at Anchor Lodge, must have decided that it would
be more sensible to move in with us at the Mews. My
grandmother did not at all approve of my mother's other
WVS duty, known as 'scavenging', which was almost as
interesting as the camouflaging. On Saturday morning we
would go from house to house with an old pram, which
Mrs Griffin said we were welcome to borrow because what
we proposed to do was patriotic work. I had discovered
the pram in the back of a shed and supposed it had once
contained Mildred; in it we would stow any pieces of metal
offered, like old saucepan lids or bean cans, and take them
to the depot near the railway station. Though my grandfather was a doctor he remained silent when the health
hazards of such collections were discussed. He had been
brought up in the Duncairn neighbourhood of Belfast,
which had recently been flattened in the blitz, and so had
a distinctly partisan attitude to even the smallest initiatives
in support of the War Effort.

My grandmother relented somewhat when we brought
home a handsome iron kettle, saying it was far too good to
be made into bullets. She filled it with earth from the garden
and sowed marigold seeds in it, which she said would
brighten up the back step – and, anyway, who knew if all
this trash would reach a suitable destination? My father
informed her that it would be taken to Sion in County
Tyrone where the Herdmans' linen mill had been turned

into a munitions factory: this was very 'hush-hush' and we must not tell anyone we knew.

In her self-appointed role as housekeeper my grandmother did the messages about the town, calling into Maxwell & Neill's for the sparse groceries and to Thornton's for the dreaded turnips and cabbage. (Mr Neill, it transpired, ran the Wolf Cubs, in which I was duly enrolled, and Joanne Thornton turned out to be one of my classmates at Miss Logan's.) On these expeditions my grandmother discovered that a number of her acquaintances from Belfast were in the town, 'on holiday', as they said, but she knew they were here to avoid another blitz for they could well afford it: such people were called 'escapees' to distinguish them from 'evacuees', who were the unfortunate people from the shipyards area of the city who had to go wherever they were sent. One of her friends was Miss Rudd, whom she met in the Food Office and who was staying with Mrs Bristoe on the Bryansford Road. Miss Rudd told her that she was enjoying the year-round sea-bathing, which proved that she was not there for a week's holiday but was an 'escapee'. Encounters such as this were reported round the dinner-table. My father was rarely present, taking his dinner at the officers' mess in what used to be the Donard Arms.

We were visited by Zane. She stayed for a fortnight with Mrs Griffin because there was no room in the Mews but she crossed the backyard every morning to spend the day with us. She had come all the way from Smithborough on the Great Northern train so had not seen the destruction in the centre of Belfast. I told her about the houses whose fronts had fallen off. Later, when I was sitting on the twist of the stairs above the living room, organizing the coloured pencils in my school-bag, I heard her chiding my mother in her gentle way for letting us see such horrible things. My mother said there had been no alternative and, anyway, she found that children did not understand the implications – we had not witnessed human suffering, only physical devastation. Zane was not so sure. She thought we should have spent money on a guesthouse and travelled to Newcastle next day on the Great Northern.

The fine spring days stretched into the summer and it never occurred to me that some time they would have to come to an end – 'like all good things', as Miss Hogan had once portentously remarked. One morning, when I was in bed recovering from what was described as 'a chill', a dozen soldiers appeared in the yard below and started unloading large wooden packing-cases from a truck and heaving them into one of Mrs Griffin's outhouses. These turned out to be the furnishings from our bungalow in Trichinopoly. When the men had finished their work they stood around drinking tea, using cups borrowed from Anchor Lodge because we did not have enough to go round. Our Fitz-Simon grandmother – Gaay – was staying with us that week, the Killen grandparents having temporarily migrated to roost upon some other relatives, and she was amused when the men waved jovially up to her at my window. 'They think I'm the nanny!' she said, clearly flattered. The packing-cases were not opened; in fact, they must have remained in storage at Anchor Lodge for another three years, reappearing when we were living in a dilapidated mansion on the side of a mountain in County Clare, whole worlds away from the bustle of Newcastle.

Gaay brought us a second-hand copy of *Alice's Adventures in Wonderland* and *Through the Looking Glass*, bound in one volume. While I was in bed with the chill I read the whole book to myself, enthralled by the dreamlike changes of scene, especially where the sheep's little dark shop changed into a boat and Alice found herself rowing the sheep, who by now was knitting with fourteen pairs of needles, and the brook became the dividing line between this adventure and the next and had to be crossed in order to reach another chapter. At the end of the book there was a poem that exactly conveyed the melancholy feeling brought about by being left to one's self on a long summer day, while also re-creating an hour's trip we had taken the previous week in a hired rowing-boat on the Shimna:

> *A boat beneath a sunny sky*
> *Lingering onward dreamily*
> *In an evening in July –*
>
> *Long has paled that sunny sky:*
> *Echoes fade and memories die:*
> *Autumn frosts have slain July.*
>
> *Still she haunts me, phantomwise,*
> *Alice moving under skies*
> *Never seen by waking eyes.*

Julia Butler had had her appendix taken out in a Dublin hospital, and Peggy brought her to stay with us for a week by the sea to convalesce. We were told that if the air-raid sirens sounded we were not to say what it was because Julia had just been through a frightening experience and this would upset her. I was quite sure it would not, but we did as we were told. While we were playing on the strand one afternoon the sirens did go off so we looked at each other and said nothing. Instead of running indoors for our gas masks we stayed outside, which might have been quite dangerous, but then nobody really believed the Germans would ever think of bombing Newcastle when Belfast was such an enticing target. Fortunately the all-clear sounded about five minutes later: so *that* was all right, as Alice would have said.

My father had a dreadful toothache and had to go to the army dentist when everyone said he would have been much better off with Mr McClintock, in Main Street, who had such a good reputation and was so gentle. He came back, one side of his face swollen as if he were concealing a boiled sweet or a big prune in his cheek – but he was not at all downcast because he'd just collected a letter at the Army HQ telling him that he'd been promoted to lieutenant colonel. This meant that he would have the crown and star sewn on to his shoulder-strap. It also meant that he would be commanding a battalion of the East Surrey Regiment and that it would probably be somewhere else – everything was very hush-hush and he was not allowed to tell us where. While Peggy Butler was full of congratulations on his achievement my mother seemed dismayed. I asked her if it meant we would be leaving Newcastle? 'Well, not yet,' she said. 'We'll be here for the rest of the summer at least.' So there was nothing really to worry about, for the moment at any rate.

My eighth birthday party was a picnic on the strand beyond the Slieve Donard Hotel. There were sandwiches filled with banana spread, which came in a carton costing ninepence and was made from parsnips with vanilla flavouring, according to Mrs Griffin, but that didn't matter because none of us knew what real bananas tasted like. The party was spoiled because my mother invited some bigger boys, sons of one of my father's fellow officers, who were on their half-term holiday from Mourne Grange, a boarding-school down the coast at Kilkeel. They brought along several of their friends, all wearing blazers and school caps, and cricket was organized. Neither I nor Nicky nor John Hinchcliffe nor David Lanyon had cricket bats and, anyway, none of us knew the rules. The big boys kept hitting the ball into the scutch grass of the dunes on one side and into the waves on the other and we had to run and retrieve it – this was called 'fielding'. We felt entirely disregarded, while the batsmen and bowlers had a jolly time shouting, 'Over up!' and 'Well held, sir!' We grew intensely bored and started to quarrel among ourselves, which annoyed the big boys. Then a girl called Anne Carr threw sand in John Hinchcliffe's eyes and he cried, and I said I hoped I wouldn't ever have as horrible a party again.

My father, who had not been at the picnic, said it was time I was at a proper school, taking part in proper games, but I was perfectly satisfied with Miss Logan's – as happy, it had to be admitted, as the bees my mother had earlier described. There was a much more enjoyable birthday party in the garden of the Dower House at Tollymore for a girl called Diana, one of the older girls at Miss Logan's. There were races and competitions for prizes, and a cake with candles. Better still, in the house there was a Persian cat with five kittens, and a lady who must have been Diana's mother or aunt asked me if I would like one. Naturally I said I would. The next morning I heard a scrabbling noise under my bed and out skipped a grey kitten – my mother had cycled all the way back to Tollymore the previous night in the blackout to collect her. She had a pedigree written on a form supplied by the Persian Cat Society: her father was called Silver Arrow and her mother Melody. We decided her

name should be Silver Song but I called her Nullah for no
reason that I could explain, even to myself. 'A *nullah* in
Hindustani,' my father said, 'is a kind of dried-up river-bed
– and why would you want to call your cat a watercourse
or creek?' I said I didn't know and everyone else could call
her Silver Song if they liked, but to me she was Nullah.

There was another picnic for the four of us on the same
strand, near the railway station. Nicky and I were told to be
good and play for a few minutes while my mother said
goodbye to my father at the train, a few hundred yards from
where we were digging sandcastles. He was going away to
get his orders for when he would be in command of the
East Surreys and he'd probably be able to send for us when
he found out where they were being posted. She was much
longer than she had said, so we started walking along the
edge of the dunes towards the station. We saw her standing
on the Promenade, looking out at the waves. We went up
to her, but she didn't say anything. Then she turned and led
us back to Anchor Lodge Mews.

There were pictures in the newspaper of the King and Queen
coming to Belfast to look at the bomb damage and to thank
the people of Northern Ireland for their bravery. Shortly
afterwards the British soldiers seemed suddenly to vanish.
There were a few weeks with no soldiers at all and then the
Americans arrived. They had dozens of little trucks called
'jeeps' in which they were constantly whizzing about with
loudspeakers giving out greetings to the people of the town.
They also had real tanks with big white stars painted on
them, row upon row ranged out in Castle Park. Miss Moran
wondered if these Americans had any sense at all, showing
off like that; she said someone should tell them to be sure
to throw camouflage netting over the white stars that

proclaimed their presence to every German bomber in the sky! The Americans never came to the Forces' Library, though my mother continued to sit there for two hours on Monday evenings; nor did they stand around with mugs of tea, but they drank milk in great quantities and it was said that the local farmers had great difficulty in supplying their quota.

It was undeniable that the Yankees were much smarter than the Tommies, and it wasn't just their well-cut uniforms. They were taller and better-looking – 'gangling,' said Miss Moran – and they had far better teeth: 'All that fluoride in their drinking water is quite unnatural.' Also, it was darkly rumoured, they ate fried potatoes for breakfast and spread marmalade on their ham. Very curious, and not quite *comme il faut*, Miss Moran thought.

Certainly they were always chewing, whether it was Wrig-ley's gum or Hershey bars. They were generous with these, handing them out as Maureen conducted us on our way to school. 'Hey, good-lookin'!' one called out to her. 'Wanna go to the movies tonight?'

Maureen took no notice, hurrying us along. 'No manners! Making a show of me like that, shouting across the street in front of the whole of Newcastle!' she declared angrily: 'I wouldn't go to the pictures with *him* if his arse was studded with diamonds!' I thought this was terribly funny because that was a word you weren't supposed to use, and if his arse *was* studded with diamonds he would have found it very sore sitting down, even on an upholstered seat in the Ritz Cinema.

Miss Rudd, on her way to her morning plunge in the Irish Sea, remarked that the Americans were always doing silly things. Her landlady, Mrs Bristoe, had learned that a few nights previously, during the blackout, two of their sentries had heard footsteps approaching and called, 'Halt!' The footsteps continued, so they shouted, '*Wo gehen Sie?*' as they had been instructed. Finally they decided they had no option but to shoot. There was an inhuman cry, and when they got out their torches they saw that they had killed a donkey. 'Such a way to treat one of God's creatures!' declared Miss Rudd in disgust.

On the Fourth of July the US 11th Infantry Division paraded through the town with a brass band, carrying what Miss Rudd described as 'a thing like a barber's pole', which later revealed itself, when unfurled, as the Stars and Stripes. Loudspeakers in jeeps invited the local public to 'come and see the baseball game' in a field near Tollymore, and many people did so out of politeness, though they did not under-stand the rules, applauding at what were obviously the wrong moments. I was bored after two minutes. Fortunately there was a Sherman tank on display nearby, its gun-turret swivel-ling menacingly, and I wished we had been allowed to climb inside. Anne Carr said of the tanks that they were 'nasty blooming things', repeating this phrase several times so that I thought it was not really what she thought but something she'd picked up from an unfair adult. That evening my mother and some other ladies were invited as special guests by the US officers to a barn-dance in the ballroom of the Slieve Donard Hotel, which she said was got up for the occasion with bales of hay and pens with real cows and pigs! It was quite fun, she said, though Miss Rudd made it plain she did not appreciate being addressed as 'honey' by the colonel.

When the summer term ended at Miss Logan's, my mother decided that our education required 'continuity' so she arranged for us to share the governess of two big girls in a decrepit turreted house in King Street overlooking the harbour. Joyce and Christine Hackett lived with their mother – it was another household in which the father was abroad

– and were visited by a retired school-teacher, who came from Belfast every day on the bus. Miss Douglas was about a hundred and always wore the same black skirt and grey blouse. My mother said that she wasn't well-off and needed to earn some money to keep an aged relative, perhaps her mother. (If so, her mother must have been a hundred and fifty.) We sat round a table covered with what looked like a candlewick bedspread. The Hackett girls were far ahead of me in books. I felt there was no possibility of even trying to catch up and was therefore seen to be idle. At the end of each week Miss Douglas went through a protracted ceremony that involved pieces of cardboard, a metal ruler, a large kitchen scissors, a fine-nibbed pen and a bottle of Indian ink. This resulted in the production of four small cards on which she inscribed 'First Honour' or 'Second Honour', as the case might be, then handed one out to each pupil. I found that I was usually the recipient of a 'Third Honour' and that Nicky and the girls were much more likely to be presented with a 'First'. 'Well, at least it's an *honour*,' I said, in defence of my poor showing, 'I mean, it's not a *dis*honour.' My mother urged me to 'try harder' but I had no idea of how this could be done, for Miss Douglas was a terrible bore and there wasn't much more to it than that.

There was ominous talk of 'boarding-school'. When classes finished at the end of August it was found that Nicky had six 'First Honour' cards and I had none. The cards, signed by Miss Douglas, could be exchanged for goods at the Educational Company Ltd in Belfast: Nicky had one shilling and sixpence worth and I had only ninepence.

The ending of classes in the Hacketts' rackety house, all nooks and steps and secret look-outs, signalled the end of Newcastle for us. Clearly the US Army was in possession and there was no possibility of my father's regiment ever coming back. The weather grew stormy – 'The early equinoctial gales,' Miss Douglas explained. The oakwoods below the forest of firs on Slieve Donard began to turn yellow. Miss Rudd continued her sea-bathing – 'Nothing like salt water to clear the head!' she announced, emerging suddenly from a rocky pool. Certainly her head, with its mulberry cheeks and sloe-coloured eyes, did look remarkably clear.

'She's a tough old gull,' said my mother. I tried to visualize Miss Rudd clad in grey and white feathers bobbing on gentle billows but I could not imagine her as a seagull for she was the wrong sort of shape. She was more of a walrus – large and heavy and commanding. Walruses also had moustaches, and Miss Rudd certainly had the makings of a fine one. I observed this more closely when she was winding her towel round the handlebars of her bicycle one morning after her swim. (There were seven distinct hairs.) She said it would be nice if I and my friend Gineen Bland – who was distinguished in Newcastle because she had a Sudanese nanny, the first black person ever seen there – would come to Sunday lunch; Mrs Bristoe would enjoy that so much. She would call for us at Anchor Lodge Mews after her swim and we'd all three cycle out to Bryansford.

There was no sign of Miss Rudd on Sunday at the time she had proposed. My mother said it had probably slipped her mind and if she failed to turn up by two o'clock Gineen could stay and have Spam and fried potatoes with us. I slipped down to the strand to see if Miss Rudd was still in the water. It was blustery and the tide was in. The tops of the posts designed to prevent the landing of enemy aircraft could be seen sticking out of the waves. On one of these posts, quite far out to sea, sat a large seal.

I was about to return to the Mews when I noticed that the

US Army band was preparing to give its Sunday-afternoon recital for the people of the town, not many of whom had turned up. Those who did were holding their hats down because of the wind. There was also a group below the bandstand on the beach and in the midst of this was Miss Rudd, enveloped in a huge bathrobe. She appeared to be changing into her swimming costume rather than out of it. The costume was made of a thick woven material the colour of lichen, trimmed with an arrangement of white string resembling the ropes that festooned the gunwales of the local lifeboat. She asked a man for the loan of his umbrella and he was obviously so surprised that he could not say no.

Miss Rudd strode into the sea. I had never seen a person going swimming with an umbrella so I moved closer. From the remarks of the onlookers I gathered that after taking her morning swim she had noticed the stranded seal and nothing would dissuade her from rescuing it. At the point where the strand shelved into deeper water Miss Rudd started to swim. The people below the bandstand stood aghast. They remarked to one another that the weather was much too squally for a woman of that age to go out swimming, least of all in an effort to rescue a seal, which might take a notion against her. Resolutely breasting the foam Miss Rudd churned onwards, the furled umbrella appearing and disappearing at every stroke. A man said they should send for the fire brigade; another said it would be better to hire a rowing-boat from the pier; but nobody moved, so riveting was the scene. Miss Rudd reached the pole on top of which flapped the seal. It looked down at her and they seemed to be having a conversation.

'She must be treading water,' a woman said, as Miss Rudd poked awkwardly upwards at the seal with her umbrella.

'She won't be getting much leverage,' a man replied.

The sound of Miss Rudd's voice came in gusts across the waves. 'Shoo! Shoo!' she cried.

'Them seals can turn vicious,' said the woman. 'A bite would leave you with lockjaw.'

Suddenly the seal seemed to overbalance. It flopped into the water, making a splash that could not be heard over the noise of the waves. The crowd by the bandstand applauded. 'Isn't she the quare brave woman?' said the man, who would clearly not have undertaken such an escapade himself for a pound note. Miss Rudd made for the shore, hampered by the umbrella yet clearly determined not to cast it aside – the woman in the crowd said that its owner had probably paid a good price for it, and its owner agreed. Unaware of the incident unfolding before them, the band of the 11th Infantry Division played a selection of Sousa marches. Some people in the crowd went as far as to remove their shoes and socks to assist Miss Rudd out of the water. The woman who had been worried about the seal's demeanour advised her to take a good strong cup of hot Bovril. Miss Rudd said she was perfectly all right – her only wish had been to cherish a distressed member of the animal kingdom.

I hung about the bandstand, pretending to listen to the music, to give Miss Rudd time to dry herself and put on her clothes before reminding her of our delayed lunch appointment. I was about to approach her when I noticed that she had suddenly paused in fastening the buckle of her sandal – something had caught her attention out to sea. We saw the waves, and the gulls, and the posts thrusting up through the water, and there, on top of the same post, calmly sat the seal.

Some time in the early autumn we left Anchor Lodge Mews. We were going to stay with the Butlers at Maidenhall, my mother said. Perhaps later she might join my father for a bit, wherever he was. My kitten Nullah travelled with us on the train in a bicycle-basket with a lid. The Newcastle summer was over.

Like Alice, I wondered if it had all really happened.

> *Ever drifting down the stream –*
> *Lingering in the golden gleam –*
> *Life, what is it but a dream?*

## Maidenhall, Bennettsbridge, County Kilkenny

We were met at Bennettsbridge station by Peggy Butler in a trap drawn by a whimsical pony called Minnie. Julia was there too, and Joe Hone, who had been living with the Butlers since they left Annaghmakerrig, and settled in Hubert's family home, Maidenhall. Nullah was mewing in the bicycle-basket and they were all dying to see my kitten but I said that if we opened the lid Nullah might jump out and run into the hedge and be lost for ever. The plaintive voice continued to be heard as we trundled through the village past the Co-operative Creamery and the Garda station, with its two crenellated towers – Peggy said the plans for a barracks had become mixed up at the time of the British colonial regime, and Bennettsbridge had got the one intended for the Khyber Pass – or so she had heard. There was a little shop called Wall's and a pub called the Nore Bar, after the name of the river. Then Minnie stopped. 'When she sees a hill,' said Julia, 'even if it's a mile away, she stops.' This hill was the steep approach to the river bridge and we had to get out and walk because Minnie knew exactly what would be too heavy for her.

The five-arched stone bridge over the Nore rose to a greater height than some of the houses in the village street. From the parapet you could see over the spreading surface of the river, which divided downstream, one of the channels leading towards a six-storey mill, the only tall building in a landscape where all others were low-lying and where even the church had only a little spike of a belfry. We paused to look over the swirling water.

'Do you know what that is?' asked Joe.

'It's a waterfall.'

'No, it's a weir. That's the mill-race and it drives the waterwheel that drives the turbine that makes the machinery grind the grain into flour.'

We descended to the west bank of the river where there was a cluster of houses, one belonging to the Mosse family who owned the mill – 'But Pam and Berry Mosse, whom you'll meet because they come for lessons every day with Miss Mahon, live further down the road, at Annamult where the Nore joins the King's river,' said Peggy. 'Lovely situation, dreffy damp house.'

Horse-chestnut trees, now almost leafless, bordered the road to the mill and we bumped along behind Minnie for the last quarter-mile to the gate of Maidenhall – an unexpected entrance that looked as if it led to a farmyard rather than a big house. Peggy was telling my mother that had it not been for the broad two-storeyed extension, which Julia's grandparents had built in the early 1900s, and for the white-columned porch, which they had added to the front of the old house at the same time, Maidenhall would look unusually tall and stark, a narrow four-storeyed building teetering on the side of its hill. The alterations gave a sense of the house spreading comfortably into its surroundings in the way that the trees, which had been planted generations before,

spread comfortably into the hillside round about. Peggy said
it was most unusual for Victorian or Edwardian additions to
blend with what had gone before. Sunlight illuminated the
porch for most of the day; when the sun was not shining
the porch was still a place where you could sit out, its deep
canopy and enclosed ends providing shelter when the weather
was less inviting. There was an assortment of old wooden
and wicker chairs, logs piled ready for burning, daffodil and
hyacinth bulbs drying out in autumn, croquet hoops and
mallets and sundry garden implements. This was the porch
of a real country house, not of a fashionable gentleman's
residence. My mother said to some visitor or other that if
Chekhov had placed one of his plays in Ireland this house
would be the setting.

The interior was different from other country houses
where we had lived or had visited – quite unlike the zeal-
ously broomed and beeswaxed rooms of Annaghmakerrig,
where every piece of ormolu or marquetry and every gilt-
framed portrait was irremovable from its allotted place, or of
Hollywood, where brooms and mops were out of favour and
tattered pieces of bedroom furniture had strayed nonchalantly
into the dining room. There was a feeling at Maidenhall that
the furniture was arranged this way or that to make changes
that were pleasing to the eye and undoubtedly further changes
would take place, if not today then next week. Tradition was
merged with innovation. Hubert had lined the walls of the
drawing room with white wooden bookcases, which gave it
at once a bright and cosy look. Over the chimney-piece he
had hung a wooden image of St John the Baptist, which he
said was a Russian icon, probably painted by a very famous
artist of the fourteenth century called Andrei Rublev. He
told us it had been given to him by a writer, Leonid Leonov,
after he had translated his novel *The Thief* into English,

because Leonid couldn't afford a fee – and, of course, it was far nicer to have the icon. I thought St John looked somewhat demented and in need of a good meal, and Hubert said this was the way he was usually portrayed, the dishevelled saint whose voice was heard crying in the wilderness.

There was a big desk in the drawing-room window where Hubert did much of his writing, though sometimes he spread his papers all over the heavy Victorian table in the dining room next door. Peggy had sent for the pattern books from the new Irish Carpets factory in Kildare, choosing a green sisal Tintawn for the stairs and landings and a dark cherry-coloured rectangle in the same material for the drawing room. Rugs and mats of distinctly ancestral mien were deftly scattered cheek-by-jowl with those of unmistakably Balkan origin. She bought a plain tea-set manufactured in Carrigaline by the new pottery that had been set up with help from the Free State government; it chipped very easily and the handles had a way of breaking off, but it looked stylish and modern. Electric lights – their current supplied by a wind-charger on a pole situated on the hill beyond the yard – were of the marbled mixing-bowl type that threw much light on the ceiling and little elsewhere; the power was not strong enough to boil a kettle or make a piece of toast, but to have electricity to any degree was a remarkable accomplishment outside the towns. Before our arrival Hubert and Peggy had 'brought up' the kitchen, abandoning the basement to the storage of unwanted furniture and the barrowloads of apples that were gathered from September to Christmas.

The new kitchen was the chief topic at the time of our introduction to Maidenhall. It was built out from the back of the house so that it did not interfere with the Georgian symmetry unless you peered very closely through the horse-chestnut boughs and saw that its windows were of the

metal-framed kind that opened outwards, like those at Whinsfield. This kitchen contained the latest convenience, an Aga
cooker, which kept a steady heat by day and night and burned
glistening black anthracite from the mines of Castlecomer
only twenty miles away. 'Hubert! Have you filled the Aga?'
was Peggy's nightly reminder, and then we would hear a
tremendous rattling noise as the ashes were raked out with
a metal hook that connected to a cog-wheel, followed by
the scrunch of the fuel falling from the hopper into the
ironbound furnace at the stove's heart.

Bringing up the kitchen had evidently caused considerable
controversy in the Butler family, Hubert's younger brother
and his sisters disapproving of anything that changed the
pattern of life hallowed by a century and a half of custom
and practice. As his brother and sisters were living, respectively,
at Scatorish, the neat farm half a mile across the fields, in
Wales and in Ceylon, my mother felt it was hardly civil of
them to criticize changes in a house they rarely visited. Peggy
was not greatly interested in *cuisine* and employed a cook,
Nelly Wemys, who could not possibly have coped with the
immense stove in the old basement kitchen, which had
needed a full-time yard-boy to stoke it; and Nelly would
certainly have given notice at the time of year when
wellington boots had to be worn because of a mysterious
spring that regularly flooded the basement to a depth of six
inches. The new upstairs kitchen, with its bright, cream-
coloured stove, was clearly a great improvement and the huffs
and pouts of Hubert's relatives were, my mother surmised,
occasioned by envy.

I had been reading Enid Blyton's *Five on a Treasure Island*, a
present from Bunty Worby, in which the father of one of
the children was a distinguished scientist who required

absolute silence in the house while he was working. He was given to bursting out of his study in an absolute fury when disturbed by the smallest sounds of laughter or by the bark of the heroine's mongrel. ('"*Woof!*" said Timmy.') Knowing that Hubert was a writer I was prepared for the same, and when he disappeared in the morning I thought we should all keep very quiet – but I soon learned that he was exactly the opposite to the glowering parent in the book. When immersed in papers or battering away at the black Royal typewriter he did not appear to notice external noise at all, and when interrupted he was always ready to attend to the needs of some visitor with a horticultural enquiry or to respond enthusiastically to a plan for an excursion to some place of local historical interest – such as the ruined cloister of Jerpoint Abbey, where I found a sculpture of St Christopher that Hubert said had been created by a local stonemason in the fourteenth century, or Kells Priory, with its enormous fortified enclosure that made it look more like a castle than a place of spiritual contemplation. ('It was a bit of both,' said Hubert.) Hubert was waging a campaign to have the Norman tower-house known as Foulksrath Castle preserved – the general view was that if money was collected and spent the building would deteriorate again in no time so it wouldn't be worth the bother, but he persevered and, after much writing of letters and speaking at meetings, Foulksrath was converted into a hostel for hikers and cyclists. In spite of many dire warnings that no one could possibly want to hike or bicycle to such a place, it drew visitors from all quarters. ('Hearty outdoor types of indeterminate sex in khaki shorts subsisting on bully-beef,' said Peggy.)

With Hubert we inspected the great earthen circle of Sheestown, at least a thousand years old, he said; it was thought to have been built as a place of religious ritual but

Hubert had an idea that there was a much more practical explanation, an enclosure for cattle, because cows were used as money in those days and there were always marauders trying to steal a rich man's herd. Sheestown was believed to be named in honour of the People of the Shee, or *Sidhe*, as it was written in Irish – the Fairy People – but again Hubert had a more practical theory, which was that one of the leading families or tribes was called Shee, or O'Shee, the same as the modern name O'Shea.

The castle in Kilkenny was closed because the Ormond Butlers who owned it had gone away, but Hubert said the Ormonds didn't like visitors anyway. You could see its towers from many of the streets and there was a riverside view of most of it from St John's Bridge – a view I recognized from *The Spirit of Ireland*, one of the books that had belonged to my great-uncle John at Eldron. It was strange to think of the vast bulk of the castle with its formal gardens and grounds standing unused and unappreciated in the centre of the city. At the other end of High Street was St Canice's Cathedral, which was usually open and had a much older round tower; the church authorities had improved the wooden staircase so that visitors could pay sixpence and climb up to see the view. From the top you could look down on Smithwick's brewery, with its puffs of steam and rising smell of fermenting hops, and next to it the gleaming daffodil-yellow Savoy cinema and beyond that High Street joining the cathedral to the castle like a spine, with streets leading off, like ribs and limbs. Inside the cathedral the floor of the chancel was paved in the four colours of Irish marble – black from Kilkenny, pink from Midleton, green from Connemara and grey from Antrim.

The most spectacular place we visited from Maidenhall was the Rock of Cashel, a ruined castle and cathedral standing

on a craggy outcrop in the midst of the lush pasturage of
Tipperary. There were spiral staircases inside the walls leading
up to nowhere. My mother signalled to us to come down
*at once!* when she spied us emerging on the top of the roofless
tower. From this vantage-point we could see the grey slated
roofs of the town of Cashel below and the remains of five
more abbeys scattered about the plain. When we came down
she was very cross and said we must *never* take such a risk
again, the masonry could easily collapse under our weight
and it was ridiculous that there was nothing to stop people
clambering about in such a dangerous way – there should
at least be a person in charge at a place that must certainly
attract sightseers. Hubert said that national monuments were
the responsibility of the Board of Works but they hadn't any
money to do anything other than put up notices saying
'*Fógra!* Commit no nuisance.' (My mother remarked that
people falling from the battlements would certainly be a bit
of a nuisance.) We tried to get into Cormac's Chapel but
the iron gate was locked. Hubert said it was the masterpiece
of Hiberno-Romanesque architecture and had been inspired
by monasteries on the Rhine but the style of sculpture was
very Irish, which meant that King Cormac – if indeed it
was he who had had it built – had employed local craftsmen.
Looking through the bars, we could just discern the snaky
carvings that Hubert said were typically Celtic. King Cormac
had died because a fishbone had stuck in his throat so he
never saw the completion of his monument.

'We're on our *uppers*,' said Peggy gaily to my mother. 'Selling
apples is absolutely *de rigueur* if we're to keep boring things
like bread and butter on the table.' Every autumn day when
it wasn't actually pouring with rain we went out to the
orchard, Hubert climbing a ladder and the rest of us picking

whatever we could reach. The apples were put in boxes, bags and baskets and stowed in the pony-trap. It was Peggy who marched into the shops in Kilkenny to sell them. 'I don't suppose you'd have any use for *apples*?' she would say, as if she were suggesting something not quite respectable, and the shopman would come out and doubtfully inspect what was on offer, sometimes taking a bag, sometimes not. Visitors to Maidenhall were set to pick whatever fruit and flowers the garden had to offer, depending upon the time of year, to sell in the shops or in the market that the Irish Countrywomen's Association had established in the yard behind the Kilkenny courthouse. Peggy found that daffodils were particularly good sellers, because 'every little suburban lady comes *panting* for tiny bunches to put in the front window under the frilly curtains'. Lunch guests were used to having basins thrust into their hands on arrival – 'Would you *ever* pick some raspberries? They're at their best just now – we're having them for pudding.'

Miss Mahon was the governess, a soft-spoken lady from Portarlington who was as unlike the fearsome Miss Roberts of Annaghmakerrig or the pedantic Miss Hogan of Eldron as one could wish. She supplied us with nature-study books that had a plain page on one side for drawing and a lined page opposite for writing descriptions. I did a piece on a hedgehog after we came across one in a brambly part of the orchard and it drank a saucer of milk without the least fear. Miss Mahon said it would lie on its back, spike a windfall apple, and then walk off triumphantly to its lair, but though we watched for ages it didn't give us a demonstration. I also wrote up the story of how the wind-charger flew off its pole in a storm, and drew a picture of it with its nose buried in the ground, like a crashed Dakota DC3. Miss Mahon told us all about the harvesting and processing of sugar-beet, which all the farmers were growing because there was no sugar-cane coming from Cuba any more, and I drew that story too, showing how I imagined the beet was distilled into sugar in the factory at Carlow. Julia was sure her uncle Gilbert wouldn't mind if we took a root of beet – or perhaps two or three in case the experiment didn't work the first time – from a heap awaiting collection in his farmyard. We chopped one up and boiled it in a doll's saucepan on the schoolroom fire until it turned to mush. Then the thing was to distil the steam that came from further boilings but whatever steam was left in the saucepan lid showed no inclination of turning into crystals. We tasted the mush in case it was on the way to becoming sugar but it was nearly as gruesome as the *carraigín* that had made us sick at Ballyconneely so we said nothing to Miss Mahon in case she advised us to eat it all.

Miss Mahon released us from lessons at noon but Pam and Berry Mosse had to stay on till one o'clock, because they were older, and Nicky and Joe didn't have to do any lessons at all, which I thought very unfair as they were now almost six and I'd had to start lessons when I was four. There was an arrangement that Hubert would tutor me in Latin once a week but he was either too busy or forgot and I wasn't going to remind him, so I learned only as far as the Fourth Declension of Nouns – *consul, consul, consulem, consulis, consuli, consule*. This was to be in preparation for my going to a 'real' school where Latin would be important.

Nicky's sixth birthday came in November, and there was a party with a wonderfully spooky magic-lantern show in the darkened sitting room. The lantern had been discovered in a cupboard on the top floor, and Hubert thought his grandparents must have bought it to amuse his father when he was a little boy. It was made of shiny wood and its metal parts were brass; the glass slides were square and contained in boxes labelled *The Sleeping Beauty* and *The Babes in the Wood* and *Sinbad the Sailor* in old-fashioned print. The pictures projected were in very bright colours and the wicked people had frightening faces with big red lips and slanty eyes like wolves. In *The Babes in the Wood* the parents were shown dying in a four-poster bed; their faces were completely white, they looked about a hundred years old and the babes were being lifted up to kiss them goodbye by a fat nurse in a mob-cap with big blobby tears streaming out of her eyes while two evil robbers peeped in through the lattice window.

The person who was showing the slides was supposed to read the stories from a dog-eared pamphlet. Hubert hadn't really sorted the slides or, indeed, studied the book, so when he was reading out, 'The roc seized Sinbad in its scimitar-like beak by the hem of his garment, O best beloved, and bore him off to its nest on the highest pinnacle of the Beauteous Mountain, intending him to be devoured by the little rocs who were screaming for a tasty meal of human flesh,' the picture that appeared on the bedsheet that Peggy had drawing-pinned to the wall showed the Archdeacon's widow in a wheelchair being pushed into Ennisnag Church.

Miss Mahon organized a game of Forfeits. Berry Mosse had to kiss the cat but no cat could be found and Peggy lifted up the aged Pekinese that she had inherited from her parents-in-law and said, 'Kiss beauffy old Fan Tan instead!' but Berry only pretended to kiss Fan Tan because she was really quite smelly. Joe was told to sing something, which I would have hated to do, but without hesitation he sat himself down on the sofa and sang the song Delia Murphy was forever broadcasting on Radio Eireann:

*I'm a rambler, I'm a gambler,*
*I'm a long way from home,*
*And if you don't like me*
*Just leave me alone;*
*I'll eat when I'm hungry,*
*I'll drink when I'm dry,*
*And if moonshine don't kill me*
*I'll live till I die . . .*

Everyone clapped, including all the adults, and someone's mother said it was quite moving, knowing the circumstances, whatever she meant by that.

Mrs G came to stay from Annaghmakerrig but she got congestion of the lungs – probably from the cold of the house, my mother thought – and Bunty was sent for, after which there was much bustling about with bowls of beef tea and hot compresses until she recovered. Peggy bought a pig's head at the pork butcher's in Kilkenny because it was going for next to nothing – no one else would buy it – and Nelly served it on a huge platter. It looked like the centrepiece of a prince's banquet in an old story except that you could see the bristly inside of its ear and the twisty look in its eye. Peggy said we were *not* to say what it was in front of Mrs G and I thought that as Mrs G wasn't completely blind she might notice the outline on the dish even if she couldn't see its nostrils or its teeth, but she didn't.

'Mum, will you have *ham*?' said Peggy, and we all started sniggering.

'What *are* they laughing at?' asked Mrs G.

Abruptly Peggy said, 'Christopher and Julia, *do* be absolute angels and get the glasses from the pantry cupboard and, Mum, will you have cabbage? And spuds?' so that got us out of the room and the business of serving the meal seemed to make it unnecessary for Peggy to answer Mrs G's question.

Another day, when Hubert was slicing a stuffed vegetable marrow – we had our dinner at one o'clock, all of us seated round the big dining-room table – a clip-clop clip-clop was heard and a pony and trap with two ladies passed the window. 'Oh!' cried Peggy. 'It's Joyce Tottenham and Aunt Maisie. I'd forgotten I'd invited them to lunch!' and we carried our plates back to the kitchen while two extra places were laid and Hubert delayed the ladies' entrance by asking them to drive round to the yard where Jimmy Lawler would see to the pony.

People often came from Dublin to speak to Hubert about talks he was going to give on Radio Eireann or articles he was writing for the *Bell* magazine. Sean O'Faolain, the magazine's editor, came with a dumpy-looking woman called Honor Tracy who, people were saying, had written a very funny book about Ireland. Before she arrived Hubert read out some bits in which she had said that on enquiring at the Cork Tourist Office what entertainments were available in the evening she had been told there was a choice between a performance at the Opera House of *The Pirates of Penzance* by pupils of the Mercy Convent or a lecture in the Metropole Hotel on the Sacred Shroud. He said some of the people she described were easy to identify, though it was obvious the names had been changed. It was clear that Peggy didn't like Miss Tracy, or perhaps didn't like her book, for she only poured a tiny dribble of sherry into her glass when everyone else's was filled to the top. The playwright Padraic Colum, a little man like a hobgoblin, came another time and was suddenly sick on the sitting-room floor. He said, 'Sorry!' and Peggy got a basin and cloth and wiped up the mess without any fuss at all. I thought that if Miss Tracy had vomited there would have been a lot of running to and fro and Peggy would have said, 'Shall I send for the doctor?' or 'It must have been something you *drank*', and Miss Tracy would have been asked if she'd like a taxi to take her to the station.

There were visits from several foreign people, among them Erwin and Liesl Strunz, whom Hubert had helped to leave Vienna just as the war was about to start. They were Jews but they didn't have big noses, nor were they a bit like the Jews pictured in *My First Book of Bible Stories*, which Mrs G had given me two birthdays ago; naturally I wasn't expecting them to be wearing robes and headdresses like Abraham, but the fact was they looked disappointingly like everyone else. They had started a restaurant in Dublin called the Unicorn and they were saying how they were attracting 'the international set' and also 'the Bohemians' and this was quite unexpected because they hadn't imagined such people existed in Dublin. They never stopped telling us children how they wouldn't be in such a happy position had it not been for Hubert and they described with great enthusiasm to the grown-ups how members of the diplomatic corps met each other at the Unicorn, people from Germany and Italy, Britain and the United States, who could not possibly have mixed socially – or, indeed, at all! – in their own countries. They said they were aware that their restaurant had taken on a reputation as a meeting-place for spies but they didn't give countenance to such gossip – though indeed some quite *shady* characters were sometimes seen digging into Liesl's *Linzetorte*. Members of the White Stag painters' group were regulars, many of them conscientious objectors who had fled from warlike England, and the actors from the Gate Theatre, like Mr MacLíammóir and Mr Edwards, who, Erwin thought, were very frustrated in Dublin and were looking forward to the time when they could be touring again in Europe. 'In the evenings we are like a little League of Nations!' he said, with a satisfied laugh.

There was also Alexander Lieven, a Russian prince studying at Trinity College. On his visits Alexander shared our room at the top of the house; he was studying Irish folk tales and kept me fascinated with true ghost stories, none of them, unfortunately, to do with houses we were likely to visit. A dance teacher called Erina Brady came to stay. She was from Bad Homburg in Germany and wore a leopardskin coat and a black beret. She gave junior and senior tuition each week at the Desart Hall in Kilkenny – my mother thought it must be a dreadful step down for her to be running classes in provincial towns in Ireland and dancing the part of a squaw in a semi-professional production of *The Merry Widow* in Dublin – but, then, it would be worse to be living in Germany where nobody had much cause to dance at all. Miss Brady was producing a dance-drama called *Elfin Hill* with her senior pupils in Kilkenny. Julia and I went to her junior class so were not included but she sat on the sheepskin rug in front of the sitting-room fire at Maidenhall and told us how she was approaching the production, which involved a scene where it slowly became daylight, and this would be achieved by someone picking slides one by one off an electric lantern. I thought this would make for a rather jerky dawn, but I didn't have a chance to see the play, for, by the time it was produced, we were on our way back again to Northern Ireland.

Nullah was accepted into the circle of Maidenhall cats – Smoky, Pully-Molly and Forget-me-not – without the angry growlings and hissings we had anticipated, probably because he was so young. Pin Win, the frisky Pekinese who had eaten Mary Burns's hen, kept barking at him but he didn't seem to mind and Pin Win's aunt, the aged Fan Tan, didn't appear to notice him at all. I had to get used to calling him 'he', for when we had stayed for a few days at Seaview on our way to Maidenhall my grandmother – who had met Nullah as a kitten at Newcastle – said he was *definitely* a tom. 'Look at the big head! And the jowls!' Bridie Donoghue, the Seaview maid, was entranced. She had never seen such a coat on a cat, and my grandmother explained that he was pure-bred Persian, 'with a pedigree as long as today and tomorrow'.

The truth was that I was sorry he was a he because I liked the idea of a lady cat who would have kittens of her own. He slept in my mother's bedroom where there was a huge curtained bed but she never let him into it in spite of my suggestion that he would be like an extra hot-water bottle – my mother always took two of them to bed for, she said, she had never experienced such cold in her life. She kept a tray of earth for Nullah to use as a lavatory; the other cats were not so well trained and Forget-me-not, a wistful-looking black and white female, made a mess accompanied by a very explosive noise in Hubert's waste-paper basket, after which all cat life except Nullah was banned from everywhere indoors except the old pantry, where there was a hole in the wall they could use as a door.

Nullah, though only six months old, had a sense of his own importance. He would prance into any room where he knew there would be an audience, his tail floating aloft like a banner, his demeanour stating, 'I am here! Disregard me if you can!' and, of course, everyone present exclaimed at his beauty and regality. '*Uaisleacht*' was how a Free State army officer, who had come to give Irish lessons to Hubert in exchange for tuition in Russian, described him. In the damp days of early December Nullah caught a cold, and when this turned to a wheezing cough my mother sent for the vet, who said he had cat flu – well, it could hardly have been *dog* flu, she said – prescribing aspirins crushed in milk. My mother covered him with an old jersey, for the room was quite cold. One morning when I looked into her room I said he seemed very still and my mother said he was sleeping so I mustn't disturb him. That evening when I was having my bath she said that a very sad thing had happened: poor Nullah had died. I was shocked and cried for hours. Why had the vet not cured him? It was all Miss Mahon's fault: she had tonsillitis and had passed it on to him.

'When did he die?'

'This morning, quite early.'

'Why didn't you tell me?'

'I didn't want to spoil your day.'

'*Spoil my day!* Where is he?'

'Jimmy Lawler very kindly buried him.'

'Where?'

'In the garden, I suppose. I didn't ask.'

'I should have been there. There should have been a funeral.'

My mother said that I might have taken more interest in him, for it was she who had fed him and changed the earth in his 'garden' while I had only played games with him. Then I felt very guilty and wondered whether he would not have died if I had been more attentive.

Next day Julia and I went looking for places in the garden where the earth had been disturbed so that we could decorate Nullah's grave with flowers, but we didn't find anywhere. Somehow I couldn't bring myself to ask Jimmy Lawler for I had a sense that there was some sort of connivance between him and my mother and he'd only say something stupid like 'Ah, sure I can't remember at all.' I was bereft. I had lost my dearest friend and no one would ever take his place. And then my mother said I'd have to pull myself together, everyone had to die and it was just a pity that he had died so young. I wrote a poem about him and decided to show it to Miss Mahon, but then I didn't in case she thought I was being silly. I considered writing a letter to Diana in Newcastle but I remembered that she had been sarcastic when I'd asked her to hurry up writing out his pedigree, though she had done so in the end. I thought how unfair it was that Nullah should have come all the way from his lovely home at Tollymore Park, had grown up at Anchor Lodge where he had been the centre of attention, had been much admired by Bridie Donoghue at Seaview and now had been cruelly taken away. I thought that if I concentrated on him very hard he would know I was missing him so I often talked to him in the middle of the night. Then I had an idea that he was watching over me and would be on hand whenever I needed guidance, as in the words of the hymn,

> *Through the darkness, be thou near me,*
> *Keep me safe till morning light . . .*

Shortly after the time I was mourning for Nullah, my mother started behaving as if some other sad thing had happened. One afternoon we were peeling apples on the porch and she was telling me about the time a monkey had jumped through the window of our sleeping-compartment in an Indian train and had sat down opposite me in my cot and she was afraid that if I made a sudden move it would bite and I'd get hydrophobia and die, but the minute the engine whistled for departure the monkey got up and jumped out of the window and then she saw there were dozens of monkeys doing the same thing and this was quite usual. Near the end of the story she broke off and I thought she was going to cry, so I said, 'But the monkey *didn't* bite me and I *didn't* die,' and she said, 'No, I was thinking of something else. I had a letter from your daddy and he thinks he'll have to leave the army.' Having said that, she stopped looking so upset and finished the story. 'Your grandfather was in the next compartment and I told him what had happened and asked if *he* would have hooshed the monkey away and he said, "I'd have looked into the cot and the first thing I'd have done was ascertain which of the two was the monkey!"'

A few days later she said that because my father had chronic sinusitis, probably brought on by breathing all that sand in the desert, he was going to have an operation, but he might never be fit enough to go on active service again so he might have to leave the army. She said he was far too young to retire – he was forty-five – but he'd have to find another job and that mightn't be all that easy. 'What annoys me most is that the army is his life. Anything else will be second rate to him.'

I said he could be a farmer because he liked animals, or a horse trainer, but she said that was hardly the point.

It was not surprising that when we made subsequent visits to Maidenhall we found that Hubert had revived the long inactive Kilkenny Archaeological Society and that its programme embraced all kinds of activities not necessarily connected with archaeology. The Ulster Naturalists Field Club wrote to him saying that they intended to pay a visit to Kilkenny. They would hire a bus and travel on a Saturday to visit the Dunmore Caves where there would be a lecture in the afternoon; they did not usually go such a distance on their annual outing and would therefore be spending the night at the Club House Hotel in Kilkenny where they would hold their annual general meeting, and they would be grateful for suggestions for the Sunday.

'They'll have to be given time to go to church,' said Peggy, her knowledge of Ulster ways to the fore. 'Protestants in the North always go to church so as not to be seen as ungodly by their Romanist neighbours, unlike Protestants here.' Hubert felt that some of them might well be Romanists – these naturalists were known to be of ecumenical disposition. A leading member of the Archaeological Society, Mrs Lanigan, was consulted. She said she had just been talking to Major Briggs of Swifte's Heath and perhaps the Ulster visitors would like to look over his house – the major would certainly be delighted to give a talk on its architecture and associations, in fact nothing would stop him if he got the chance – and perhaps we should provide a picnic lunch in the grounds. Peggy remarked that as the major was somewhat eccentric it would give the visitors an eye-opener on social mores in the South, and as the address on their writing-paper was 'Larne' they certainly wouldn't be used to anything even remotely *outré*.

On the appointed Sunday we spread rugs on the rough grass that passed for a lawn at Swifte's Heath, Major Briggs directing the operation as if it were a bivouac at Mons. It was clear that horses had been present not long before but, judiciously placed, the rugs concealed most of the evidence. The major had agreed to emphasize the scientific aspects of the neighbourhood in his talk because of the interests of the visitors – 'You may take the term "scientific" in as broad a connotation as you wish,' Hubert had told him, several times, on the telephone as if he were deaf – but because the poet Yeats had once been to the house the major had also invited Mr Sibthorpe, a well-known local writer who had originally come from Yorkshire as manager of the Kilkenny Gasworks, to read suitable poems. We children were deputed to carry chairs from the dining room, which we arranged in a semi-circle by the sundial.

At noon a blue bus crept slowly up the potholed avenue. The Ulster naturalists descended, smoothing their dresses and fixing their ties; they spent much time photographing each other and their bus with very expensive cameras. Members of the Kilkenny Archaeological Society murmured among themselves that perhaps they should not be wearing old tweeds and flannels for the outing, but Peggy said the Ulster folk would take it that we were being informal and welcoming.

Major Briggs ushered the group to the seats of honour by the sundial. When sat upon, the chairs slowly sank up to their mahogany hocks in the moist turf, but everyone was very polite and pretended not to notice. Mr Sibthorpe was the first speaker and he said that it was not generally known that 'the poet *Yeets* had spent a night in this very house and had written a poem in one of the bedrooms' – though he was not sure what poem or which bedroom. He said that Yeets had inscribed his name on the window-pane – or perhaps it was Swift: he had been unable to find that out either, and then he looked to Major Briggs for guidance. 'I never heard that one,' said Major Briggs, 'but then I haven't been in some of the bedrooms for donkey's years!' Mr Sibthorpe read a poem, which he called 'The Hosting of the Sidy'. We looked at each other because we knew that he meant the *Sidhe* and we supposed that the Ulster people would think it was the 'Hosting of the City' because they pronounced city 'siddy'.

When the chairs had been pulled out of the ground and their legs rubbed down with wads of grass, Major Briggs invited us into the house for the scientific talk. There were many admiring remarks about the furniture, but the ragged carpets, the wallpapers soiled by damp and the curtains bleached by the sun did not pass unnoticed, as the nudges of the visitors, their eyes raised to the ceiling in disbelief, disclosed. A mummified rook lay in the fireplace and a trapped bluebottle buzzed incessantly on the dining-room window-pane. 'Perhaps he's looking for Swift's signature!' Major Briggs remarked. The throng stood wedged between the huge centre table and a number of heavy, unpolished tallboys and sideboards.

Our host told us that a relative of his had designed and built a small bi-plane in which he proposed to fly to Dublin and land in the Royal Dublin Society's grounds during the Horse Show. The aeroplane had been dragged to the top of the battlemented Foulksrath Castle by a team of plough-horses attached by ropes to a winch but at the last moment its designer decided that the butler, rather than he, should pilot the inaugural flight. The butler sat into the cockpit, and the catapult that was to launch him on his journey to Dublin was drawn back. A small crowd of well-wishers urged on the horses and shouted advice to the pilot. Seconds later the plane had tumbled into the moat with a noise that was heard two parishes off.

'Fortunately the moat was quite dry,' recalled Major Briggs, 'although the flying-machine was a total write-off.'

'What happened to the butler?' a voice from the back of the room enquired.

'Oh, I think he sustained a few broken bones,' replied the major. 'I'm sure he was carted off to the infirmary.'

Everyone from the Ulster Naturalists Field Club marvelled at the very idea of anyone designing an aeroplane as far back as – when was it? Nineteen *twelve*? Then someone mentioned

Leonardo da Vinci and another voice said, 'But his didn't work either,' and there was muffled giggling. There were many enquiries from the local people, most of whom had never been in the house before, about the antiques with which it was so richly furnished.

'These pieces of furniture would have been familiar to Jonathan Swift, you know,' said Major Briggs. 'He went to Kilkenny College and often stayed here as a child.' Hubert then contributed the information that the future metaphysical philosopher George Berkeley had been a classmate of Swift in Kilkenny, as had the playwright William Congreve.

Major Briggs said that the Swiftes of Swifte's Heath continued to spell their name correctly, with an *e*, but that did not rule out their being related to Jonathan Swift's family, which was really a minor branch. He said that the ancient sideboard to his right had originally belonged to Jonathan Swift's people.

An elderly patron of the Kilkenny Archaeological Society, Elaine, Lady Bellew, spoke up loudly to contradict the major about the sideboard. 'It couldn't possibly have belonged to those Swifts,' she declared. 'Your mother bought that sideboard for a knock-down price at my auction in Jenkinstown!'

'Indeed, she may well have done,' said the major, 'but, you know, it could have reached your husband's family via the Swifts, centuries ago.'

'I dare say,' replied Lady Bellew tartly, 'but that is *most* unlikely as it's Victorian.'

The visitors from Northern Ireland were bemused by this example of upper-class repartee in the Free State. Major Briggs then asked the crowd to follow him into the library, which, in spite of its name, was singularly devoid of books.

'I know that as naturalists you'll be interested in this tigerskin,' he said, indicating a somewhat worn pelt on the floor before the hearth. 'I rose up from my tent at six thirty and shot him before breakfast!'

There was an impressive silence, broken by a question from a tiny lady swathed in shawls who appeared to be Lady Bellew's companion.

'Was that here?'

'No, it was in Malaya,' replied the major, without any indication of surprise. I visualized tigers, lions and leopards roaming the forests of Foulksrath and thought what a pity it was that there weren't any – but if there had been, as I remarked later to Julia, I certainly wouldn't have shot them, either before or after breakfast.

'And now,' announced Major Briggs, in a tone that should have been followed by a flourish of trumpets, 'if you'll all step this way into the tack-room I'll show you the actual propeller!'

## Milltown House, Strabane, County Tyrone

'Strabane is universally known as "the town of dreaming spires",' Miss Hogan had once informed us. My mother thought she was getting a tiny bit confused – surely that was Matthew Arnold's description of Oxford? – but she couldn't find a copy of Arnold's poems to check who was right. Miss Hogan was certainly correct in so far as Strabane did have a spiky skyline. The Great Northern train, as it slowed for the railway station, disclosed a panorama not unlike a topographical print, with the spires arranged diagrammatically from left to right. They began with the most venerable, the massive square tower of the Protestant church in Lifford, situated on the left bank of the river and therefore in County Donegal rather than Tyrone. Then there were trees and a lot of grey roofs building up to the Victorian Gothic steeple of Christ Church. Next, the merry little cupola of the town hall and close to it the squat polychrome spire of the Presbyterian church, which, we were to discover, was all that remained of a building that had been accidentally destroyed by fire one Christmas morning only a few years back, leaving the congregation nowhere to worship but an anonymous-looking hall on the Derry road, the interior of which would shortly become familiar to us. On the extreme right, balancing the Lifford tower but quite surpassing it in splendour, was the soaring, heavily decorated steeple of the Church of the Immaculate Conception.

When my father had been diagnosed by the military doctors as suffering from an acute form of sinusitis he was allowed to nominate his own consultant surgeon. He decided upon my grandfather's first cousin, Dr Jim Killen of Derry. A lengthy convalescence was anticipated and we were billeted in a house on the outskirts of Strabane, fifteen miles south of Derry.

When our move to Strabane was announced it was followed by the disagreeable reminder that Miss Hogan was living there in retirement and had very kindly agreed to give us lessons every morning at Milltown House, where we would be staying with a Mr and Mrs Harpur. We came to know the dreaming spires and their surroundings quite intimately during the spring of 1943 while my father was recovering from his operation and we went for long, exploratory walks on dull afternoons, Miss Hogan's duties in what she called 'the schoolroom' – it had once been the servants' hall and was allocated to us as a sitting room – having finished at one o'clock when she walked back to her lodgings in Patrick Street.

The only way of approaching Milltown House was through an area of tumbledown cottages, many of them with corrugated-iron roofs like shanties, clustered round the Immaculate Conception Church. Our hostess, Mrs Harpur, referred to this neighbourhood as 'the slums'.

'These people are completely improvident!' she remarked, of Milltown Road's inhabitants. 'Seven or eight or even nine children in every family! And in many cases only one bedroom! And their Church does nothing for them. In fact, it encourages them.' Mrs Harpur was forced to pass through this seething mass of Roman Catholic riff-raff when she walked into the town, for with the petrol rationing she was denied use of the family car. Fortunately for her, Mr Harpur had a disability allowance as he was diabetic and deemed medically unfit to walk to his hardware shop in Main Street, so she was able to take a lift with him if need be.

'The first time I noticed that man with no legs,' said Mrs Harpur, 'you know, you often see him on a little cart made from an old pram, he pushes himself along with his hands, well, I understood him to be an ex-serviceman, honourably wounded, so as we drove past I threw him sixpence out of the car. He threw it back at me and dented the mudguard! Those people have no moral understanding. Imagine rebuffing an act of charity!'

Milltown House, which was to be our home for several months, was perched on an eminence where a rocky outcrop of the Sperrin mountains descended steeply to the river Mourne. The western windows of the house did not take in the magnificent view in the way they should, for between them and the cliff there was a dense shrubbery dominated by yews, but if you went into the brick-walled kitchen-garden you could look down on the river valley stretching to the distant factory chimneys of Sion Mills from where, it was said, the finest linen in the world had once been supplied to the crowned heads of Europe. Below the garden a mountain stream tumbled to meet the river; some ruined buildings and a weed-covered waterwheel, once powered by the torrent, were all that remained of the little mill that gave the hamlet its name.

My father said the house was 'of vaguely Jacobean inspiration, as if some Victorian bigwig had wanted to draw attention to himself'. He was just about right, for we later learned that it had been built in the early nineteenth century for the Marquess of Abercorn's land agent. It was all gables with roofs and dormers at unexpected levels and in curious relationships to one another. Designed in much the same style, but in miniature and distinctly prettier, was its *cottage-orné* gate-lodge, occupied by the family whose male members dug and raked feverishly in the Harpurs' garden and grounds. We had not been installed in the main house more than a few days when Mrs Harpur told us that one of the marquess's agents had been a Major Humphreys whose daughter, Cecil Frances, was the author of many famous hymns. Did we know '*There is a green hill far away, without a city wall*'? As a matter of fact we did. Everyone knew it. 'Well, then,' continued Mrs Harpur, 'if you look out of the smoking-room window you are looking straight at that very hill!' This statement created a number of issues, for surely that hill was supposed to be outside the walled city of Jerusalem, at a place called Golgotha? Mrs Harpur explained that the green hill at Milltown had made Miss Humphreys *think* of Golgotha. ('The place of a skull', I said in my own mind, remembering many Easter readings of St Mark's Gospel.) But then, there was the question of Great-aunt Zane's story that the green hill was inspired by one of the Seven Hills of Armagh. Who should be believed? I told Mrs Harpur that I had heard that the idea for the hymn came from Armagh and she said that was an easy mistake to make because Miss Humphreys had later become the wife of Archbishop Alexander of Armagh and it had been widely – but erroneously – reported that she had written the hymn after her marriage upon observing the view from the Archiepiscopal Palace; but the *real* green hill was here at Strabane.

What a triumph for Strabane – and for Mrs Harpur. The

interior of Milltown House was exactly what one would
have expected of the home of the wife of a successful busi-
nessman, who had bought this handsome and historic
dwelling with the fruits of his own industry. To the right of
the lofty entrance hall was the drawing room, which
contained several stiff armchairs covered in a rich floral
material in lime-green and mauve. There was a walnut grand
piano with a tapestry cover. The window embrasures were
half concealed by swagged velveteen drapes. This room was
entered only on Sundays. Across the oak-panelled hall was
the smoking room, which was used every day and in which,
I suppose, one was expected to smoke, though nobody did.
A huge sofa with its back to the front window was covered
in grey corduroy and was referred to as 'the chesterfield'.
Here we had afternoon tea at three thirty when Mr Harpur
returned for a brief break from his hardware shop, the early
hour explained by his having to eat at very regular intervals.
('Dinner' was at one and 'tea' at six thirty, the last meal of
the day.) At the foot of the stairs was the dining room, which
had a second door leading to the extensive kitchen quarters
from which Mary the maid kept appearing with trays laden
with substantial dishes. There was a heaviness in the furnishings that complemented immense roasts of beef with Yorkshire
pudding and boiled potatoes – these were for dinner, as tea
was very much the same as breakfast with a plentiful array
of fried foods and several varieties of bread – farls, baps,
bannocks and scones. The deprivation occasioned by war or
by the social ills so evident on Milltown Road might have
been a thousand miles away or in another era, but this was
justified in a verse of another hymn by Mrs Cecil Frances
Alexander, *née* Humphreys, also familiar to us, called 'All
Things Bright and Beautiful':

*The rich man in his castle,*
*The poor man at his gate,*
*He made them high or lowly*
*And ordered their estate;*
*All things bright and beautiful,*
*All creatures great and small,*
*All things wise and wonderful,*
*The Lord God made them all!*

It was in the bedrooms that Mrs Harpur's taste in decoration was seen to best effect. My parents had the sunniest room in the house – in fact, the only room on either floor with a southerly outlook. It was well that this was so, for the dark furniture and the wallpaper of copper-coloured foliage luxuriating over an umber trellis did its very best to create a noonday gloom. The smaller room with its dormer window and yew-tree view, which had been assigned to 'the little laddies', as Mrs Harpur insisted on calling us, was papered in a pattern of what I took to be Alpine peaks, though at times I wondered if they were not Japanese. I would lie in bed in the mornings trying to work out how many chasms and summits were involved, but I never came to a correct count, so numerous and repetitive were the snow-capped mountains. Far from creating a sense of space and distance this landscape had an oppressive way of making one feel closed in, especially as the prevailing colour was brown.

In his bed in the Londonderry City & County Hospital my father had a chance to listen to the BBC news on the progress of the war from which he was for the time being excluded. The Allies under General Montgomery were besieging Tunis, and it was presumed they would shortly invade Sicily, then mainland Italy. At Milltown House we did not see a

newspaper, nor did we think of asking for one; in any case
the Harpurs were the kind of people who would consider
it a bit forward for children to take an interest in such things.
On a more personal note Mrs Harpur often spoke of General
Montgomery, to whom she referred admiringly as 'Monty'.
She also spoke of his mother, whom she had met, it seemed
quite frequently. 'Lady Monty' was now a widow, her husband
the bishop having died quite a while back, living all on her
own – with a few servants, of course – at New Park, the
family home across the border in disloyal Donegal. The
bishop – such a distinguished old gentleman! – had devoted
a lifetime's study to the problem of how and where the
Israelites had made their famous crossing of the Red Sea.
My father, Mrs Harpur urged, should certainly call on Lady
Monty when discharged from the hospital: she would be
greatly interested to meet someone who had served in the
Western Desert.

One day we went to Derry on the Great Northern. We
met our Killen grandparents for lunch in Foster's restaurant.
They were spending the winter looking out at the Atlantic
waves from a boarding-house at Portstewart, only an hour
away on the London, Midland and Scottish Railway, which
had somehow insinuated itself into County Derry. After
lunch we all went for a walk round the ancient city walls
and then we visited St Columb's Cathedral, where we saw
a huge iron cannonball on a specially built stand. The verger,
who was warming the bishop's robes at a coal fire in the
vestry, told us that it had been fired at the city by King
James's troops in 1689. It weighed 270 pounds and he showed
us a little hole in it that had contained a letter offering
favourable terms to the besieged citizens if they gave in – but
they did not, even though they had to eat rats and mice.
'No surrender!' they heroically replied. We were told that a

similar cannonball had landed on a house and demolished it completely, killing all fourteen people inside. My grand-parents then went to call on the surgeon Jim Killen at his house on Lawrence Hill while we went to the hospital across the road. When we came into the small private ward, my father was resting his forehead on the stone chimney-piece – he said it was cool and helped his headache. His nose was covered in cotton-wool held on by plasters, but apart from that he didn't look bad at all. Later, there was much subdued conversation between my mother and my grandfather about the probable consequences of the operation, but my grand-mother took us for a walk down to the river so we didn't hear how this might affect our future.

The river Foyle, a quarter of a mile wide at Craigavon Bridge, was the scene of intense naval activity. There were submarines tied up side by side in such a way that you could almost cross the river by jumping from one to the next, and indeed we saw a sailor doing just that. An elderly bystander on the quay told us that these were captured German U-boats and that the battleships and corvettes with which the river was thronged were part of the North Atlantic Fleet. It was no secret, he said, that hundreds of German prisoners were locked up in the old barracks and they were delighted to be there instead of submerged in those tin cans with nothing to do but think about how they were likely to be blown to bits under the water. 'A bad end that'd be for young men only out of school,' he said, 'and a sad one too, forby, even if they are Nazis.'

If Great Britain was short of agricultural and dairy produce, the Free State was woefully in need of manufactured goods. People in Northern Ireland who could afford the price of a rail ticket and an overnight stay in Dublin flocked south at weekends for a surfeit of steaks and omelettes and also – though they usually didn't admit it – to see the lights, for while the streets of Belfast and Derry were blacked out at night, Dublin was once again ablaze with electricity and neon as if to emphasize its internationally accepted state of neutrality. It was said that groups of Northerners could be seen standing on the corner at Trinity College marvelling at the changing colours of the Bovril sign. The reverse side of the picture was that those who lived in the South were restricted to half an ounce of tea per week – enough to make one pot – and coffee was unobtainable; newspapers were reduced to a front and a back page, folded to make them look like four. There were curious scarcities – such as candles, because they had traditionally been imported from Birmingham. One enterprising Dublin butcher started manufacturing them from the fat of sheep; the homes of people thus illuminated could be identified by a pervasive smell of mutton stew.

Knowing that Great-aunt Zane was much discommoded by a lack of candles – for she liked to read when sitting alone at Eldron in the long winter evenings – my mother grew into the habit of buying a packet in Strabane and cycling across the Foyle bridge to Lifford to post them within the Free State jurisdiction, the officers at the Customs post never having been known to stop cyclists or pedestrians; but my mother concealed the candles in her corset *just in case*. She became acquainted with a Mrs Simms who lived in a handsome Georgian house on the Lifford side of the bridge, and there she left the candles until there were enough to fill a large biscuit tin which she would then dispatch by parcel-post to Eldron. Mrs Simms was the wife of the State solicitor for Donegal and my mother felt certain qualms about involving her in a felony, but Mrs Simms did not seem at all concerned. 'So very Irish!' remarked a British brigadier, who came to tea at Milltown House.

Mrs Harpur was a party to these transactions, warning my mother on one occasion that a Lady Searcher was reported to have been seen at the Customs post. This proved to be correct, for a young woman wearing an official-looking cap was standing on the bridge when my mother made her next foray bearing contraband. She decided that the better part of valour would be to dismount and enter the Customs hut as if in search of some information or other. 'Can you tell me, please, what steps need to be taken if one is moving house from Northern Ireland to the Free State?' she asked the officer in charge. He found a number of forms and showed her where to fill them in – this one was for a list of furniture, this other for the value of the goods exported, another was a declaration of the reason for change of residence. He was most helpful, telling her how his wife's sister had been facilitated with no trouble at all when she explained that her mother was dying of bad rheumatics in Ballybofey and needed the family round her. The implication was that the quickest way to get approval for the importation of dutiable goods would be to discover a relative who was close to death. Thanking the Customs man for his advice my mother made her exit, nodded to the Lady Searcher and pursued her journey. The delay, however, had allowed the candles to melt and she and Mrs Simms spent the best part of an hour scraping them off her torso and remodelling them. Aunt Zane wrote on a postcard that she was delighted with the candles, though some were a very peculiar shape.

On one of his sojourns at Milltown House between his discharge from the hospital and visits to England, my father discovered that the riding establishment attached to

Londonderry Girls' High School had been evacuated to Strabane along with the boarders and staff even though Derry was well out of range of German raids – unless, of course, the Bosch were to develop a long-distance bomber, which was quite possible since the destruction of the HQ of the British Atlantic Fleet must have been at the very top of the Luftwaffe's wish-list. At the High School a pony was available for hire by the hour on Thursdays, and it was decided that Nicky and I should take a weekly riding lesson. My father had been 'born in the saddle' and my mother had taken to horsemanship in Egypt when they had both been members of the Club at Heliopolis.

The minute I was on the back of this pony I knew it was not the place for me. I was not in the least afraid of falling off – I had tumbled out of quite tall trees without a bother on me – but there was something about the suspicious glint in the pony's eye that told me it knew I was not looking forward to the lesson and how uninterested I was in the rituals of buckling girths, strapping stirrups, fixing bridles and reins, not to speak of placing the bit that disclosed two rows of hideous yellow teeth and a fearsome puce tongue. I pointed out that this pony didn't have blinkers like the horses at Annaghmakerrig and was told not to be silly because only plough- and dray-horses had those. Round and round a grassy enclosure we went, as boring for the pony as it was for me. I could see wooden jumps in the next field and would not at all have minded having a go at them, but it appeared that you couldn't do that until you had 'mastered the basics', which evidently was going to take me a long time. When it was Nicky's turn on Dobbin he immediately assumed the look of a trained horseman.

I would wake on Thursday mornings with the feeling that something dreadful was going to happen but I was not adept at thinking up sustainable reasons for staying away from the riding lesson. Certainly there lurked at the side of my mind the notion that if I did not try my best I was somehow letting my father down. It was with the greatest relief that one Thursday we arrived to find that Dobbin had saddle-sores and that no other pony was available that day. A huge weight was lifted from my mind for another week and I felt like dancing through the slums of Strabane as we made our way back to Milltown House.

My parents, being interested in family history, made a trip on the Strabane & Letterkenny Light Railway to Convoy, where distant relatives of my mother ran a small woollen mill. I resented not being taken on this outing for I loved railway journeys, but Miss Hogan had said I was 'falling behind' and could not afford to miss a morning's lessons. They returned bearing a length of grey tweed with which my mother had been presented by the miller. Braced by the success of this excursion they planned a visit to Ballygawley to seek the home of certain ancestors of my father. It was a much longer journey, necessitating sandwiches enough for two picnics and taking their bicycles on the train to Omagh from where they would explore the by-roads of the south of the county. They set off on an early train and were expected home by bed-time. When they did not appear Mrs Harpur surmised that they must have missed the return train at Omagh. She told us that everything would be all right and she would put us to bed. We could put ourselves to bed, I said, without intentional discourtesy; but she looked in the door of our bedroom quite late and said there was still no sign of Daddy and Mummy. She told us we were not to worry, but it had not occurred to us to do any such thing.

Next morning we were told that our parents would not be down to breakfast as they were very tired, as well they

might have been. The previous night Mr Harpur had telephoned the Great Northern station at Omagh and also the
police barracks there, but no couple answering his description had been seen. It did not seem to occur to my parents
that their absence might have caused alarm for they had not
attempted to telephone to say they had miscalculated the
amount of terrain to be covered, and having missed the train
from Omagh by two hours decided to cycle on to Strabane,
arriving after one o'clock in the morning. Mr Harpur
thought it odd that a military man, used to reading maps,
should have made such a grave error. When they appeared
in the schoolroom at eleven, as we were having cocoa with
Miss Hogan, my father said they had cycled nearly sixty
miles!

On the Sunday next to St Patrick's Day my mother said we
would go to the service at Christ Church because there was
little likelihood that the old Irish hymns would be sung in
the Presbyterian hall, which we had become accustomed to
attending as part of the Harpurs' entourage, with its pedal
organ, stacking chairs and a reading-desk in marmalade-
coloured varnished wood instead of a pulpit. Christ Church
had pitch-pine pews and pointed arches dividing the aisles,
and plenty of colourful glass with scenes from the Bible
stories. All the hymns chosen that morning were in the
section of the book headed 'Hymns from Ancient Irish
Sources'. One was called 'The Breastplate of St Patrick':

> *I bind this day to me for ever,*
> *By power of faith Christ's Incarnation,*
> *His baptism in Jordan river,*
> *His death on cross for my salvation;*
> *His bursting from the spicèd tomb,*

*His riding up the heavenly way,*
*His coming at the day of doom:*
*I bind unto myself today . . .*
*I bind unto myself today*
*The virtues of the starlit heaven,*
*The glorious sun's life-giving ray,*
*The whiteness of the moon at even;*
*The flashing of the lightning free,*
*The whirling wind's tempestuous shocks,*
*The stable earth, the deep salt sea,*
*Around the old eternal rocks.*

'*We* certainly did not sing any "Ancient Irish" hymns!' Mrs Harpur said, when, as was customary, the nature of the services attended was discussed over Sunday dinner. She then declared that she didn't know there were any such things. My mother explained to her that these were hymns that had been translated from the Irish language; they were 'literature' as well as being 'devotional'. Mr Harpur remarked that he didn't know anything about literature but he liked a good hymn with a good tune. His favourite was

*There is a Fountain filled with Blood*
*Drawn from Emmanuel's veins,*
*And sinners, plunged beneath that flood*
*lose all their guilty stains . . .*

and he went on to say that as well as having a good tune there was meaning to it. His wife, dishing out the braised tripe and onions, declared that the hymns of Mrs Cecil Frances Alexander were by far the best because they had a meaning for *all* religions, whether you were Presbyterian, Methodist, Unitarian or Church of Ireland – she did not include Roman Catholic in her list. My mother offered the thought that Mrs Alexander had actually translated 'The Breastplate of St Patrick' from the Irish, and that she and my father had chosen it to be sung at their wedding in South Kensington. Mrs Harpur couldn't imagine anyone as well bred as Mrs Alexander *knowing* Irish, let alone being in a position to translate it, and she was sure my mother must be mistaken.

'Oh, no,' said my mother, warming to the topic, 'there was a tradition of Celtic scholarship in the Church of Ireland during the nineteenth century. That was when many local churches were renamed in memory of the Irish saints, like St Phelim in Donegal and St Macartan in Monaghan.'

'We Presbyterians don't recognize saints, except the evangelists, as you know,' said Mrs Harpur. 'How did you come to learn all that?'

'I went to Alexandra College in Dublin. Miss Macardle, our English teacher, was greatly interested in the translation of Irish texts. I think she made some translations herself.'

'Was this Miss Macardle one of the – the other sort?' Mr Harpur enquired.

'What do you mean?'

'Was she RC?'

'I expect she was Church of Ireland. I must say I never thought about it. She belonged to the brewing family in Dundalk – you know, Macardle's Ales, you can see the factory from the train. Miss Macardle went on to write a book called *The Irish Republic.*'

'She couldn't possibly have been a Protestant,' said Mrs Harpur. 'I think you must have got it wrong.'

My mother let the matter rest there – for, after all, we were guests at the Harpurs' table – but she said later it was lucky my father was away because the Harpurs must have noticed that he never went to any church at all and they would have been quite taken aback to learn that he was a Roman Catholic even if, at that time, he didn't go to Mass.

The theological discussions at table were witnessed in silence by a Swedish lady, Mrs Kripps, who had recently joined us. Her husband was a colonel in the Swedish Army and, like us, she had been assigned to Milltown House because the Harpurs were apparently deemed by some official in the Ministry of Supply to have 'an excess of unused private accommodation'. Mrs Kripps had a baby daughter called Yoscelyn who was looked after by a woman from Donegal, called Nanny Kripps. We never saw Colonel Kripps. He was always away on what my father called 'hush-hush tours', for Sweden was not in the war and his presence would have caused 'a powder-keg reaction' if it were to become known – we were instructed never to breathe his name. In the mornings Mrs Kripps wore a long turquoise garment with a zip from top to bottom. Mrs Harpur liked everyone to be properly dressed at breakfast – her son Ian, when home on holiday from Campbell College, always wore his school tie – but there could not really be an objection to Mrs Kripps's attire because the turquoise rig-out was certainly not a nightdress or even a dressing-gown.

Mrs Kripps received mysterious parcels delivered by a military driver. She described the contents as 'the necessities of life' – there was always a packet of coffee-beans, which she ground in a machine that she screwed to the kitchen table, and she kept a pot bubbling all morning on the wood stove in the dining room. Mr and Mrs Harpur declined her offers of fresh coffee but my mother gladly accepted. 'Oh, it brings me back to Cairo!' my mother said. 'The aroma!'

It was difficult to have the routine of the household

disordered by all these strangers, Mrs Harpur confided to a friend who came to see her garden – but, then, one had to make sacrifices to assist the War Effort. (I was not actually eavesdropping, but 'playing' by the herbaceous border while these ladies were in conversation.) 'At least the Fitz-Simons and the Krippses are the families of high-ranking officers,' said Mrs Harpur. 'That does compensate somewhat. I was very much afraid that we'd be landed with evacuees from West Belfast, possibly even from the Falls Road!'

Her friend nodded sympathetically. 'I know what you mean – hanging religious pictures on their bedroom walls and japping holy water around the place.'

'I do find Mrs Kripps a bit too *continental* in her ways,' Mrs Harpur pursued, as her friend paused to admire some peonies, 'but, then, what would you expect? She comes from the continent. Though you don't think of Sweden as being *continental*, do you?'

'Not like France,' remarked her friend.

'Oh, no,' said Mrs Harpur, 'not a bit like *France*! Now the Fitz-Simons are from some place down in the Free State but *she* was originally from Belfast. Very respectable – she mentioned to me that they used to live in one of those avenues off the Malone Road, College Gardens, I think. But she does have some strange ideas, picked up in Dublin, no doubt. All the same, I quite like her.'

I slunk away into the rhododendrons.

## Annaghmakerrig Again

With the Butlers now living at Maidenhall, Annaghmakerrig had become a very different place from the one we had enjoyed during the early years of the war when the Butlers' ever-changing gathering of paying guests and refugees made for an intensely lively household. 'Quiet' was the word used by Susan Murray, the cook. We thought Susan must be Scottish because of her accent, until she told us she had come back from Glasgow to be near her elderly parents who, it turned out, lived in Smithborough. Susan had trained as a waitress and liked nothing better than to dress in her restaurant outfit on Chrissie Morgan's day off and serve at table, which she did with a flourish, balancing five plates at once on her elbows and ostentatiously clearing unused cutlery and condiments after each course rather than leaving them to be removed at the end of the meal.

'She's letting us know she's properly trained,' said Bunty Worby.

My parents made an arrangement with Mrs G to stay as paying guests while my father searched for a job for himself and a boarding-school for us. He made sporadic visits to his parents in Dublin to help them settle into their new home at Kilgobbin. We accompanied him on one of these trips to find our grandmother putting down a line of gooseberry and blackcurrant bushes while our grandfather sat indoors studying the *Irish Times* and *Dublin Opinion*, and each evening starting on a fresh bottle of Jameson Ten.

Mrs G invited our grandmother, whom she had not met before, to come for a week to Annaghmakerrig to recuperate from severe blood-poisoning, the result of a bite from a horse-fly while she was removing a blockage from her new septic tank. My mother said she had 'nearly died', but she did not seem in the slightest bit frail, and she added a welcome gaiety to the Annaghmakerrig dinner table – Nicky and I were now promoted to dining with the grown-ups at midday – though it was evidently a disappointment to Mrs G and Bunty that she did not play bridge. She told me that she would like nothing better than for all of us to come and live with her at Kilgobbin, but unfortunately the house was just that little bit small. In the fullness of time, she thought, this difficulty might be overcome, but she did not say in what way. She came with Nicky and me to meet the Daley girls – two of them now going to secondary school in Clones – and with them we showed her over the old yard and outbuildings. She observed what a fine farm it must have been once. She pointed out a hen that, judging by its furtive behaviour, was probably 'laying out', and sure enough, when we followed its circuitous and very leisurely journey round to the back of the byre, we found a nest with eleven eggs in a briary sheugh. A few days later the hen, her demeanour altered to one of ostentatious pride, walked into the yard with eleven chicks scuttling around her feet.

The Daley girls lived in the pretty lattice-windowed house in the ivy-covered terrace that started with the dairy, the ironing room and the laundry and ended with the stable and the motor-house. Eddie Daley was still the farm steward and had under him Brian McGoldrick and Seamus McGorman. Between them they did all the ploughing, sowing, harrowing, mowing, turf-cutting and milking. Eddie had come to Annaghmakerrig from his family home at Drumary, which was only a mile away but hidden by trees and hedges and situated across the Newbliss road from the prominent pink two-storeyed house belonging to the Scotts. 'Strong farmers' was the phrase Mrs G used for their like. Eddie had married Annie Scott, who had been quickly absorbed into the Annaghmakerrig routine and put in charge of the dairy.

The dairy had a flagged floor and shelves made of polished limestone, which were meant to keep the butter cool. Earthenware crocks contained the milk that was to be skimmed for cream and, after churning, the sweet buttermilk. There was a big wooden churn like a boat slung on trestles, unlike any churn I'd seen before: you pushed it to and fro instead of winding a handle, and after a very long time the milk turned to butter. Mrs Daley suffered from an excess of weight – semi-blind as Mrs G was, she could still make out the contours of Mrs Daley as she reclined on the sofa in her front room, describing her naughtily to Bunty as 'looking for all the world like a distant view of the Mountains of Mourne'. Once a week Mrs Daley would sit at one end of this wooden contrivance, pushing it rhythmically while humming snatches of popular hymn tunes to herself, sometimes breaking out into the words. The bare interior of the dairy amplified the sound and also caused an echo so that strange harmonies were produced as the notes hit against one another in the stone-built space. On hearing this music anyone returning to Annaghmakerrig from elsewhere would immediately make the mental observation, oh, yes, it's Churning Day.

Most of the five Daley children were older than the rest of us and were viewed with the distanced respect that age confers. They were Lillie, Susie, Ethel, Lora and Joan, and after leaving the national school down the road at Crapagh they each went on to secondary schools in Clones, with the teaching, secretarial and nursing professions in view. There was a kind of mystique about the Daley girls when they were going to Crapagh, for theirs was a complex world from which we were excluded because we were taught by governesses. They spoke of their terror on the day when the inspector came and asked them hard questions, they told us of heroes from the past of whom we had never heard because we mostly read stories from English history, and they learned Irish. Peggy Butler said that of course every young person in the Free State should learn Irish but our governesses had no knowledge of it.

The Daleys recited action-songs in Irish, some of which I learned from them at second hand, going through the movements that accompanied the words and making the whole thing seem like a stage performance:

> *Is maith liom a bheith i mo sheasamh,*
> *Is maith liom a bheith i mo shuidhe,*
> *Is maith liom ag tabhairt bualadh bos,*
> *A h-aon, a dó, a trí . . .*

There were elaborate standings-up and sittings-down and hand-clappings. Mrs G told us that the Daley parents had not attended school after the age of thirteen and she thought it was splendid how the younger ones were taking to secondary education with such a sense of purpose. Once after a heavy fall of snow Lillie and Lora walked with their bicycles all the seven miles to Clones to find the High School closed because of the weather. The headmaster, Mr Wheatley, was amazed to see these two girls trudging up the path at nine o'clock when all the other pupils had taken it for granted that there would be no school that day.

My parents decided that because of the difficulty of finding a new governess when they could not offer any degree of permanence, they would take on our schooling themselves. The upstairs sitting room that had been Hubert and Peggy's became our classroom. My father taught us Arithmetic, Geography and Latin, my mother English and History. History was learning the dates of the Kings and Queens of England from William the Conqueror to George VI, and of famous events such as the Battle of Bannockburn and the South Sea Bubble, which my mother set out in columns of heavy handwriting, and reading from *Little Arthur's History of England*, which Mrs G said she had read to Tony and Peggy when they were our age and must surely still be on a shelf in the Morning Room – which proved to be correct. There were a lot of outstanding historical stories, some of which I already knew, like King Alfred burning the cakes and Sir Walter Ralegh casting his cloak on the street so that Queen Elizabeth would not have to step in a puddle. I was poor on memorizing the dates and took to writing them out on scraps of paper, which I hid behind a pile of books when it was time to recite them.

I had no difficulty at all in memorizing verse. Mrs G drew our attention to a collection of *Poems Patriotic and Nautical*.

Very quickly I learned the six stanzas of Thomas Campbell's 'The Battle of the Baltic', which was patriotic and nautical in equal measure:

> . . . *'Hearts of oak!' our captains cried,*
> *When each gun*
> *From its adamantine lips*
> *Spread a death-shade round the ships*
> *Like the hurricane eclipse*
> *Of the sun . . .*

In more melancholy vein there was Lord Tennyson's poem about Sir Richard Grenville's little ship the *Revenge* in its doomed action against the Spaniards off the Azores:

> . . . *So Lord Howard passed away with five ships of war that day,*
> *Till he melted like a cloud in the silent summer heaven;*
> *But Sir Richard bore in hand all his sick men from the land*
> *Very carefully and slow,*
> *Men of Bideford in Devon,*
> *And we laid them on the ballast down below;*
> *For we brought them all aboard,*
> *For they blest him in their pain, that they were not left to Spain,*
> *To the thumb-screw and the stake, for the glory of the Lord . . .*

When Tony Guthrie came on one of his visits from England I said I'd like to recite the 118 lines of this poem for him. He stood, all six foot six of him, inclined against the marble chimney-piece of the drawing room, listening attentively. 'Bravo!' he said, when I'd finished. 'I heard every word, which is the most important thing when you're addressing an audience, but you must achieve this without having to shout.' He told us that these poems were masterpieces of Victorian sentimentality, and if there were still such a thing as verse-speaking competitions in England, Campbell and Tennyson would continue to hold their own. As it was, verse-speaking remained a component of Irish cultural life – he was about to adjudicate at the Feis Cheóil in Derry and had set the contestants some poems translated from Irish during the Victorian age by Thomas Davis and James Clarence Mangan – 'superior as literature and just as rousing as those English boys'.

Arithmetic continued to be what Miss Hogan had once described as my 'Achilles' heel' – a preliminary to telling at length the story of Achilles being dipped in the water of immortality. My father had much less patience than she, developing a painful habit of pulling the short hairs on the back of my neck when I was being particularly slow to make a calculation. The geography lessons were more enjoyable when he showed me how to trace outlines from maps, then to copy in the names of places. We covered Spain and Portugal in this way, and then India, all of them countries in which his old regiment, the King's Own, had played an important part. For Latin he had bought a mean-looking little book called Hilliard and Botting's *Shorter Latin Primer*, which was really a grammar. He recalled his teacher at Earlsfort House in Dublin making the boys recite poems which were supposed to make you remember the conjugations of verbs, and he passed on this knowledge to me:

> *-bam, -eram, gives was and had,*
> *-bo, -ero, gives shall, shall have . . .*

He was generally in bad humour and I was glad when he had to go away to be interviewed for jobs such as a BBC announcer and the governor of a prison in Cumberland, though we never heard anything more about either. It was difficult for a civilian – as he now was – to be granted a permit to travel to Great Britain. On one occasion Tony Guthrie wrote a letter for him saying it was *essential* that he should travel at once to rehearse for *Hamlet* at the New Theatre in London's West End, so the permit was granted. He attended rehearsal as an extra and wrote to my mother to say that the language used by Tony was more colourful than he had been accustomed to hearing on the barrack square. He wrote that many of the actors seemed to be degenerates and nancy-boys who had failed the call-up test for the forces so the only employment open to them was crowd-work in the theatres. He told Tony that the soldiers on the battlements of Elsinore, who should have been marching and presenting arms in a manly display, were *mincing*, and Tony set him the task of drilling them like real soldiers. As one of the Four Captains called upon by Fortinbras at the end of the play to bear away the corpse of the Prince of Denmark in procession, to drumbeats and distant trumpet calls, my father found that on nights when there was a warning of V2 rocket bombs the members of the cast who were assigned to fire-duty left early, so that quite often fewer than four Captains stepped forward. On one night when he found he was the only Captain left on stage he had to drag Robert Helpmann into the wings by himself, to the 'choice' language, uttered in a distinctly audible stage whisper, of the recently deceased prince.

If Annaghmakerrig now had fewer residents there was no lack of visitors. One or other or all of the Butlers, with Joe Hone, came quite often. A lady called Nettie Irwin came every summer from Kent – like a swallow from the sunny south, said Susan Murray – and once when she was at

Annaghmakerrig on the date of my birthday she gave me a tiny purse made of knitted threads with a silver clasp and a silver threepenny piece inside. My mother said it was a real heirloom and I should keep it very carefully. A lady called Miss Walpole came from Strokestown Park with a very old dog that died while she was with us. Miss Walpole borrowed the pony-trap to go to Clones to make arrangements with Mr Lendrum, the stonemason, to carve a gravestone for it. Tony and Judy Guthrie came on several trips from London, the Old Vic theatre company having returned there from its exile in Burnley once the War Office indicated that the German bombing was unlikely to be continued and London 'required' more serious drama.

'Cream!' Judy shouted when, on coming down to breakfast, she noticed that the milk jug had a quarter-inch of very thick cream floating on top. She said they never saw cream in England where the milk was actually blue and, indeed, there were shortages of everything imaginable. In Burnley she had wanted to buy a kitchen sieve and had been to every hardware shop in the town without success. In one of them the owner told her in a hushed voice that he had actually *seen* a sieve in a little general store in the suburb of Gawthorpe, but it was *very* small.

'How small?' asked Judy.

'Tiny!' said the shopman.

'How tiny?'

'*Teenshy!*'

My mother remarked that it was very odd the way people were going to the theatre to see the kind of plays Tony was producing, when in wartime you'd expect them to want something light. Tony said it was completely the opposite of what had happened in the first war when musicals and variety shows had done particularly well; perhaps it was because the bombing made this war a part of everyday life that the public seemed to want something more, what? Uplifting? Something to connect them more immediately to concerns such as Mortality and Fate and the Brevity of Time. He said he had been quite taken by surprise by the huge public response to *The Cherry Orchard*, 'not a piece one would have expected Cousin Tom and Auntie Milly from Streatham to come rushing in to see'.

I had never seen a play but I'd leafed through the illustrated books and programmes that Tony brought from London. On his visits to Annaghmakerrig he would describe to his mother what was in the pictures because she could only see them as shadows, explaining who the actors were and who had designed their costumes. Bunty would read aloud whatever magazine articles and reviews he sent in the post or brought with him, and both ladies would groan and sigh and tut-tut when any of Tony's work was mentioned unfavourably.

'That horrid Mr Hobson,' said Bunty. 'How can he ever have got a post on a respectable paper like the *Sunday Times*? And that Mr Trewin in the *Illustrated London News* is just as bad, if you ask me, though he puts it in a nicer way, if you could call it nice, and I certainly don't.'

'Quite beastly,' Mrs G agreed.

'No point in getting in a sweat about them,' said Tony. 'Rise above!'

Bunty said it was all very well trying to 'rise above' when the whole world was reading the nasty things that were printed.

'The best one can say is that the Almighty has provided them with opinions which He in His boundless wisdom would not wish to suppress, even if He has also fallen short on endowing them with any discernible degree of intelligence,' said Tony. '"Mere" and "meagre" are terms that come to mind.'

Over a period of a dozen years almost all our Christmases were spent at Annaghmakerrig. When the house was full there was a huge cast available for charades, and my mother took to writing sketches that we would learn and perform. One year she wrote a play called *The Stolen Princess* in which Pamela Cullen was a royal baby in a cradle spirited away by her sister Jennifer as the envious Fairy Queen. Jennifer was cast as the Fairy Queen because she was the only good singer and my mother wrote new words for her, set to the "Londonderry Air". Joe Hone was given the role of the Prince who had become a Professor because he was able to put on a pompous voice. Nicky was the Robber, Blood McGrew, Lora Daley was the Witch who brewed helpful potions, and her sister Joan was an officious Lady-in-waiting. Julia played the distressed Queen who promised extravagant wealth to anyone who would restore her daughter to her, and I was the mean-minded King who spoke in a selection of regional accents, one of which was South Ulster:

> *Whisht, wumman! Don't be promisin' all thon stuff:*
> *A few wee hens'd be quite enough.*
> *A good thing I've me money tied up tightly –*
> *We'll make him Duke of Aghabog, and that'll do rightly!*

Joe had the best lines and got all the laughs from the audience of the entire household and the people who lived on the estate – they even laughed at things we didn't know were funny. Mrs McGoldrick, who lived in the Lake Avenue Lodge and came to do the washing every Monday and the ironing every Wednesday, was in kinks of laughter throughout.

Tony told her that she should be paid handsomely to sit out front at all his productions to applaud and laugh – at the notion of which she burst into further streels of laughter.

Joe's opening speech was:

> *I am the Prince Augustus Brown,*
> *Much the most famous prince in town;*
> *I've been to several colleges*
> *And studied all the -ologies –*
> *I speak Italian, Urdu, Greek,*
> *And once in Dublin for a week*
> *I occupied the Chair of Mineralogy . . .*

For several days Eddie Daley, while milking the cows or harnessing the horse to the harrow, would exclaim, 'Blood McGrew!' and Tony remarked that if you had that kind of word-of-mouth after an opening night you were into big business.

For years now petrol rationing had dictated travel by train, Bob Burns driving the pony-trap to Newbliss station to meet whoever was arriving or to deliver the parting guest to the vagaries of the Great Northern Railway. Sometimes we cycled to the station, loading our bicycles into the guard's van and rushing to pull them out again when we reached our destination in case the train moved on with them still inside. Social visits in the immediate neighbourhood were reduced to those houses that could be reached by bike or trap. Marcus and Catherine Clements lived with their parents and their governess, Miss Bishop, at Ashfield, situated above a bend of the river Finn near Cootehill, five miles away. This distance was about the limit of what could be managed either as cyclists or as pony-driven excursionists. We quite liked the visits of the Clements children to Annaghmakerrig because they seemed to leave behind them the pall of good behaviour that we found so oppressive when we went to Ashfield. We would introduce them to the Daley girls and go climbing in the rafters of the hayshed or the branches of the copper beech, conscious that everything was rather rougher than they were used to, though Marcus, a boy with glimmering dark eyes and black hair that flopped lazily over his forehead, always declared that they found whatever escapades we led them into to be 'very jolly'.

The constant use of the word 'jolly' placed the Clementses in a world that really belonged to another time, a world of adventure stories handed down in ragged books that had probably belonged to Tony Guthrie before the Great War, yet not at all unlike that inhabited by the children we were now reading about in the stories of Arthur Ransome, children who spoke in a way that was very old-fashioned even though the stories were supposed to be taking place today. I thought the children in *Swallows and Amazons* were desperate goody-goodies and when I mentioned this to my mother, who was reading the books aloud to us, she said she thought the real word for them was 'smug'.

Would Marcus and Catherine like to try their balancing skills on the rotting footstick bridges of the Annaghmakerrig bog garden? 'Oh, rath*err*!' Another currant bun? 'Scrummy!' While the visits of the Clementses were enjoyable enough, there was an undeniable sense of dread when an invitation was received for us to go over to Ashfield. When the Butlers and Cullens were at Annaghmakerrig, 'party clothes' would be discussed. This was easy enough for the girls, who seemed to have an adequate store of pretty frocks, but I had only two pairs of trousers, brown corduroy and grey serge, both of them much worn, and a selection of rather bulky woollen pullovers knitted by Zane. I did not own a jacket, let alone a suit.

Peggy would usually drive the trap, which she handed over to a man who always appeared miraculously the minute she called, 'Whoa!' to the pony at the Ashfield front door. Introductions having been made, the grown-ups were quickly absorbed into the drawing room, or on to the lawn if it was summer, while Miss Bishop took control of whatever children were in our party and we would go either upstairs to a large playroom where we instantly became rigid with shyness or – which was certainly greatly to be preferred – down by the steep slope that led to riverside paths meandering in and out of shrubberies and thickets. Miss Bishop asked if any of us *sang*, and when even Jennifer could not bring herself to answer that she *did*, Miss Bishop told us that Marcus and Catherine now had quite a selection of songs. So, as we walked along under the alders, they gave us 'The Bonnie Bonnie Banks of Loch Lomond'. When they had finished I thought one of us should say something so I tried, 'That was really quite nice!' which, as I said it, sounded dreadfully haughty, not to say smug.

Tea was in the dining room watched over by a number of family portraits, which my mother had once told me were painted by very famous artists and were certainly very valuable. The grown-ups sat at a long table with Mr and Mrs Clements. She was a thin lady with a loud voice, and he was sturdy-looking with extremely dark hair, much blacker and thicker than Marcus's. We children sat round a table in the window in absolute silence. When we had finished eating some very delicious cress sandwiches and coffee cake, Mrs Clements announced that we might now 'get down'. We did so, bounding about the room and out into the grand hall with its marble busts and handsome staircase, but the Clements children remained seated and did not join us in the playroom for quite some time.

'Why did Marcus and Catherine not leave the table when their mother said they could?' I asked, as Peggy guided the pony across the Finn bridge and out through the Ashfield gates.

'Because they're so well behaved. Even when someone says they can do something, they remember that they've been instructed otherwise, and they don't depart from the rules. Someone must have told them never to leave the table until all the grown-ups have done so.'

'But Mrs Clements *said* they could!'

'She saw that you were all looking restive and might need to leave. But she was very pleased when her own two behaved correctly.'

Jennifer said she had never seen anyone with such black hair as Mr Clements.

'That's because it's a wig,' said Peggy. 'The whole thing has to do with appearances.'

Money was needed for the upkeep of Aghabog Church. The rector, the Reverend Grey, wondered if a summer fête would help their finances. Evidently Mrs G, as the most prominent parishioner, felt it would and it should take place outdoors at Annaghmakerrig, so preparations began. On an afternoon before what Bunty referred to as 'the great day' Mrs McCaldin, who kept the drapers' shop in Newbliss, was invited to tea to advise on the pricing of home-knitted socks, scarves, cardigans (which she called 'corrigans') and any other goods of which she might have a passing commercial knowledge, such as crocheted egg-warmers, satin tea-cosies and nightdress cases that could have the initials of the purchaser embroidered on them if returned in due course to their manufacturer, a single lady in Cootehill. Bunty had laid out the donated goods all over the drawing-room furniture and on the curved seat in the bow window so that tea had to be taken in the dining room – this was such an unusual departure, except for Christmas parties, that it became clear the fête was going to be a really extraordinary occasion. Mrs McCaldin favoured prices that were just a fraction below the next highest shilling; she said that customers would hesitate before buying a woollen pixie bonnet for three shillings but would hand out two shillings and elevenpence without a thought. I, with Julia and her schoolfriend Eleanor Arkell, wrote the prices on little white tags, which we tied to the items for sale. Afterwards my father mentioned that if Mrs McCaldin had been less scrupulous she could have proposed much higher prices so that people would put off buying anything until the next time they were in her shop. As it was, she was very generously undercutting her own business by suggesting such low figures, and neither Mrs G nor Bunty seemed to have thought of that.

Peggy Butler had driven from Maidenhall with Julia and Eleanor, clutching a two-month-old billy-goat kid between them in the back seat. ('There was *such* a funny noise all the way from Kilcock,' said Peggy, as she drew up at the front door. We found that the running-board was dragging on the road.) People were to pay tuppence a line, or sixpence for eight lines, to guess the kid's name and write it on a card and the first person to get the name right would take the kid home. There were to be stalls for flowers and vegetables on the lawn and a stall in the garage for all sorts of useful objects, such as the mysterious leather satchel with straps and buckles that had hung in Bob's storeroom for many years – someone would undoubtedly recognize its purpose and wish to buy it. My father said it was definitely not a piece of military equipment; Mrs G thought that perhaps it was something to do with her father's scientific explorations in New Zealand; Peggy said it should unequivocally be described on the label as a 'period *garde-carton*'. There were to be two hour-long concerts in the End Room, with local talent and a well-known lady entertainer from Enniskillen as the star turn. There was also to be a fancy-dress parade for which people would pay a shilling entry fee; the poster, which was fixed to telegraph poles from Scotshouse to Drum, promised 'Very Valuable Prizes!' and it was rumoured that people were sitting up all night throughout the parish and, indeed, further afield, creating imaginative costumes. Those of us who had recourse to the Annaghmakerrig dressing-up box were firmly instructed by Bunty not to make use of it as we would have an unfair advantage over everyone else. We were all to pray for fine weather as otherwise no one would come and the church funds would not benefit a single bit.

The day turned out to be fine. At two o'clock the flute and drum bands from the Orange lodges in Doohat and Drumalane were heard approaching from opposite directions, causing quite a tremor of anticipation among the early-comers who were making a quick round of the stalls in search of bargains. ('But the bargains'll be at the *end* of the day, to get rid of what they can't sell,' remarked the fore-sighted Mrs Burns.) Mrs G had spoken to the band-leaders and asked if they could possibly manage some tunes that were not hymns – 'though of course hymns will be *most* welcome too!' It appeared that the repertoire was as limited as she had feared, for by the time the bands were approaching the house from the Doohat and the Lake Avenues respectively and quite a crowd had assembled, both stopped playing because, it was later explained, the two sounds 'mightn't mingle right' – which was indeed true because one was playing 'Stand Up, Stand Up for Jesus!' and the other 'Onward Christian Soldiers'. There was no possibility of persuading the two bands to play together so one was directed to the pond garden and the other to the space in front of Daley's Entry where the solidity of the house intervened to prevent the sounds from mingling at all.

Bob Burns had laid out trays of multicoloured coleus, which he had grown from seed in little pots at half a crown a plant. When I asked him what the packets of seed had cost he made a face and said, 'Sssh!' My father said he reckoned that if Bob had paid sixpence per packet and each packet contained twenty seeds, the church funds would benefit by almost a thousand *per cent* a packet! The coleus plants sold within minutes, and then Bob went away to prepare for the fancy-dress competition.

The contestants, about thirty of them, were marshalled by my father outside Bob's Motor-house. There was much giggling and nudging as they paraded round the Half Moon, ending up at the front steps where the entire assemblage of visitors was by now gathered. Someone went to tell the band-leaders to stop playing because the Enniskillen Lady, who was to judge the costumes, would be inaudible over the noise, which could be heard on the steps from both quarters. There was no mistaking who was the guest-of-honour, for the Enniskillen Lady was attired in a bright floral dress that accentuated rather than disguised her ample proportions. Peggy wondered why she was 'wearing the parlour curtains from the Creighton Hotel in Clones, and why she had decided to swathe her neck in a white material that made her head look as if it was peeping out of a meringue'.

The Enniskillen Lady had already mingled among the contestants and noted in an exercise book what each was wearing so that she would not have to make up her mind at the last minute. She whispered to my father that she thought it very curious that a palsied old woman with a stick should want to be in a fancy-dress parade and, anyway, as she was not *wearing* fancy dress she ought to be disqualified even though it might be distasteful to do so. 'That's not a palsied old woman,' said my father, 'that's Bob Burns, the Annaghmakerrig chauffeur!' The Enniskillen Lady replied that, that being the case, Mr Burns should certainly get an award for such a convincing impersonation. Julia and Eleanor had swathed themselves in towels snatched from the bathroom and were appearing as a young Arab couple – Julia, astride a hastily borrowed donkey, being the bride. My father observed that if they had been *real* Arabs the woman would be walking and the man seated serenely on the ass.

We waited, transfixed with expectation, as the Enniskillen Lady made her speech. She said that the lovely wee goat had been won by a man who did not require such an animal and he hoped it would not be taken amiss if it was returned to its donor. I noticed Peggy making a funny face, probably at the thought of having to drive back to Maidenhall with the kid scattering currants all over the back seat. The Enniskillen Lady then praised the generous participation of the two bands, remarking, in conclusion, that she had never heard anything quite like them. Then she turned to the contestants in the fancy-dress parade. 'There has been a wonderful selection of costumes – ingenuity vying with imagination at every turn! I have much pleasure in awarding the prize for the most original costume to the lady who appears before us as the well-known Andrews Liver Salts advertisement.' There was applause as a woman dressed neatly as a housemaid carrying a dustpan and brush and a placard that read 'Inner Cleanliness Is Important Too!' stepped forward and received a little parcel done up in crêpe paper. 'The prize for the prettiest costume goes to the young lady over there dressed as Red Riding Hood – any wolf would be glad to eat her!' Everyone laughed as a very shy little girl was pushed forward to take her prize.

'I thought I would have a very difficult decision to make for the principal award. But, as it turns out,' she continued, gesturing towards Julia, Eleanor and the donkey, 'I have no hesitation in presenting the first prize to the Holy Family!'

The blushing Julia and Eleanor made their way to the steps, casting apprehensive glances towards Bunty, whose face was a study in annoyance. They received their glass paperweight and a box of Cadbury's Milk Tray with rather less grace than was normal for them.

'If they've any sense,' my father said, 'they'll get up on that donkey and make a speedy departure for the Promised Land.'

Between his visits to England in search of work my father made it his business to study the prospectuses of several boys' boarding-schools. My lack of proper education had become a matter of intense concern, and as Nicky was now seven my father was clearly bothered about his future as well. There was a school called Elm Park at Killyleagh on the way to Armagh, which we had often seen from the train. Its prospectus said that pupils were given 'a great grounding in English'. I liked English but whatever 'a great grounding' may have been it did sound a little extreme – goodness only knew what dire methods were employed for other subjects – but Elm Park was dismissed because it might be 'a little out of the way' if we went to live somewhere else. Brackenber House in Belfast was considered, until my mother heard from one of her relatives that 'on no account' should we be sent there for there had been 'trouble' with one of the masters and a number of parents had withdrawn their sons. It must have been bad trouble because no one would tell us the nature of the erring master's misdemeanour. Then Mrs Crawford of Hollywood told us she had heard from her friend Mrs Magee, the widow of a former rector of Ballinode, to say that she had bought an old terrace house in Bangor, overlooking Belfast Lough. Mrs Magee had passed on the information that there was a school with a very good reputation on the other side of the harbour. The main import of Mrs Magee's letter was that she intended to divide her house and would be looking for a tenant for the lower two floors.

My parents decided to inspect the school and the house. They gave us two days off from lessons, though I was encouraged to draw a map of Ceylon and learn the dates of the Kings of the House of Hanover during their absence. They stayed in Belfast with my mother's cousin, Professor Brice Mayers, who conveyed them to and from Bangor in his car. One of his arms had been shot off in the Great War so he had to let go of the wheel every time it was necessary to change gear. To their surprise the trip to Bangor was accomplished without accident, and the professor advised that he felt both the school and the house formed an attractive proposition.

On their return my father elaborated on this, drawing a plan of Mrs Magee's house for us. Both the drawing room and the dining room looked across the road at the sea. There was a big bedroom that they would share with Nicky, and the two tiny bedrooms were for me and Mrs Magee's elderly maid, Bessie, whom we would inherit because Mrs Magee would not need her help in her little flat on the top floor. But who was going to use the other big bedroom? 'Oh,' said my father, 'that will be for your Killen grandparents. It looks as if they'll be spending the whole winter with us.'

My mother said they had been shown over the school by 'a nice Scots cook'. The boys all wore red blazers and caps and grey flannel shorts and shirts and looked very smart indeed. They'd had a long talk with the headmaster, Captain Wilfred Hutton, who had been allowed to leave the army because his teaching partner and founder of the school, a much older man, had died. My father evidently liked Captain Hutton, who came from Dublin where his family owned the firm of Brooks Thomas, the largest hardware company in the city. He told Mrs G and Bunty that the Huttons were 'the kind of people you could invite to dinner'.

It emerged that I had been entered for a vacancy in September of next year, by which time Mrs Magee would have found a builder to convert her house, but there was no vacancy for Nicky until the following January, more than a whole year away. We were given a copy of the prospectus, which said that Garth House was 'a boarding and day-boarding school which prepares boys between the ages of seven and fourteen for the Public Schools and for the Royal Navy'. One of its principal precepts was 'strict attention in the classroom – the essential to concentration and a habit of industry'. Concentration! The very word that Miss Hogan kept declaring was a quality I singularly lacked. The prospectus went on to say that geometry and algebra were begun 'as soon as arithmetic has reached the stage of money sums and weights and measures'. Money sums! I, who could not reckon the change to be expected when proffering half a crown for two tuppence-halfpenny stamps without counting out loud and using my fingers, would hardly make rapid progress, if I made any progress at all. The prospectus also said that football was the winter sport, with cricket and tennis in the summer. I had watched Uncle Marcus and Aunt Mat playing tennis at the club in Monaghan, but football and cricket were near mysteries. What chance would I have of survival in such a place?

September 1944, however, was nine months away, and, with luck, things would change, as they'd had a habit of doing. Until then my father would be taking a temporary position in England that would keep him there till we all met again in Bangor. In the meantime I would be going to a day-school in Monaghan town run by a Mrs Bradley and staying with Uncle Marcus, Aunt Mat and my cousins John and Margaret at their house, the majestic Aviemore.

Aviemore, Hill Street, Monaghan

Whichever direction you looked in Monaghan there was always the sense that Aviemore was the most important house in the town. The homes of the wealthy business people, the McCaldins, the Pattons, the Greacens, and the residences of the chief medical officers in the hospitals, the McArdles at the County and the Coynes at the Mental, were larger but situated on outer roads surrounded by gardens rich in lilac and laburnum and could not possibly be counted as anything to do with the real town. In all my explorations on foot or by bicycle through the intricate laneways and thoroughfares of Monaghan with Nicky and my cousins, I never came across a house as imposing as Aviemore, either in its situation or its design.

Anyone travelling from Dublin to Derry, or Belfast to Cavan, on the highways that crossed at the Diamond in the town centre could not fail to note Aviemore's presence at the head of Mill Street, watching the passing traffic and the comings and goings of the local people. If you stood on the wide limestone steps leading up to the front door

– or, better still, if you looked out from one of the upper windows – you could survey the entire townscape, the slim steeple and little attendant pinnacles of St Patrick's Church dominating the rooftops of the foreground, to the right a glimpse of the pillared portico of the Court House, in the middle distance the stubby spire of First Monaghan Presbyterian Church. Was there a Second Monaghan? I wondered, until I learned that the pretty, barn-like building on the road to Lamb's Lough, which had no spire at all and was usually referred to as Ballyalbany Church, was unfairly reduced by its correct title, which was probably why the members of the congregation did not use it. On the southern side of the town, at the top of the hill that was complementary to Aviemore's, was the crowning spectacle of St Macartan's Cathedral. My Presbyterian relatives were wont to point out – somewhat snidely, I thought – that it would not have been there at all were it not for the relentless campaign for Catholic Emancipation undertaken by my great-great-great-grandfather, Daniel O'Connell. St Macartan's Cathedral was 'ostentatious', 'affected' and 'unnecessarily dominating'. I, who had been leafing through Arthur Mee's *Book of One Thousand Beautiful Things* at Eldron, found it to be a glorious manifestation of Victorian Gothic, its soaring spaces of marble and coloured glass creating a kind of concealed portal to Paradise, unknown to our circle in Monaghan because in some mysterious way its interior was illicit territory.

How my uncle, Dr Marcus Killen, had come to live at Aviemore was explained to me by my grandmother. After he graduated from Queen's University in Belfast and had undertaken initiation into his profession as medical officer on an ocean liner, it had seemed only natural that he should go into partnership with his bachelor uncle, Dr John Elliott of Eldron, expanding the practice to include Monaghan town. Marcus, like my mother, had spent many school holidays at Eldron; he and his uncle shared an enthusiasm for field sports and had come to know every lough, bog and spinney for miles and miles. Then Marcus became engaged to Matilda Olivia Pringle, daughter of the leading lawyer in Clones. Great-uncle John and my grandfather helped him to buy Aviemore and, after they were married, Mrs Pringle helped Marcus and Mat to furnish their very large new home.

'Then a very sad thing happened,' my grandmother said. 'Uncle John died unexpectedly. Their grand plan to work together was only just beginning.'

There was a framed photograph of Uncle John on a round table at Eldron. He had a kind face and a neatly cut beard, and did not look at all like someone who was going to die. 'He may have had a weak heart, but if he did he never said anything about it,' my grandmother said. 'Your aunt Janey was very upset because from then on she had to live at Eldron alone.'

I said she'd always had Lizzie for company.

'Have a bit of sense!' said my grandmother.

Fortunately for Mat the previous owner had 'brought up' the Aviemore kitchen from the immense basement and a 'modern' kitchen with a gas cooker had been created from one of the four reception rooms at entrance level. The smallest reception room was converted as Marcus's surgery, where he attended to a queue of patients every day; the dining room was where they waited to see him, reading old copies of the *Field* and this week's *Northern Standard*. There was a big drawing room on the first floor, and on this and the floor above, seven bedrooms, most of them twice the size of a bedroom in an ordinary house. Two bathrooms with Roman tiles in key patterns had been added in the Edwardian era in a specially built return. Below the bathrooms an insignificant door in varnished oak opened on to a staircase that was used as a repository for carpet-sweepers, mops, slop pails and big tins of floor polish, and if you chose to pick your way through all these you could descend to a labyrinth of abandoned pantries, larders and sculleries as well as to the old vaulted kitchen where a dead iron range presided gloomily over the domestic debris of earlier centuries. I thought the most impressive feature of the house was its curved staircase rising up three storeys around a central well – this was true grandeur and I imagined myself as a duke or, better still, a king, descending graciously to receive the homage of my subjects.

While I was staying at Aviemore and attending Mrs Bradley's school, Mat decided it was time that her comparatively new kitchen should be renovated. There was much discussion with Mr Hamill, the Painter & Decorator in North Road. Mr Hamill was impressed by my aunt's choice of colours and by the decisive way in which she selected linoleum for the floor and a pretty oil-cloth for the shelving, which she cut out herself in a pattern that left a lively little border of crescents festooning the edge of each shelf. Mr Hamill clumped about the kitchen in his heavy boots, his white overalls becoming more and more colourful as he climbed ladders and slapped paint on the walls and ceiling, occasioning warnings from Mat to mind the surface of the gas cooker and not to leave wet paint lids where the cat would step on them. Sensing that I was not a member of the family he commented on the great size and unusual design of the house and on my aunt's executive approach to its management.

'She has a good eye, yon Mrs Killen. She sees things the

way they should be.' He paused in his task to consider further the supervisory qualities of his employer. 'She misses nothin', yon Mrs Killen. She'd see a midge on a mare's arse in Tyrone.'

At one period my cousin Margaret, attracted to wildlife from an early age, kept a hospital in the basement for wounded mice, jackdaws and whatever other ailing animals she came across. When she was only five she had a big tabby cat called Wilfred, which she used to dress in doll's clothes – pinafores and bonnets and pyjamas – pushing him around the house in a doll's pram. Her father's patients, arriving for consultations about their swelled ankles and bad backs, would bend down politely, irrespective of the pain, to admire the wee girl's dolly and then get the fright of their lives when the coverlets were drawn aside and they were confronted by two gleaming golden eyes and a complaining 'Miaow!' Some, no doubt, wondered if they should not be consulting Dr Coyne at the Mental.

My aunt Mat said that in the eighteenth century Aviemore had been the town-house of the Hamiltons of Cornacassa, a country mansion destroyed in the Troubles of 1922. She thought they probably had another town-house in one of the Georgian squares in Dublin. Aviemore had changed hands many times and had once been a ladies' seminary, or private school. Some time in the mid-nineteenth century the front had been 'done over', with plaster arabesques added below the parapet and heavy plaster decorations round the front door and windows – but the most obvious difference was in the windows themselves, where the original twelve panes had been replaced by two-paned plate glass, which made the house look Victorian instead of Georgian. She showed me that the windows at the back of the house had not been changed. Among them was the very handsome round-headed window on the staircase.

Life at Aviemore was very different to that at Eldron, six miles away, which was characterized by its rustic calm, interrupted only a few times a day by the passing trains on the Belfast line, and just as different to Annaghmakerrig, nine miles away, where there was a peculiar sense of self-sufficiency, with the dairy farm, orchards and vegetable garden, and no need for anyone to travel outside its gravitational centre, except for unusual assignations like a tooth extraction or to buy a wet battery for the wireless. Aviemore was immutably connected to the life of the town of Monaghan by the eminence of its situation and by the daily visits of the halt and the maimed, and connected to the wider county by my uncle's visits to the rural sick in the public dispensaries at Smithborough, Scotstown, Ballinode and Golan Murphy. My aunt went about her daily urban round to Mr Gillanders, the butcher, Mr Black, the chemist, and Messrs J. & J. McCaldin, the grocers, calling at the Round House for fruit and vegetables and the Egg Store for half a dozen new-laid eggs for boiling and the same number of cracked eggs – they were a halfpenny cheaper – for baking. On this brisk itinerary with her shopping-bag she replenished the kitchen cupboard, exchanged words with other ladies on similar errands and was back in forty minutes to help Maggie or Rita or Bridie or whoever was the current maid to prepare the lunch. She played bridge and received other bridge-players to the house of an evening and she and my uncle played golf at Rossmore Park and tennis at the lawn-tennis club beside the railway station. They went out into the world daily and the world came daily in to them.

My earliest memory of Aviemore was spending a night there when my grandmother was taking me from Belfast to

deliver me to my great-aunt Zane at Eldron. I was two and
a half. Possibly she had decided not to make the journey in
one day so as to give me a little extra time in her familiar
company before introducing me to a completely new house
and its occupants. I remember the shimmering light on the
gauze curtains in the sitting room and standing between
them and the window from where I could see the line of
houses descending, in steps as it were, to Church Square. At
this time Aunt Mat had a little baby called John. Then there
was a new baby who was christened Margaret at a ceremony
in the upstairs sitting room performed by the Reverend
Noble Huston, a relative from County Down. This minister
told me that it was he who had baptized me nearly four
years previously at my grandparents' house in Belfast. Before
coming to Margaret's christening Zane taught me to kneel
down with my hands together 'like church windows'. Later,
there was never a visit to Monaghan from Eldron or Annaghmakerrig when whoever I was with did not stop at
Aviemore to say hello, and perhaps take a cup of tea. John
and Margaret's birthdays were so close together they shared
a party every year. John became interested in carpentry and
was given a set of tools, which were much admired, indeed
coveted, by the rest of the party-goers. 'Where's wee Walter
Greacen?' enquired Mat, noticing the absence of one of John's
friends. Walter was found in the sitting room sawing the leg
off a settee.

It was my aunt Mat who had suggested that I might go to
Mrs Bradley's new school in Monaghan until the vacancy
occurred at the big school in Bangor. She mentioned that
Mrs Bradley had already attracted twenty pupils from families
dissatisfied with the Protestant national school. Mrs Bradley
had been a teacher herself and was taking up work again
because her husband, an inspector with the Department of

Education, had been killed in a motor accident. 'He was run over by a priest. They say the priest was drunk – but that didn't come out at the inquest, you may be sure.' Heads were nodded, and lips pursed.

Mrs Bradley's twenty pupils were squeezed into the dining room of Glenbeg, her semi-detached house on the Cootehill road. She would deal with one class – she called them 'groups' – setting work to complete while she moved on to the next. We did Latin but instead of Hilliard and Botting's *Shorter Latin Primer*, with its enervating tables of declensions and conjugations, there was a book called *Latin for Today*, which had pictures of Romans in their houses going about their daily business in the atrium and peristyle, descriptions of their gods and goddesses and the wars that were fought to extend their empire. Mrs Bradley taught Irish history, which I'd never supposed was anything but some vague adjunct to the endless lists of kings, queens and battles that comprised English history. It turned out to be full of heartrending stories about people dying in the cause of liberty. My group was reading the chapter on the Insurrection of 1798 and how the Protestant patriot Theobald Wolfe Tone was captured by the English on a ship in Lough Swilly and brought to Dublin in chains, where he did the only honourable thing, slitting his wrist with a penknife in his prison cell, thus robbing the English of the public trial to which they were eagerly looking forward.

My arrival at Mrs Bradley's spoiled the composition of what was called the Graham Group – Margaret Graham of Ballyleck and her cousin Florence, whom I already knew, two other Grahams, Alan and Noreen, who lived on a big farm on the Armagh side of the town, and yet two more Grahams, Robert and Bertie, who were no relation to the others and cycled to school every day from some remote

place that no one had ever heard of and whom we never
visited because of the distance. After school finished at three
o'clock I would call for my cousins at Aviemore – their
junior school having finished earlier – and we would cycle
out to see the more accessible Grahams, or other friends
such as the Bretts and the Greacens, and rampage through
their farms or gardens until sent home by some anxious
adult with the comment that Dr and Mrs Killen would be
wondering where we were. As it happened, Dr and Mrs
Killen seemed to trust us not to roam too far or to disobey
the Rules of the Road. I credited this sense of freedom to
the fact that I was now nine; it was wonderful to be able
to cycle to places on my own and often I would take a
new route from the school to Aviemore just to see what
was round a certain corner or beyond some bridge or other.
Then Mat would remind me that I had homework to do
and I was banished upstairs, where I would sit for an hour
at my window overlooking the town, occasionally allowing
my attention to stray from the magnificent view of St
Macartan's Cathedral to the Roman Empire or the Battle
of Ballinamuck (where the Irish and French were unfairly
outnumbered by the English) or to Oliver Goldsmith's *The
Deserted Village*, which I had no difficulty in learning by
heart.

My mother and Nicky were installed again with Great-aunt
Zane at Eldron, six miles away. My father had a temporary
job in Preston, pending the big, decisive move to Bangor. I
went 'home' to Eldron from Aviemore for the weekends,
sometimes cycling and sometimes on the train, which only
took twelve minutes. When the old black engine with its
two carriages rounded the hill between McEntee's farm and
the Eldron orchard I would press my face to the window,

for Zane would always be there, standing at the stile, waving as the train slowed down for its final half-mile into Smithborough station.

My mother and Nicky had been to see a Georgian house on a grassy hill between Monaghan and Smithborough that was for sale. It was called Aughnamala and it came with outhouses and several acres of meadow. The farmer who owned the land was looking for four hundred pounds for the dwelling-house. Nothing would stop me from going to see it too, so on a bright Sunday evening, as I was setting out from Eldron to return to Aviemore, my mother accompanied me on her bicycle for the three or four miles. There was a gate-lodge where a woman gave us the key to the house, which was up a gently curving avenue bounded by daffodils. Aughnamala looked very fine from the road, but when we approached I could see that it needed several coats of paint, and the plaster was falling off the walls and chimney-stacks. Inside, water was running continuously in the lavatory and the inside of the bath was all rusty, but the house had a comfortable feeling. 'I think it would take another four hundred to make it habitable,' my mother said, in a voice that put all thought of living there out of the question.

We locked the front door and stood looking at the unspectacular but pleasant view of the surrounding woods and drumlins. There was another large house on a hill at the far side of the road just above the line of hawthorns that marked the remains of the Ulster Canal. 'That's Drumaconnor,' my mother said, 'where Oscar Wilde's half-sisters were burned to death at an evening party.'

'Were you there?'

'Oh, no, it was years before I was born. Oscar Wilde later became a very famous writer but he was at boarding-school in Enniskillen at the time of the fire.'

We freewheeled down to the gate-lodge and gave in the key. I asked how the sisters had been burned.

'I'll ride a bit more of the way with you,' my mother said. 'Well, these two girls from Dublin were staying with their uncle and aunt at Drumsnat rectory – that's the tower of the church over there. It was New Year's Eve and they were invited to a ball, but it can't really have been a ball because Drumaconnor isn't big enough, but that's how the story was handed down. Snow was on the ground, drifting against the ditches, so they walked round by the road instead of along the tow-path of the canal. There was dancing. One of the girls twirled too close to the chimney-piece and a spark caught her dress. It was made of some kind of flimsy stuff, muslin perhaps, and immediately caught fire. Her sister rushed to try to put out the flames by beating her with a cushion but her dress caught fire too. Apparently there was a lot of screaming while people went to the kitchen to get jugs of water to throw over them but a sensible man shouted to someone to open the hall door and he and other young men carried the girls out and rolled them in the snow.'

'That would have put out the flames?'

'Yes, far more effectively than throwing water over them. The snow put out the flames but the girls had been very badly burned so they died.'

'And were other people burned too?'

'Some of the men who carried the girls out were, but only slightly. They were very lucky the house didn't catch fire.'

'And what happened then?'

'I suppose the girls' uncle had to get a message to Dublin to tell Dr Wilde that his daughters were dead. Canon Robinson, who lives in the rectory now, once told me that people remembered Dr Wilde's groans as his little girls' coffins were let down into their grave. They said it was the most dreadful sound they had ever heard.'

My mother turned back for Eldron at Ballyleck bridge. The following Sunday I asked if we could go to church at Drumsnat instead of Smithborough to see the grave of the Wilde sisters. My mother enjoyed what she called 'expeditions' so we endured a long and very dreary sermon from Canon Robinson and at the end of the service asked him where we would find the grave. He led us a few steps towards a briary hedge and there it was. The inscription read,

*In memory of two loving and loved sisters*
*Emily Wilde aged 24 and Mary Wilde aged 22*
*who lost their lives in this parish November 10th 1871*

My mother said, 'That's astonishing!'

'Oh, it was a terrible tragedy,' said the canon. 'They'd lingered, you know, for several months. They didn't actually die on the night of the fire, the poor things, may God have mercy on their immortal souls!'

'I mean, I'm astonished that they were in their *twenties*! The way I heard the story they seemed like young girls!'

'That may have been the perception. They were farmed out, of course. The Wildes didn't want them in Dublin.'

'I think you once told me that their father was dreadfully upset at the funeral?'

'Oh, indeed,' said the canon, 'and witnesses were quite sure it was genuine grief. But I fancy it was grief tinged with remorse – or guilt.'

When we were cycling down the lane that led from the overgrown graveyard to the road I asked what Canon Robinson meant by the father's guilt.

'Oh, well, you see, by that time Dr Wilde was married to

another lady and Mrs Wilde probably didn't want step-daughters, whom she knew nothing about, in her house. So the girls must have been sent as paying guests to the rectory here.'

I knew all about step-mothers and how cruel they were from the fairy stories I used to read. My mother said that Mrs Wilde probably wasn't a bit cruel but people looked at things in a different way at that time – and, of course, the rectory at Drumsnat would have been a lovely place to live, with the canal and the lake and all that. The young ladies probably quite enjoyed being there.

'It was the olden days,' I said. 'People in the olden days were very stupid.'

For as long as I could remember I had been prone to what were called 'sick headaches'. These usually announced themselves by flashing lights or – much more unpleasantly – half vision where I could only see a portion of the object I was looking at. After a short time I would be violently ill. Zane attributed these attacks to 'something I ate', the earliest on record having occurred after the Reverend Noble Huston had shot a snipe that Lizzie had served on a dainty platter of boiled potatoes. Instinct told me that eating was not the reason. Later, while we were at Newcastle, I was taken to see a specialist in Belfast who diagnosed 'acidosis', prescribing six spoonfuls of sugar in a glass of hot water nightly. This was quite the opposite to what I felt I should be taking for I'd discovered that I could sometimes fend off an attack by eating a very sour apple or even tasting a drop of vinegar. The Aviemore household was enthralled by the spectacle of my nightly drink of lukewarm syrup and also by the fact that I was usually sick on a Sunday evening after my arrival from Eldron. Mat was sure I had migraine, from which she also suffered; she, too, was invariably sick after travel. Marcus felt I could safely ignore the advice of the Belfast doctor so the sugared water was discontinued. He possessed what my mother called 'the bedside manner', which was quite surprising because he was outgoing in a sporty way and you'd think he wouldn't trouble to suppress his naturally extrovert manner when ministering to the ailing. One time when I was lying in a darkened room feeling that my head was going to fall off he sang an amusing ditty 'to take your mind off the headache', which it certainly did, supporting his theory that migraine was 'partly psychological'. The song had become popular on the wireless as sung by Bing Crosby,

> *Would you like to swing on a star,*
> *Carry moonbeams home in a jar,*
> *And be better off than you are –*
> *Or would you rather be a . . .*

and there followed a list of what you might like to be – a mule, a pig or a fish.

I heartily wished I could magically transform myself into one of these animals when, at an outdoor sports event in aid of the Red Cross, Joe McArdle, the county surgeon's son, challenged me to a pillow-fight on the greasy pole. I had sensed a migraine all afternoon and was wondering if I could reasonably go back to Aviemore and lie down; but that would show me up as a softy – a type despised in the mettlesome Killen household, so I took my pillow, which seemed to be stuffed with lumps of lead, climbed on the pole and aimed at McArdle's head. He was surprised by the suddenness of the onslaught, hitting mightily back while I fended off his succession of well-aimed blows. Then I noticed there was only half a McArdle opposite me and this partial-person was encompassed by a nimbus of coloured light not unlike the heavenly glow that surrounded the saints in the stained-glass windows of St Macartan's. I was now only automatically making what must have appeared to the onlooking crowd as half-hearted, not to say feeble, lunges at my opponent. All at once my stomach lurched, I toppled off the pole and voided what must have appeared as several substantial meals over the sward. Stewards ran forward – there was an appropriate attendance of Red Cross personnel – and I was assisted to the First Aid tent. Voices were saying that risky games should not be allowed and others that the child had obviously been overeating and his people must have been *out of their minds* to let him enter a sporting event of any kind. My mother and Mat appeared. Everyone apologized to each other – the nervous Red Cross people for introducing a game they had not realized might be dangerous, my mother for their needless fright and concern and I for spoiling the grass of St Louis's Convent sports field. Of Joe McArdle there was no sign. I envisaged him telling his friends about the cissy he had so easily defeated on the greasy pole.

Mrs Bradley kept us in touch with world events. In January 1944 the Allies landed at Anzio and she marked the progress of the troops up the leg of Italy on a wall map. There was respectful interest when I said my father had been in on the beginning of the campaign that had pushed Rommel back along the coast of Africa, whence the invasion of Italy was projected. Nicky walked from Eldron to Mr Kerr's shop in Smithborough every morning to collect the *Belfast News-Letter*, which had detailed maps marked with arrows to show where there were advances and stars where there were battles – 'strikes', they were called. Everyone in Smithborough was congratulating Mr and Mrs Kerr because their daughter, a nurse in the Royal Navy, had been decorated by the King for bravery when a destroyer in a convoy in which she was serving on the hospital ship was torpedoed in the Mediterranean.

Mrs Bradley said it would not be long before the Allies invaded France or the Netherlands – the Germans would know this and were probably neglecting Italy and keeping a large force to watch the English Channel. She said there were now very few American soldiers left in Northern Ireland – we'd probably noticed that the numbers on weekend leave crossing the border to enjoy the bright lights of Monaghan had dwindled to nothing. They were undoubtedly massing at this very moment on the coast of southern England.

*There'll be bluebirds over*
*The white cliffs of Dover*

sang Vera Lynn on the wireless. Mrs Bradley said there'd also be warplanes flying over the white cliffs of Dover.

In the days coming up to my birthday on 9 June she tuned in her dining-room-classroom wireless for us to hear the latest BBC bulletins. If the Germans had been unsure as to where precisely the invasion of Europe was going to take place they must now be in no doubt because imminent landings all along the coast of Normandy were reported for the whole world to hear. Mrs Bradley said this was to confuse the Germans so that they'd take it the invasion would be somewhere quite different and defend the coasts of places like Brittany or Holland – but it turned out that the broadcasts were true and the British, American and Canadian soldiers had landed in Normandy after all. The city of Cherbourg was soon taken by the Allies, then Bayeux and Caen.

'Berlin's the goal!' announced an excited commentator with a plummy English voice. Mrs Bradley said that once Berlin was captured the war would be over.

Marcus observed that, with the Allied advances in Europe, it was curious the way things seemed to relax in the Irish Free State, a non-combatant country. Identification cards ceased to be needed for cross-border visits so the only border officials left were the Customs men. Passengers' baggage on the Great Northern line had to be searched but this had nothing to do with the war, Marcus said. It was designed to stop people from Northern Ireland coming to places like Monaghan to buy our cheaper goods, though naturally the shopkeepers were delighted that so many Northerners braved the system. Mat's aunt Zoë came across the border from Aughnacloy and bought a woolly cardigan and four pairs of combinations, which she put on in Mat's bedroom; then she went home on the bus looking considerably larger than she had been that morning.

A special train hired by Duffy's Circus stopped at Monaghan station for the obligatory Customs examination. One of the animal trucks was inadvertently opened and a lion stepped out on to the platform. Marcus read us the report in the *Northern Standard*, which said that 'The intrepid Chief of Customs and Excise smote the King of Beasts on his countenance with his cap of office.' Apparently the lion meekly returned to its wagon. A man from Armagh was said to have bought a suit in Harpur's Gents' Outfitters and went into the WC on the train to put it on, intending to throw the old suit out of the window into a field where a neighbour would retrieve it. In his hurry he parcelled the trousers of his new suit with the old one and stepped down on to the Armagh platform wearing only a jacket.

It was decided that when the summer term finished at

Mrs Bradley's we would all go for two weeks to Arnold's Guesthouse at Dunfanaghy in Donegal. This meant passing through Northern Ireland and out the other side, so we would be searched by the Customs four times. Marcus said there should be a system whereby people moving from one part of the Free State to another should not be searched, but Mat pointed out that a smuggler travelling with a case of whiskey or a loin of lamb could easily buy a ticket to Donegal, say, but get off the train in Omagh to sell his goods there. My mother added that it was such a *business* travelling by train to anywhere in Ireland she supposed few would have the energy to do such a thing.

In the week before we went to Dunfanaghy posters appeared, announcing that Duffy's Circus would be at the Fair Green for two days, admission sixpence and a shilling. My mother was badgered into taking us. We crowded on to the wooden benches while she decided to splurge a shilling for the comfort of a seat that was covered with a kind of brown matting. A small band played for ages and then a troupe of horses trotted in, turning and stopping and turning again when the ring-master cracked his whip. Then a lady in a spangly blouse swung to and fro on a trapeze, but as the tent was not very large she did not have far to fall if she failed to reach the safety of her crow's nest on the central pole – John said that she probably wouldn't die, only break her leg. Then another lady rode around the ring standing on a pony's back, stopping here and there to place a red or white handkerchief in a series of little boxes; then the horse had to go to each box in turn and pick out only the red handkerchiefs, which it successfully did. Next, a clown changed round the white and red handkerchiefs, putting his finger ostentatiously to his lips as if to say that we mustn't tell the horse – but the horse still picked out the red handkerchiefs and we all cheered. After this a man came on in a blue costume that clung to his body like a swimsuit. He seemed to be made of rubber for he contorted himself in a fascinating way, ending up walking on his hands with his legs twisted round his neck so you couldn't make out which end of him was which.

'His balls must be up his nostril,' remarked John.

Three ladies came on with accordions and played tunes for us to sing – 'Deep in the Heart of Texas' and 'This Is the Army, Mr Jones'. Then the whole company assembled and sang 'Wish Me Luck, As You Wave Me Goodbye!' There were really very few of them, so the performers must have been doubling up on their acts. Perhaps the clown had also been the contortionist, for there was no sign of the latter in the line-up. Outside, some of the circus animals were on display. A woman with a red face, who, my mother said, should have known better, went up to a horse and gave it a few slaps on the haunch whereupon the horse kicked her in the stomach. The woman fell on the ground and screamed while her friends shouted, 'Och, Maisie, are you hurted?' and 'Will I get on the bike and go for the doctor?' but the ring-master, now wearing a very old pair of corduroys and a lumberjack's shirt, came out and said, 'Ah, it was only a wee kick!' He assured the woman that a kick from a horse was never serious and he'd make sure that the animal was given a good beating. When we were leaving the Fair Green we did indeed see a man lashing the horse with a pair of reins but my mother said that, by the looks of him, he was only pretending and certainly the horse didn't seem to mind.

My mother kept scratching, first her leg and then her stomach, finally contorting herself to reach her back. She said she must have picked up something from the upholstery of the seat, which was quite hard anyway and she'd have been better off sitting with us on the wooden bench. When she got home she shook out all her clothes, but the flea – or fleas – must have hidden somewhere for she was still scratching next day on the train.

'Are we near Dunfanaghy?' Margaret asked, as the train slowed at the bridge over the river Bann and the brown and yellow brick station of Portadown came into view.

'No, we're getting further and further away from it!' her father replied. 'To get to Dunfanaghy you have to go all over the place.'

We pulled our bicycles out of the guard's van and stacked them ready for loading on to the Strabane train, but when we learned that there was a two-hour delay we decided to hold races up and down the deserted platform until John crashed into a pigeon-coop at the door of the Military Transport Office and a furious second lieutenant rushed out and told us to get the bloody hell out of it. He then bent over the coop and made cooings and other soothing sounds to quell the astonished fluttering inside. Marcus thought it strange that the British Army was using carrier pigeons when surely there must be more up-to-date methods of transmitting messages, such as Morse code.

'Or semaphore,' my mother suggested.

At Strabane we had to change to the County Donegal Joint Committee's narrow-gauge line, on which a Toytown type of train carried us by a circuitous route to Letterkenny. There, in lashings of rain, we found a decrepit Lough Swilly bus, which dropped us an hour later at the guesthouse door – *what* would it have been like, my mother wondered, if the guesthouse were somewhere more remote and we had to reach it with all our bags and boxes balanced on the handlebars and back-carriers of our bikes? Well, she really did not like to *think*. The journey had taken seven hours. A crow – or one of the British Army's pigeons – would have flown the ninety miles in a quarter the time.

The Lough Swilly bus was crammed with people from the villages of north Donegal returning from a day's outing to their county town, with holidaymakers, like ourselves, and students going to the Irish-language summer schools. If there had been such a thing as an inspector he would have removed half the passengers because of overcrowding. There was a pervasive odour of damp tweed and Wills' Woodbines cigarettes. It was especially uncomfortable for my mother because the flea from Duffy's Circus was still travelling around in her clothes.

I was stashed between her and a language teacher, who was travelling on, he told us, to Gaelscoil an tSamraidh at Gort a' Choirce. He spoke of the strides the Revival was making, informing us that more and more people who had never thought of learning Irish were now taking it up – and not at all because knowledge of the language was a stepping-stone to a good job in the civil service, which he was aware was the general perception. Irish had all kinds of advantages nowadays, he said. Several Irish classics had been translated into other languages, like *La vie de Peig Sayers* and *Mon petit âne noir*, and a number of renowned foreign books were now available in Irish, such as *Eachtraí Searloc Holmes*.

My mother became irked by the insistence of this monologue – possibly she was tired, for I had heard her defending the Revival when we were staying at Milltown House, but when this bus passenger informed her enthusiastically that you could now read Dickens in Irish she exclaimed, 'I really have no compelling wish to read Dickens in *any* language!'

and that, as she said later, put a stop to his verbal diarrhoea. She thought it curious that members of the language-revival movement always wore dark suits and overcoats even when on holiday and always had a row of fountain-pens in their breast-pockets and a Pioneer pin in their lapels, which meant that they didn't drink. 'Killjoys,' she said. 'The real Gaelic culture was never like that.'

In the days following, we cycled by way of sandy, fuchsia-fringed lanes to the hidden coves and strands of north Donegal. While splashing in the waves of Marble Strand on Sheep Haven we watched, mesmerized, as an American battleship silently glided into view and stopped – it was near enough for us to see the sailors hurrying about on deck and I thought we should swim out to it, but was immediately told this would be highly dangerous and I should put any such notion out of my head if I wanted to return to the shore alive. We waved and shouted, 'Welcome to Donegal!' but no one on the ship waved back. It was still there when we were leaving, this grey floating fortress bristling with radio masts and guns, behind it the yellow shore and the lazy hayfields of Fanad. Mr Arnold at the guesthouse said that kind of thing had happened before, a battleship mistaking the entrance to Sheep Haven for Lough Foyle, where it would have been routed to the international naval base at Derry. It was most likely that the ship we had seen did not have enough space to turn round and was waiting for high tide so that it could reverse back into the open sea. Marcus said he pitied the captain, who would undoubtedly face court-martial on arrival at Derry, but Mr Arnold said if he had his wits about him and kept quiet no one would ever know a thing about it because there was no Irish military or naval presence in the neighbourhood of Marble Strand to report the incident as a breach of our neutrality.

'All the same, it'll make him late for Normandy,' said Marcus.

> *And all the monkeys aren't in the zoo,*
> *Every day you see quite a few,*
> *So you see it's all up to you,*
> *You could be better than you are,*
> *You could be swingin' on a star.*

# 144 Seacliffe Road, Bangor, County Down

We arrived off the train in an opal-coloured dusk, the harbour enveloped by a pale sea mist tinged by the expiring glow of the setting sun. There were no lights in the shops as we cycled cautiously down Main Street, for the blackout was still observed. My mother said this was now quite unnecessary – 'but the powers that be in Northern Ireland like to do everything by the rules'. The gas-lamps on the quay gave out no light, serving merely to indicate the line of the pavement. Hushed singing was heard ahead, women's voices. Presently we overtook a platoon of the Women's Royal Navy Service marching on crêpe-soled shoes to the tune of

> *Wish me luck, as you wave me goodbye,*
> *Cheerio, here I go, on my way . . .*

Then they turned left on to the pier and disappeared into the darkness of the bay.

Inside number 144 the wooden Venetian blinds were closed

and thick curtains pulled across them – 'Just to be sure,' Mrs Magee said, as she descended the stair to welcome us. The rooms were lighted by old-fashioned gasoliers on brackets on either side of the chimney-pieces. 'When the war's over I'm going to install electricity,' said Mrs Magee. 'More modern and much cleaner. And as tomorrow's Sunday,' she continued, without pause for change of subject, 'I'm going to cycle over to Groomsport for the Harvest Thanksgiving, if any of you would like to come with me?'

I volunteered.

Mrs Magee was a tall, angular woman, who wore steel-rimmed glasses. She was interested in everything, and made even the smallest expedition to the grocer's seem like a journey of discovery. As we rode along the seafront next morning she explained the geography of Bangor as the bay opened up to view. Corvettes and destroyers were at anchor out in the lough. The widest of the bays was Ballyholme, with Caproni's Ballroom and Ice-cream Parlour at the near end, then rows of terrace houses looking straight out to sea and then the grand mansions of Dufferin Villas. Mrs Magee said that the American soldiers were the greatest patrons Caproni's had ever known but those young men were now on the march in France and Belgium. 'If they'd gone to church in the numbers that went jitterbugging in that place our parish debts would have been paid off like billy-oh!' she said, with a laugh.

I was fascinated to see roads named Baylands First Avenue and Baylands Fifth Avenue but Mrs Magee said they'd been there long before the arrival of the US troops. 'There's also a Broadway and a Beverly Hills, I don't know why, someone on the Borough Council trying to show off what they've learned from the talkies. Hollywood, you know, and all that. Perhaps Baylands is set out like the ideal American suburb.'

Here was a complete new world of neat homes with privet hedges and mown lawns and I would be living in the midst of it. It had a friendly, sociable feel.

Fields of fresh stubble with corn-stooks ready for threshing came into view in the flat land between Ballyholme Bay and Groomsport Bay, and then we saw the pretty village church, which was our destination. Mrs Magee explained that all the neighbourhoods of Bangor had their own churches – there was the old Abbey Church on the Newtownards Road, St Comgall's in the centre of the town and St Columbanus's in Ballyholme. Comgall had lived in the sixth century, she said, and had founded a great monastery at Bangor. He was a very holy man and drank only water and ate bread made from withered barley. I wondered why he waited for the barley to wither before making the bread and Mrs Magee said it was probably that he let everyone else eat the good barley and he took what was left in the bottom of the barrel. One of his students was Columbanus, who went to convert the pagans of northern Italy; he was terribly interested in choral music and organized the choirs in such a way that there was continuous singing at the monastery in Bobbio throughout the day and night.

'Imagine that!' said Mrs Magee. 'I'm sure all the monks died young, from insomnia. Quite what they would have made of the divisions in the Church today I can't bear to think,' she continued, as we found a wall in the churchyard to lean our bicycles against. 'The Presbyterian churches in Bangor now far outnumber the Church of Ireland ones. There's also a Methodist chapel on the seafront and a small Roman Catholic church at the back of the railway station – and you'd be hard set to count all the other so-called Places of Worship. Nothing more than shacks, most of them. Look, there's one with – what is it? – "Elim Pentecostal

Hall" over the door. Needs a bit of paint, doesn't it? Who goes there, I wonder? Not anyone I've ever met.'

Groomsport Church was decorated inside with sheaves of corn and wheat, big bursting purple and orange dahlias, slim blue and mauve Michaelmas daisies and loads of baskets of apples and turnips and beet, just like at Aghabog but with far more of everything. The clergyman spoke of the Lord's bounty and of better times to come. He said that if he were a betting man – which he hastened to add he was not – he would wager that when we all met under the same roof in a twelvemonth there would be no more talk of air raids and no more sad telegrams delivered to the homes of North Down. He ventured to add that it would not be premature to join in singing the hymn 'The Strife Is O'er, the Battle Done'. I noticed in the hymn-book that it was not one of those attributed to St Columbanus.

The clergyman trusted that we could all look forward in Jesus's name to a happier year, but I was apprehensive of what was coming the following *week*, when 'proper' school started. I wondered if it was going to be like *The Fifth Form at St Dominic's*, which my Fitz-Simon grandfather had picked out for me from his shelf of old school stories, or *Fellow Fags*, which Bunty had given me for my last birthday, both of which were full of nasty, mean characters and boys being unfairly expelled for crimes they had not committed. I thought that for me the strife might only be beginning.

My mother may have sensed my anxiety, for she decided I should meet one of my fellow pupils before term started. We called on one of her oldest friends, Eileen MacNeice, who had been one of the six young ladies from Belfast who had gone off together to school at Le Chaud de Fonds near Neuchâtel shortly after the end of the Great War. 'Eileen's little boy, Denis, goes to Garth House and she tells me he loves it,' she said, as we walked past Caproni's to the MacNeice home on Baylands Fifth Avenue.

Denis turned out not to be a little boy at all but quite tall and I guessed he must be about twelve. He was in the garden with two of his pals, Ledlie and Lorrimer, all three engaged in fixing a rope to the branch of a tree. I realized immediately that I must appear an oddity in my old corduroys and the white *báinín* pullover knitted by Zane, for my new acquaintances were uniformly dressed in grey.

When the rope was successfully attached and strenuous efforts made to climb it I was able to demonstrate that I could do so with ease and, furthermore, that I had far less difficulty than they in clambering about on the thin branches. I judged mentally that if I had lost points for dress I should have gained on prowess; yet there was a sense that I had actually lost further points for being a show-off. The only remark that was passed was that I ought to watch out that I didn't get my white jumper dirty. This made me wonder how I might appear before the whole school, but my mother had foreseen this and produced a set of clothes bought from the mother of a boy called Hyde, who had outgrown them – so it was in a correct if well-worn and too-large outfit that I presented myself at Garth House School the following Monday.

The school was only a few minutes away, cycling along the Queen's Parade past the seawater swimming-pool at Pickie Point and up Tennyson Avenue. I arrived to find a mêlée of grey and scarlet boys coming and going through a side door of the surly orange-brick Edwardian mansion, stowing bicycles in a shed next to a building that looked as if it might once have been stables but was now classrooms. A very wide playing-field took up most of the property, with dark fir trees round the perimeter. There was something unassailably daunting about the scene, yet at the same time something that made one feel magnetized into it. I followed the lead of others in leaving my bicycle in the shed and then heard a crabbedy female voice calling out, 'New boys over here!' An ancient hag in a drooping green knitted dress was consulting a little notebook through round-lensed spectacles.

'Wot's yer name?'

I told her my surname, guessing that to give my first would be shameful – and I was right, for when another newcomer said his name was Hugh, she replied, 'Hugh wot? We don't go in for Christian names here, you know!' and there was a laugh of derision from some older boys.

'Fitz-Simon, you're in Form D. You'll report to Miss Gallagher after Prayers. You'll find a hook for your coat and cap with your name above it in the corridor inside that door. And you're in Platoon One. This is your platoon captain, Cook, and your platoon corporal, Ellis.' Captain Cook was a big boy with a lot of fair hair who looked as if he should already have gone on to Public School (or the Royal Navy, the alternative destination referred to in the school prospectus). He said, 'Hello,' quite civilly. The bespectacled Corporal Ellis, who was much smaller and resembled the highbrow Dick Callum in the Arthur Ransome stories, told me in a slightly affected tone that I must *repair* to the Boys' Hall at the end of morning class and then I'd be told where to *proceed* next. I hung up my coat and cap in a long tiled corridor smelling of Jeyes' Fluid and whatever was being cooked for lunch – cabbage, it would seem. I expected to be stared at as a newcomer but no one took the least notice of me. A bell clanged and I saw Corporal Ellis pulling on a rope. I asked him who the old lady was.

'Miss Swanson. Our revered former headmaster, now

gathered unto his fathers, bequeathed everything he had to the school, including his sister,' he said, with what I took to be the nearest he could approach to a conspiratorial wink.

I followed the crowd into the big classroom and almost immediately there was a chorus of 'Good morning, Miss Gallagher, good morning, Miss Logan, good morning, sir, good morning, sir, good morning, sir,' as the members of the staff trooped in. The masters all wore black gowns. Captain Hutton, a squat man with a squashed face like a boxer's and black hair greased across the bald part of his head, could be identified because he took his place behind a large desk. He wore a droopy brown suit, the trousers held up by a knotted club tie. He welcomed us to 'another year' and said we would start by singing the hymn 'Awake, my soul, and with the sun/ Thy daily stage of duty run'. This was accompanied on the piano by a middle-aged master with a polished head and pursed lips, introduced after the hymn as Mr Peyton. Mr Peyton, the headmaster announced, would be choosing members for the choir during break and all new boys must assemble in this room, where he would test their voices. All these clear instructions made everything very simple: we were not going to be left awkwardly standing about. Captain Cook read a passage from the Old Testament, we said the Our Father and then there was silence as the staff trooped out. Miss Gallagher stayed in the room with what turned out to be my classmates and I got to know their names very quickly.

I duly sang a scale for Mr Peyton and was instantly enrolled in the choir, whether I wanted it or not. When the bell clanged for lunch we all went to the Boys' Hall, which was really a kind of changing room with lavatories and showers. (If you wanted to go to the lavatory while in class, you said,

'Please, sir, may I go to the Boys' Hall?') Its ceiling was reinforced by beams supported on wooden pillars, for this was where the boys and staff took shelter when the air-raid warning sounded. Football togs were stashed in open pigeon-holes under the bench that ran round the room and here we sat in our platoons, waiting for the call to lunch, while the corporals examined our hands and sent us back to the wash-basins if there was so much as a tiny speck of ink or a grubby fingernail. On the first day Miss Swanson read out the list of names for seating in the dining room. I was placed at a table where the matron, Miss Hill, and the cook, Miss Gault, presided over the vegetable dishes – I made conversation by mentioning to Miss Gault that she had shown my parents over the school, enquiring politely if she missed Scotland. She said she had never been to Scotland in her life. She was from Ballymoney.

The dining room was decorated with pictures of the Royal Family. The late King George V was seen on the deck of a ship in the uniform of Admiral of the Fleet. Hanging near him was Queen Mary, wearing a long and very grand dress. She had a wide blue ribbon diagonally across her front like something Miss Ulster would be presented with at a bathing-beauty contest. King George VI was shown in a black-and-white photograph speaking into a microphone. His wife, Queen Elizabeth, was seen in a long coat with trailing furs attending a garden party at Balmoral. The little princesses, Elizabeth and Margaret Rose, were seated beside a wireless-set listening, the caption said, to one of their father's broadcasts – possibly even the one shown in his picture. Miss Gault told me that all the works of art had been chosen by Miss Swanson, who had given a lot of her time to cutting them out of illustrated magazines like *Picture Post* and the *Sphere* and having them artistically framed at Woolworth's.

Miss Hill went round the tables distributing Adexolin and Redoxin tablets, which she said were 'to supplement the war-time diet'. I thought of the brimstone and treacle administered to Nicholas Nickleby and supposed we were better off. There was a kind of stew, made largely of potatoes and turnips, in which pieces of fat attached to particles of meat could be discerned, and then a semolina pudding with a dot of jam on the middle of each white heap. No matter how energetically I stirred the jam into the pudding I still found the texture and taste nauseating. 'Don't you care for it?' Miss Hill enquired, the surprise in her voice indicating that I was rejecting the most appetizing dessert in the world. 'Well, you have to eat it or you'll be made to stay behind until you do.'

A diversion was caused by Captain Hutton calling, 'Quiet, please!' and reading out the names of the teams for football practice. I was to be in the junior game on the team called 'Whites'.

'What's Whites?' I asked the boy sitting next to me.

'You wear your white jersey. If you're in "Colours" you wear your red one.'

'I haven't got a jersey,' I confessed.

'You'd better tell Mr Lucas, the ref.'

A period known as Quiet Life ensued, when we were supposed to borrow a book from Miss Swanson's library and read it for half an hour. I picked one of the Arthur Ransomes that I hadn't come across before, *Swallowdale*. I was irritated as usual by the way these children kept pausing to eat 'rations' of chocolate while trekking over the Cumberland fells when it was quite obvious that they would have finished a whole month's ration in one morning. They also had this way of never doing anything wrong and of always pleasing the grown-ups, which I found more than a little far-fetched. I kept wondering what Mr Lucas would say when he heard that I didn't have a white jersey.

In the Boys' Hall Mr Lucas and Mr Sheppard were supervising the changing for games. When I approached him Mr Lucas said he was sure Batley would lend me his jersey because he had a cold and wasn't allowed to play. 'Have you got shorts?'

'No, sir.'

'Boots?'

'No, sir.'

'What kind of parents are they sending us nowadays that don't know how to fit out their offspring?' he shrieked, in a way that I knew was meant to be a joke. 'Well, I'm sure the ailing Batley will lend you his entire outfit.'

Batley was sent for and agreed without demur. It was evident that there was a kind of understanding about the mutual loan of sporting gear.

No one had told me the rules of soccer, nor had I troubled to enquire. I believed you simply kicked the ball towards the other goal and if you scored that was one up to your team. I knew nothing of 'offside' or 'corners' or even the names of the positions on the field. The captain of the Whites for the afternoon was a little English chap with a face like a clenched fist called Brogden. He told me he was putting me at 'right half', and as someone else was assigned to 'left half' I positioned myself on the opposite side of the field and watched what he was doing. There was a lot of barging and shuffling and Brogden kept appealing to Mr Lucas, who was continually blowing his whistle and calling instructions. Suddenly I saw the ball flying towards me through the air. The natural reaction was to stop it, which I did by putting up my hand. 'Foul! Foul!' screamed Brogden, apoplectic that a member of his team should have let him down in such a way. Mr Lucas blew his whistle and awarded a penalty.

'Sorry, Brogden,' I said, genuinely dismayed, 'I didn't know.'

'Fool! Fool!' shouted Brogden, and Mr Lucas told him to shut up and have a bit of sense.

At 144 Seacliffe Road that evening I said I needed football gear but forbore to disclose my humiliation on the field. For a few days I continued to borrow Batley's outfit, which grew muddier and muddier, and then my father returned from a trip to Belfast with a beautiful new pair of football boots, white and coloured jerseys and a pair of blue shorts. The shorts were a bit on the small side but the total effect was exceptionally *snazzy* – my mother's word – and my father said that the price had nearly ruined him. I restrained myself from saying that if that were the case I would be very happy not to play games at all. The boots impressed the other players no end when I appeared in them the following afternoon – so much so that I was told they would have to be 'christened' and I was led to the muddiest spot in front of the goal where my team-mates stamped in the squelch and then stamped on my boots. This was my second sporting humiliation, but no one seemed to perceive it as such, possibly because I pretended to be amused.

Next day at games time I could not find my new boots. No one else I could see was wearing them so I informed Mr Lucas. He told me to look in every boot locker – a misnomer, for there were no locks – which I did. Then he said I should borrow boots for today – which I did. If I was quite sure they were lost, I should report the fact later to Captain Hutton.

'Sir, I can't find my new football boots.'

'What? Have you looked everywhere?'

'Yes, sir.'

'Was anyone else wearing them?'

'No, sir.'

'Do you believe they've been filched?'

'I don't know, sir.'

'But you *suspect* they've been filched?'

'I've no idea, sir.'

Of course, I was quite sure they had been *filched*. Next morning Captain Hutton announced at Prayers that a new pair of football boots had gone inexplicably missing. They could hardly have *walked*, he said. All boys must look for them during break and if they were still missing he would have to assume they'd been *filched*. 'You know what that means! If no one owns up there will be Punishment Class for the whole school!' I thought this was quite a clever way of dealing with the matter, for Captain Hutton was giving the thief the opportunity of secretly returning the boots and then they would be 'found' – but it did not happen like that.

The whole school was detained after class for forty-five minutes. What was curious was that nobody showed any sign of animosity towards me – I was expecting at least to be 'sent to Coventry', if not actually beaten up behind the bicycle sheds like in the school stories. Yet I felt humiliated all the same and certainly I could not tell my father that money he could not afford had been squandered. Henceforth I either borrowed boots or rummaged in the heap of discarded sports gear in the Boys' Hall till I found a worn-out pair that nearly fitted, and when I grew out of the shorts and jerseys I became adept at selecting second-hand clothes, like Rose in the song.

Partly because of the difficulty of being correctly togged out but more particularly because I was hopeless at football, I resorted to answering, 'Cold, sir!' at roll-call. If one had a cold one was exempted from games and was sent on a crocodile walk down the Bryansburn Glen or alongside the Carnalea Golf Course with Miss Gallagher or Miss Logan. Miss Logan went to all the latest films and during these walks would recount the plot of what she had last seen at the Tonic Cinema to the two boys at the back of the line where I and my new friend Watson always contrived to place ourselves. She told us about *The Ripper* in truly chilling instalments and *Mrs Miniver* (not half as good) and *Strangers on a Train* (distinctly dull); but the best was *Dead of Night*, which was really a film in five parts with five different people each describing an eerie experience. The most frightening was about a man in hospital who dreamed of a funeral undertaker allocating coffins to people who were not yet dead, with the spine-tingling words 'Just room for one more inside!'; when the man was discharged from hospital he was waiting for a bus and as he was about to step on board the conductor said, 'Just room for one more inside!' The terrifying thing was that the conductor had the same face as the undertaker in the dream! The man did not get on the bus, which then moved off and was involved in an accident in which all the passengers were killed. I stayed awake for several nights, not so much from fright as from delicious excitement.

When asked at home how I was getting on at games, I tried to cloak my guilt by use of the off-hand manner I had noticed my schoolmates assumed when questioned on some topic they did not wish to pursue. At least I was able to report on the Physical Training, which replaced football one afternoon a week, when a Mr Griffin came from Belfast and put us through a number of exercises that were supposed to develop our muscles and also, as he put it, our 'mental agility'. In fact, I found jumping over the box-horse quite fun and was able to describe this to my father who, as I well knew, possessed the officer's respect for *mens sana in corpore sano*. So it was that every Thursday my cold miraculously vanished and I presented myself in as hale a state as anyone, yet my indisposition on other days was nothing compared to that of a boy called Calvert who *always* had the confidence to declare a cold and never played a game of football or took part in gymnastics in all his time at the school.

The autumn term ended with a concert in the Trinity Church Hall to which all parents were invited. I was chosen to give a recitation. I learned Walter de la Mare's 'The Listeners' at the suggestion of Miss Gallagher but my mother thought it a too obviously 'school-curriculum' type of poem and intervened by some means or other, quite diplomatically it would seem because Miss Gallagher appeared to have no objection to 'The Owl and the Pussy Cat'. This was received well by the school audience at the rehearsal, and on the afternoon of the concert the parents laughed agreeably. There was an echo in the hall, which made it necessary to recite the poem rather slowly or the words would be lost, but when the audience came in the echo disappeared and I found I could speak naturally and be heard.

The hall was decorated with pictures of an uplifting nature. The best was of a Sea Scout in rather old-fashioned short pants having a conversation with a huge angel, but it was impossible to see how or where the angel's wings were attached to his body. The feathers were long and curved, resembling those of my grandmother's white turkeys. I supposed that if the angel felt cold he could shroud himself in his own wings and he might even include the Sea Scout in the wrapping.

All the other items in the concert were musical, with Mr

Peyton – he of the polished head, naturally known as 'Patey' – in charge. Mr Peyton travelled to school each day by train from Belfast. He wore a severely pressed greyish suit and in all weathers carried a smartly rolled umbrella – it was so neat he never had the heart to open it, even in a thunderstorm. On bustling past the door of the headmaster's study he would exclaim, 'Good morning, Captain,' and, not waiting to hear the reply, would continue, 'Yes! What you heard was "Good morning, Captain," yes!' so that one of Captain Hutton's nicknames was Captain Yes. He was also known as Hutty when in a good mood and as the Boiler when not. Choir practice took place during the fifteen minutes before Prayers in an all-purpose room known as the Study, which contained a huge mahogany dining-table, chairs of sundry designs no two of which were alike, an oak roll-top desk, a second-hand Blüthner piano, and a shelf supporting random volumes of Newnes's *Pictorial Knowledge*. We practised the hymn for that morning and then one or two items for the end-of-term concert, mostly two-part songs with the names of celebrated composers attached. Schubert's 'Ho! 'Tis a Sunny Morning' was proving particularly intractable. '*Ho!*' we sang. '*Ho! Ho!*' with perhaps a little too much *fortissimo*.

Mr Peyton had a way of knowing immediately if rough singing was due to failure to assimilate the subtleties of the music or to the choristers diverting themselves. 'Hark! Hark! The Lark!', by the same composer, caused a gleeful laugh when he looked over his shoulder and said there was too much larking about in the second row – but the look on his face showed that the witticism was unintentional. The second row was the altos: if you were tall you were an alto, if you were small you were placed among the sopranos; vocal range did not signify. I was in the second row and was slow to learn the alto line, reverting at times to the real tune, so

Mr Peyton would bang it out for me on the piano with one finger. We learned Brahms's 'Lullaby' and Bach's 'Jesu, Joy of Man's Desiring', and also Johann Strauss's 'Pipes of Pan' because, as Patey disclosed in a rare moment of confidentiality, some of the parents might not be up to appreciating the work of the classical composers.

The best singers contributed solos. Watson had to sing an Irish drawing-room ditty about a gossoon who was in love with a colleen who was coy about accepting his advances until he disclosed that he owned 'a ca-a-bin with pigs that number seven, And if you could be there at all, sure the place would be like he-a-ven'. The final line of this romance – which, of course, had been written by an Englishman – was 'The little pigs had done it!' This became the catchphrase of the term: whenever something untoward or disgusting happened the explanation was 'the little pigs had done it'. Claney sang a piece called 'There Is a Ladye' in which a man saw a beautiful woman whom he wished to marry but all she was ever doing was 'passing by' and as he never managed to catch up with her the song ended with them never meeting – 'and yet I love her, and yet I love her, and yet I love her till I die', he trilled, and I wondered how he managed to remember how many times to sing 'and yet I love her'. He could have gone on for hours, like a needle stuck on a gramophone record.

None of the parents, so far as I was aware, complained about the choice of sentimental songs. Perhaps, indeed, Mr Peyton's intuition was right: because they were vaguely classical they must therefore be educational. He gave a weekly class in Musical History for members of the choir and those who studied the piano. We learned of the lives of the Great Composers, from Arne to Zimmermann, and we studied the symphony and sonata form. As the school did not possess a gramophone his task was fairly daunting. I passed through the whole course over three years without ever hearing a symphony or a sonata yet I wrote about them with great fluency in the exams. Mr Peyton told us that he had come to Belfast from Cork, where there was a great tradition of organ-playing. He was now organist at St Mary's in the Crumlin Road neighbourhood of Belfast where the parish was collecting funds to buy him a Compton organ. His full name was Robert Wagner Peyton – this was printed on the front of our concert programme. Watson's mother said that people from Cork always had famous relatives.

The concert was well received by the parents. We were told that we'd all be famous and that we were well on the way to becoming pianists and singers. We might even end up training the choir of St Mary's, Crumlin Road!

After the concert the holidays began. Nicky – who was now called Nick – and I were taken to the Grand Christmas Circus at the Royal Hippodrome Theatre in Belfast. Except for the presence of Blondini, who walked a tightrope over a cage of lions, the circus was a big disappointment, for we had seen the acts in Duffy's tent at Monaghan; but the interior of the theatre building, with its three balconies and side boxes, was a revelation. The band was placed in the pit in front of the stage, which was adapted – fairly unsuccess-fully – to circus acts that, of course, should be seen from all sides. Everyone gasped when Blondini lurched and looked as if he was going to fall into the lions' den but he righted himself with the help of his green umbrella and we all applauded. My father said the lions were probably drugged, but they might not have been for there was an item in the paper some time later to say that there had been an unfor-tunate accident and Mr Blondini, the celebrated Italian tightrope walker, was no more; sincere sympathy was expressed to the Duffy family. I thought the lions were quite right to devour him, if that was what they had done, for they must have been truly vexed by all his dancing about above them and the twirlings of his umbrella, twice daily at two thirty and eight.

I had been put in Form D, the second lowest, probably because Captain Hutton supposed that having had a sporadic education with nursery governesses and schoolmarms I would be well behind the ten-year-olds who had already had the benefit of two years at Garth House, but he had reckoned without knowing how good a teacher Mrs Bradley of Monaghan had been. I came out top each week in every subject, except arithmetic, so the following term I was promoted to C2 and the term after that to C1, which looked like a spectacular advance, except that when I found myself among my true peers my results became no more than average and in arithmetic I was consistently bottom of the class. Nick, who had been attending a kindergarten run by a Miss Featherstonehaugh in a tennis pavilion at Farnham Park, was more judiciously assessed and joined Form D, which I had just vacated, in January 1945.

On Friday mornings, Prayers were taken by the Reverend Canon Good of St Comgall's, an elderly party with a far less refined Cork accent than Mr Peyton's and a face screwed into a permanent expression of displeasure. After Prayers he took the whole school for Religious Knowledge – an odd arrangement, for he had to address his remarks to sixty-eight boys whose ages ranged from seven to thirteen. There was bound to be some incomprehension, a certain degree of boredom and even some tittering as we were taken through the various forms of Divine Worship as set out in the Church of Ireland Book of Common Prayer, such as the Churching

of Women and the Order of Baptism for Those of Riper
Years at Sea. What was absolutely certain was that the canon's
demeanour indicated that he heartily wished to be
elsewhere.

One Friday, for no discernible reason, the sense of mutual
disaffection became almost palpable. A quite audible conversation about conkers was going on in the back row. The
canon called for quiet and when the murmuring started up
again he angrily shouted, 'Silence!' There was silence for a
few seconds, till a very rude noise was heard, a fart so loud
it could only have been intentional, reverberating off the
wooden bench and ricocheting round the room. Canon
Good looked as if he had just received irrefutable news to
the effect that the Resurrection and Ascension had been
faked. He stared at the assembly, and as the inevitable laughter
swelled he strode out of the room.

We laughed and laughed. Stink! Who did it? Then there
was a parley among the six captains, who decided that we
should stay in the room till the bell rang and then shout,
'Goodbye, sir! Thank you, sir! See you next week, sir!' This
stratagem was carried through, like one of Monty's clever
ruses in the Western Desert.

The following Monday when Captain Hutton entered for
Prayers his face was the colour of pickled beetroot. 'The
Boiler's about to burst!' whispered Watson, from behind his
hymnal. Prayers, the Lesson and the hymn were accomplished
with studied calm. Then the headmaster requested the staff
to leave. He said he had never been so ashamed in his life,
for only a few minutes ago he had received a letter from
Canon Good that denigrated the good name of the school.
He felt *let down*! The business was particularly *wretched* because
the late Captain Swanson had been a member of the Select
Vestry at St Comgall's. He then read out the letter in which

the canon stated that the previous Friday he had been in receipt of insult, rudeness and disrespect. He even mentioned names. 'Hall had his feet on his desk. Fryar and Blakeley were conversing on a topic that had nothing to do with the Divine Office. Walkington was flicking pellets of blotting-paper at Pedlow II.' The canon's sense of recall was remarkable – in fact, the scene he depicted was far more unruly than the actuality. We waited breathlessly for a description of the fart, but Canon Good had obviously been unable to bring himself to pen such a word.

Captain Hutton asked us if all this were true. 'Yes, sir!' we chorused. He looked perplexed, as if trying to put together some words in conclusion, but all he could say was that we would all be detained in a special Punishment Class and each of us would have to write a letter of apology. I wrote

*Dear Reverend Good,*
   *I am sorry for being rude. Please forgive me. I hope you will come back.*
   *Yours ever, Fitz-Simon I.*

The last sentence was a blatant lie. How the canon interpreted it, or the admissions expressed in the other sixty-seven apologies, was never revealed, but he did not come back, sending instead a series of colourless curates, none of whom was worth provoking; and then there came the Reverend Alwyn Machonachie, who placed the Biblical stories in their proper context for us, telling us about the geography and climate and customs of the Holy Land, and the language the people spoke and how the Scriptures had been translated and passed on, and of the adventures of the Apostles in doing so. It all became quite fascinating, and I hoped that Mr Machonachie would stay with us, but he departed at the end of the summer term to share his understanding with the benighted residents of Saskatchewan, whom he must have believed were in greater need of it than we.

With the summer term came cricket, athletics and swimming. Cricket I could have done without but I could hardly register 'a cold' when I enjoyed running and jumping and sea-bathing. I was assigned to the lowest grade of cricket practice and when I had to play the game it was tacitly understood that I was a no-no and I was placed at a position on the field that was rarely visited by the ball; when batting, it was quite certain that I would be bowled out at first ball. My difficulty was that I could not see the ball coming at me and I would make a swipe at the air with a borrowed bat and then hear the inevitable click behind me as the ball hit the stumps. 'Keep your eye on the ball, Fitz-Simon!' was the constant cry of the captain and the umpire, but I could not keep my eye on something that was invisible. The captain's hand never on my shoulder smote, as described in the poem, nor, when I made a fair enough attempt at striding manfully on to the wicket, was there a breathless hush in the close.

We swam in seawater at Pickie Pool every day before lunch, walking in twos down Ranfurly Avenue, a crimson crocodile. Captain Hutton offered a shilling to all newcomers who could swim the length of the pool without stopping and I earned my prize early on by the simple expedient of putting my foot down every few yards to give myself a hoosh on, which Hutty did not appear to notice. When changing into swimming togs a group of us observed with amusement that Hutty did not have a willy shaped like a dangling tube but a thing like a big button. We decided this was why some people referred to their 'knob' and his was certainly like something you'd pull to open a drawer. Hutty never picked me for any swimming team, and as for diving, I could hardly bring myself to jump in, let alone jump in upside-down, but I was not a disgrace at athletics and was quite adept at the hundred-yard sprint and the long-jump, which seemed to indicate that I was not a total failure.

Mr Lucas, the tall, angular Latin master (known, naturally, as Lukey Lamp-post) who coached junior games but preferred reading poems to us, left to become a housemaster at Portora Royal School whence messages came back from former Garth House pupils that he was well liked. He was replaced by a Mr Richards, who was said to be filling in time before going on to university and who declared soccer to be a cissy's game – we should be playing rugger. He had a fierce temper and was inclined to pull one's hair quite violently if one failed to recite the declensions correctly – *Bellum, bellum, bellum, belli, bello, bello* – and even tugged a tuft of Walker II's hair right out, leaving him with a bald patch. He was said to be a regular patron at Caproni's Ballroom of an evening and was often late for breakfast, sometimes not even turning up for Prayers. This enraged Captain Hutton, who marched into his bedroom one morning. 'Get up! Get up immediately! Failure to attend Prayers is no example to the boys!' he was heard to shout.

'Agh, fuck off!' came the hoarse reply.

Mr Richards was not seen again, at Prayers or anywhere else.

The spring and summer of 1945 resonated to announcements on the wireless of Allied victories in Europe. Souvenir Union Jacks started appearing in shop windows. Some boys brought paper streamers to school – you wound them into a tight bundle, threw them into the air and they floated down to the cricket pitch in a red, white and blue trail of celebration.

There were posters for the election. On Seacliffe Road, Ulster was urged to Vote Conservative and Keep Churchill In. There were fewer posters for Labour and Atlee. 'What has this Mr Atlee ever done but deride the wonderful work of Mr Churchill who got us through this terrible war?' my grandmother asked, having seen the posters when she was out buying the groceries in Mr Adair's. 'It's unthinkable that Mr Churchill should be put out.'

The groceries included tins of mock-turtle soup, which was all my grandfather would eat, for he was ill in bed and the house smelled of airing sheets and sticky medicines. A nurse came to stay up with him at night when my grandmother slept on a divan in the upstairs drawing room. During the day the nurse slept there, so we couldn't watch the convoys in the lough. Nurse Coady had been engaged through an agency in Belfast; she had frizzy reddish hair and came from Tipperary. I asked her if my grandfather was going to die, for sometimes horrible groans came from his bedroom. 'I wouldn't say so,' she replied, 'though the bronchial pneumonia is a hard man to best. With the help of God and these new 693 tablets I'd say there won't be a bother on him in two weeks' time – but for that again, you'd never be certain.'

Nurse Coady asked me if I'd like to go with her to the pictures on a Saturday afternoon. I said of course I would, but the school rules forbade the cinema in term time because we might get diseases. 'What diseases would those be, I wonder?' enquired Nurse Coady, and I said I'd heard that the American soldiers were supposed to be carrying all kinds of dangerous germs. 'But isn't it ages since there was an American in the place?' she retorted. 'And if they were still here, scattering every infection known to man around them, wouldn't I be the one to rid you of them with a jab of one of my needles?' My parents did not seem to have been consulted but my grandmother – who was always nervous about catching chills – was dubious. I said that Nurse Coady had been very good to Grandpa and it might look very ungrateful to turn down her invitation, so she gave me half a crown and said I was to pay for the seats.

That afternoon Nurse Coady and I crept to the Tonic Cinema by way of back-streets, keeping our eyes open for Miss Swanson, who might easily be spying to see who was disobeying the school rules. We saw *Meet Me in St Louis*. The tunes were well known from the wireless and Claney often played 'The Trolley Song' by ear on the piano, to Mr Peyton's discomfiture. That day I fell in love with Judy Garland, Margaret O'Brien and Peggy Ryan all at once. Claney told me next day that he had once been in love with the former school matron, Miss Crozier, and that in comparison to her Miss Hill was a cold bitch.

After the film there was a screen announcement to say that for our added entertainment Miss Louise McDonald would play the latest songs on the mighty Compton organ. At the same moment there was an explosion of music and Miss McDonald rose out of the floor wearing a glamorous spangled outfit and seated at a console that changed colour every few seconds, from turquoise to magenta to orange. The vast auditorium reverberated to the sound of some of the very numbers we had just heard in the film – 'Very thoughtful of her,' said Nurse Coady, 'and so up-to-the-minute'. The words appeared on the screen:

> *Meet me in Saint Louis, Louis, meet me at the fair,*
> *Don't tell me the lights are shining any place but there . . .*

and

*Clang, clang, clang went the trolley,*
*Ding, ding, ding went the bell,*
*Zing, zing, zing went my heart-strings,*
*From the moment I saw him, I fell . . .*

and Miss McDonald contrived to play buzzes, clangs and zings on the organ that made the music sound even better than it had in the film. I wondered if Mr Peyton's new Compton organ in St Mary's, Crumlin Road, would be able to do all these sound effects – but if it did he would surely dismiss them as 'jazzy', his favourite word for music he did not like, such as swing and blues.

Nurse Coady thanked me for taking her to the pictures and said she was now going to take me for a big tea, so we went upstairs and had fish and chips with tomato ketchup followed by cream buns in the Tonic Super Restaurant, which had wall lights in the shape of scallop shells and a chandelier that was advertised as being a replica of one in the Rockefeller Center in New York, and I agreed that Bangor's Tonic Cinema must certainly be 'Ulster's Entertainment Mecca', for where else would you find such splendour?

To everyone's surprise, Captain Hutton announced that he was going to break a school rule, though for a very special reason. The film *Theirs Is the Glory* was to be shown at the Tonic and he was going to take the whole school. We were not to consider this a frivolous treat but a Duty in recognition of the sacrifice of the men of the 1st Airborne Division, who had lost their lives after being parachuted into the Netherlands the previous autumn. No one was foolish enough to ask if we might pick up a terrible disease in the cinema while watching this type of film. I found the picture very sad – certainly not as enjoyable as *Meet Me in St Louis* but, then, it was not supposed to be.

My father said the Arnhem drops had been a disaster – nothing like as bad as the massacre at Gallipoli but certainly someone had blundered and perhaps it was no coincidence that Churchill had ultimately been responsible for both. When my grandmother said that surely Mr Churchill would be incapable of ordering such a dreadful thing he replied that those in command often took decisions that, at the time, seemed to be the right thing. He said that the film had been produced very quickly with money from the War Office to make Arnhem appear to have been less of a cock-up. I asked how was it that Captain Hutton had told us that it was a great victory in spite of the losses, and my father said that Hutton wouldn't have been aware that hundreds of soldiers had been wiped out by the SS Panzer Korps before almost two thousand others could be evacuated back to England by sea. Hutton, he said, was not a regular officer but only a member of the Royal Army Service Corps and, in any case, he had left the army before the Arnhem catastrophe. Like the rest of the cinema audience, he wasn't in a position to know the facts.

There was talk of my father taking a job in County Clare, running a country estate at a place called Mount Callan. He went for an interview and came back to say that we'd be moving at the end of the summer term. Then he called to see Captain Hutton to tell him he'd be withdrawing us from the school and to get his opinion on prep schools in Dublin as there was none in Clare. Captain Hutton pointed out that in Dublin we'd be almost as far from Clare as we were in Bangor and if my father wished for us to stay on at Garth House as boarders he'd be glad to arrange a reduction in the usual fees. I was unable to entertain the thought of having to settle into yet another school, especially as Castle Park was mentioned and I'd heard several unappetizing stories about the place, so I promised faithfully to work hard if I was allowed to stay on. My father said that 'working hard' meant working at the subjects that did not come easily to me – it was no use working hard at English and Drawing because they were not subjects that would get me anywhere in later life. I accepted the argument. We were enrolled as boarders for the following September. I did not work harder at Arithmetic, Algebra, Geometry, Geography, History, Latin or French.

Meanwhile, there was a national holiday on Victory-in-Europe Day in May, and we all received letters from the King signed *George R.I.* My father said that a special plaque should be erected on the front of the Redcliff Hotel just along the seafront from our house because that was where General Eisenhower had addressed the US officers prior to their taking part in the Normandy landings – details such as this were what History was made of. There were flags and bunting on the warships in the lough, and small aeroplanes of a kind we had not seen before streaked overhead without the heavy throbbing sound of the Lancasters and Liberators. After they had passed, trails of white vapour appeared in the sky. Bessie, now our cook-general, looked out of the kitchen window and said these were 'a sign'. Nothing would convince her that they were caused by jet aircraft. She said that God was telling the world that the war was over. If so, Mrs Magee remarked, His message had been rudely scooped by the BBC and the *Belfast Telegraph*.

Bessie had her own way of doing things. She could not abide interference. One Sunday when she brought in the tray with the pudding plates and a steaming treacle dumpling I helpfully carried the pudding from the side-table and placed it before my grandmother. Bessie snatched it away, returned it to the side-table and then carried it back to be served.

Then she stumped meaningfully out of the room, banging
the door. My grandmother injudiciously followed her out
to the kitchen whence sounds of altercation were heard. She
returned with the news that Bessie had given a week's notice.
I was mortified, explaining that I was only trying to *help*.
'Some people do not want to be helped,' said my grandmother. I offered to go out to the kitchen and apologize,
but my father said that would definitely not be the right
thing to do. I had acted in a certain way and must not show
that I now believed myself to have been wrong. It was
something to do with Churchill, Arnhem and Gallipoli.

Cycling home from school one day I noticed a bright yellow
poster with red and black letters announcing that the Council
for the Encouragement of Music and the Arts, in association
with Bangor Arts Committee, would be presenting the
Dublin Gate Theatre in three plays, *Where Stars Walk*, *A
Hundred Years Old* and *Othello*, in the Dufferin Memorial
Hall. I reported this to my mother, who said the Gate had
a good reputation but it was very expensive at three shillings
for the cheapest seat. I had never seen a play – I had only
acted in the ones she had written for us at Annaghmakerrig
– but I was quite certain that seeing a real one would be
the most exciting thing that could possibly happen, even if
it was only in the Dufferin Hall. The problem of the admission
charge must have been surmounted for I heard my mother
and grandmother discussing which would be the most
suitable play for an eleven-year-old – the Gate Theatre was
known for raciness so perhaps the modern plays should be
avoided. Because of the school rule about not attending the
cinema it was deemed appropriate to write a note to Captain
Hutton seeking 'permission to attend a Shakespeare play at
the church hall' – this wording would make it respectable.

Captain Hutton read the note and said it was perfectly in order but warned that I might find *Othello* 'rather long'.

I did not find it long. Everything was fascinating – the way the lamps were positioned and how they dimmed when the scenery was changed, the way the scenery was made to look like tapestries, which were drawn to and fro by the actors, the way these tapestries suggested Venice or Cyprus and how Desdemona's bedchamber was hung with a huge array of embroidered saints. The stage was aglow with colourful dresses and smart uniforms; in the interval my mother said that they must have been copied from the work of a Venetian painter. When the play was over and the actors had bowed to us several times I said that it would be very easy for them to roll up the tapestries and she said she hadn't thought of it like that and perhaps that was the reason they had chosen to have that kind of scenery.

Othello was played by Mr Micheál MacLíammóir, Iago by Mr Hilton Edwards and Desdemona by Miss Helena Hughes. A very funny actor called Mr Aiden Grennell was the foolish Roderigo. The actors seemed to exist in a magical world separated from us by the brightly lit red curtain – it could scarcely be imagined that they had to queue for train tickets or get their bicycles fixed at McGimpsey's or stay in a boarding-house in Hamilton Road where Mrs Magee said she had seen some of them knocking on a door.

'I knew there was murder and drunkenness in that play,' I heard my mother tell my grandmother, after I had gone to bed, 'but I'd forgotten there was fornication and a sugges-tion of other nasty things.' If there was fornication, whatever that was, I hadn't noticed it; perhaps I'd been too busy looking at the costumes.

Even more intoxicating was the visit of the Sadlers Wells Opera Company – not to the Dufferin Hall in Bangor but to the Grand Opera House in Belfast. Tony Guthrie, who directed *Madam Butterfly*, *La Bohème*, *Così fan Tutte* and *The Bartered Bride*, said that this was the government's way of thanking the people of Northern Ireland for their part in winning the war. Peggy Butler decided to come with Julia all the way from Maidenhall to see *The Bartered Bride*, which Tony had written to say was the one most likely to be enjoyed by 'the young'. It was the end of our school term. The Butlers would stay with us in Bangor and then we would all travel back with them for a few days at Annagh-makerrig before they returned to Maidenhall and we moved on to our new home, Mount Callan.

The Grand Opera House was altogether more splendid than the Royal Hippodrome next door. Decorated like the interior of a Hindu temple, it had life-size elephants' heads supporting the boxes. Tony was nowhere to be seen. When we met again a fortnight later, he said he didn't have to attend all the performances of his productions for his job was over after the first night, but he liked the idea of being with the company in Belfast, where his own professional career had begun.

Next day was the School Sports. Julia came second in the visitors' race, Nick was second in the sack race and I won the 220-yards sprint. Captain Cook's mother presented the prizes – mine was a fountain-pen – because he was Head Boy. He had won a scholarship to St Columba's College in Dublin and received a great cheer from all the boys standing on the lawn in front of the main school building where the prize-giving took place.

Cycling to school next morning for the final day of term I kicked viciously at a small black and white dog that often snapped annoyingly at passers-by, overbalanced and landed on my head. The next thing I remembered was seeing a group of people looking down at me. I kept saying, 'I'm all right, I'm all right,' though the words came out very slowly. Then Claney appeared from somewhere and said he'd see me to school. Again I remembered nothing until we were at the bicycle shed and MacNeice was saying, 'What's the matter with Fitz-Simon?' Matron was summoned and I was taken to one of the dormitories. I asked what had happened. She said I'd fallen off my bicycle, and then I asked for a basin because I knew I was going to be sick. Later, my father's face was looking at me and I heard a taxi being mentioned and when we got to 144 Seacliffe Road, Dr Hector Northey, my uncle Marcus's college friend, who was looking after my grandfather, was already there. He tapped my knees and looked into my eyes and said I mustn't move except to go for an X-ray.

Naturally the plans for Annaghmakerrig went awry but by the time we got there, two weeks later, I must have been fully recovered for I was able to row Miss Joan Cross, the Sadlers Wells *prima donna*, out into the middle of the lake to see the water-lilies. That evening in the drawing room she sang 'One Fine Day' and 'They Call Me Mimi', accompanied on the piano by Laurence Collingwood, who had conducted the performance of *The Bartered Bride* that we had seen in Belfast, and then Tony joined her in 'Lovely Maid in the Moonlight'. It was unimaginably thrilling.

## Mount Callan, Inagh, County Clare

If Mount Callan House could not exactly be described as standing on the side of Sliabh Callain, it certainly could be said to crouch in the luxuriant vegetation of the mountain's lower slopes. Architecturally it presented to the landscape neither the classical grace of a Georgian mansion nor the romantic charm of some later rustic retreat. We understood that it had begun life as a shooting-lodge for the Synge family of County Wicklow, and that at some time during the 1870s one of the Synges had built the L-shaped house in the unassuming style that could be confidently labelled as Victorian merely because it had been built during that reign. The principal rooms on the lower side of the L looked south across a lawn to dense shrubberies and woods.

Most of the windows on the other side had been blocked up, it was thought because of the notorious window tax, but that theory was put to rest by Hubert Butler when he came on a visit and said the tax had been abolished long before this house was built. He thought it much more likely that someone had decided that a drawing room in the western counties with substantial windows on three sides would have been unbearable in winter. A dank basement under this wing contained abandoned storerooms and servants' quarters. Curiously, the immense kitchen was on the ground floor, not in the basement; flagged in limestone, its centrepiece was a double-sized iron range that daily consumed two creels of turf. A back stair reached up from a cluster of sculleries and pantries to the maids' bedrooms, a bleak bathroom and the old nursery, which Nick colonized for himself for it had windows that opened on to the roof of a low extension from which you could jump into the field that descended from the mountainside.

Across the right-angle of the L there was a hexagonal porch, rather grandly inviting the visitor into what turned out to be a particularly gloomy hallway. Chunks of the internal ceiling plasterwork were constantly falling off due to damp, one just missing my Killen grandmother who was passing below with a teacup and saucer. She dropped the crockery, which shattered into a dozen fragments, but contrived to remain in one piece herself. Not at all taken by Mount Callan's unique attractions, she observed that the house resembled a second-rate girls' boarding-school in an unfashionable English resort.

At various times, woods of conifers had been planted on the mountainside but indigenous oaks flourished in the deep fern-festooned ravines that crossed the terrain, their branches reaching up to catch whatever light might be going. Synge's Glen was the deepest and most impenetrable of these hollows where cascading mountain rivulets joined to form the Inagh river, which flowed on to enter the Atlantic at Liscannor Bay. In summer the foliage was so dense the sun did not reach the torrent that gurgled in the glen's depths. Purple outcrops of rhododendron could be seen in all directions in May; other flowering trees and shrubs – magnolias, camellias, azaleas, *Pieris japonica* – had been introduced to create an extensive pleasure garden near the house so there was a constant exotic flowering from April to October, largely on account of the unusually high rainfall and the peaty soil. There was a turf bog, which supplied the fuel for the house and its dependent cottages, winter and summer.

My father had arrived ahead of us and was in the process of opening boxes and sorting furniture. He was employed by Captain R. G. Tottenham, who had inherited the former Synge property, to manage the 1,200-acre estate with its cattle and commercial timber. The Tottenhams were moving to one of their other family homes in Wicklow and left the house sparsely yet adequately furnished. There was a fine mahogany sideboard with a rope motif that exactly matched our Nelson dining-table, which had been part of Ellen O'Connell's dowry over a hundred years before and was now too large for my Fitz-Simon grandparents' considerably reduced home. It had arrived in a pantechnicon that also called to a number of houses in Monaghan where, over the years, we had deposited various belongings, among them the four-poster bed, which had reposed at Ballyleck for nearly a decade following Lady Edith Wyndham's disastrous auction, and the rocking-chair with the moth-eaten velvet seat that I had last seen abandoned in a spare bedroom at Hollywood. The pantechnicon had also travelled to Newcastle, where Mrs Griffin had been storing our overseas packing-cases in the Anchor Lodge stable. When opened, these disclosed two purple camel-hair carpets, which my parents had not seen since Cairo in the 1930s, and a dozen dun-coloured Egyptian hearthrugs and mats with geometric designs, which my mother said had been fashionable at that time because they resembled – and possibly even influenced – the *art-decoratif*, but they were now distinctly *passé*.

My father waited until our arrival to open the black wooden boxes whose contents had remained unseen since India. Here, there were treasures of all descriptions: white linen tablecloths and napkins (wedding presents from Ulster relatives), printed cotton bedspreads with Hindu symbols, soft numdah rugs, a rosewood lamp-standard of spiral design and several elegant table-lamps that my father had made when carpentry had been his hobby, a herd of green pottery horses, a crystal cat arching its back, several framed regimental and team photographs with backgrounds that ranged from Birr barracks to the Rangoon pagoda, a Palestinian coffee-grinder, brass bowls from Benares, a Kashmiri drum, and a huge brass teapot covered in Arabic inscriptions, which turned out not to be for tea at all but for use in the water-closet because Mahometans disdained lavatory paper.

The dining room was decorated not with Synge and Tottenham family portraits but with sundry trophies of the chase. Heads of elk, ibis, springbok, caribou, a number of species of native and foreign deer and some foxes in various states of decay gazed mournfully down upon us at mealtimes. Moths and other destructive creatures had taken up residence in most of them so that as we ate our breakfast or dinner, they continued eating theirs. From time to time we would hear a light plop, and a glass eye or a half-eaten ear would be found on the carpet.

The mortar with which the stone house was bonded was reputed to have been made from sea sand, which weeps, so there were many damp patches on the internal walls. It was deemed useless to paint over the discoloured patches as they would rapidly become discoloured again so no decoration was undertaken during the three years of our occupancy. This was a constant source of astonishment to our visitors, who felt the house deserved to be transformed from the dingy-looking place it was to something that, with a little thought and not very much money, might be quite splendid.

The cottages of the people who worked on the land were strung out along a mountainy lane that reached from the house to a public road, which was little more than a cart track. The nearest telephone was five miles away at Inagh but there were no shops there, only a post office and two pubs, so we bought our tea and sugar at Lipton's, and our weekly joint of meat at Casey's, in Ennis, sixteen miles away.

There were acres of potatoes for house and market. The kitchen-garden was presided over by Austin Woods, who was very well read and continued to absorb knowledge by listening to talks on the wireless. Hubert Butler described him as 'an Edgeworthian figure – had he lived a hundred years ago he would have been the archetypal hedge-school master'. Peggy thought 'the whole set-up at Mount Callan' was like a retrogression into one of Miss Edgeworth's novels. Austin Woods also maintained two magnificent hundred-foot-long herbaceous borders sheltered by six-foot-high cypress hedges through which *lonicera* vines meandered, creating unexpected scarlet gashes, like wounds.

As at Eldron, Annaghmakerrig and Maidenhall, the cows supplied the milk and butter. A colourful assortment of hens was luxuriously housed in an asbestos structure ordered from some highly advanced poultry catalogue – it was incontrovertibly claimed to be the only hen-house in County Clare with electric light, for an abundance of power for Mount Callan and its yard buildings was generated by an engine fed from a mountain stream. In acknowledgement of their first-class accommodation the hens gave generously of their eggs. They and the pigs also gave completely of themselves – a sacrifice my mother deplored and the rest of us took with a slight sense of shame, especially if it were a favourite fowl, such as Hilde or Brunhilde, or a pig rashly named Sir Francis Bacon. The people who worked on the land had no such inhibitions. Pigs were reared to be killed, salted and eaten; the rooster was for the pot, once it appeared that he was past fulfilling his normal duties. These people did not give names to their livestock and it was easy to see why: names imply relationships, so they referred unsentimentally to 'the pig with the black feet', or 'the white calf' or 'the speckled hen'.

The first people we met were Nora Scullane and Margaret Hanrahan, the cook and the housemaid. Nick and I quickly became acquainted with their families and extended families. Margaret's cousins the O'Hallorans, who had reared her, lived in the highest house on the mountain, just below the line where grazing merged into heather and furze. In the course of time one of Margaret's young cousins, Maureen, joined her on the domestic staff of Mount Callan. Visiting the O'Hallorans introduced a new world of eloquent and resourceful women. We never met the men of this house for they would be out working in the fields; we saw them when the hay was being saved or the turf footed, when all the neighbours, men and women, lent a hand and it was hard to know which of the men came from what house.

Granny O'Halloran, her daughter-in-law and granddaughters were all strikingly good-looking, with the tawny hair that our English visitors said was 'so Irish'. There was great talk among them and vivid allusions to the daily happenings, which made the terse speech of Monaghan seem devoid of colour and energy. Granny O'Halloran could remember when people had spoken Irish. She said there was no future in America for people who lacked English; and now, even though the children were learning Irish in school, they stood dumbfounded like a ewe on shearing day if you put a question to them in Irish for they didn't keep a natural word of it in their heads.

Nora Scullane's people lived a couple of fields lower down the mountain in a three-roomed whitewashed house with an attic under the slates. Her mother, Margy, was in charge of the Mount Callan dairy, situated in the farmyard next to the byre where her son John and nephew Pakky did the milking. They carried the buckets of milk into the dairy, where Margy deftly poured it into the separator, a device that was the wonder of the neighbourhood and which, true to its name, separated the cream at the turn of a handle, dispensing with the need to leave the milk sitting for days in great crocks, as in Annie Daley's dairy at Annaghmakerrig. A ritualistic air was attached to the nightly process of separation, as if Margy possessed powers with which to influence the demeanour of the machine. No such technical advances had been adopted for the churning, which she undertook laboriously once a week using an old wooden churn with rotating paddles. Anyone who happened to be passing was invited by Margy to 'give it a twisht' while she took a rest and a minute's drag on a Wills' Woodbine. Later we learned that it was unlucky for a visitor not to take a twist at the churn. From time to time Margy would lift the lid to observe the progress of the butter, finally exclaiming, ''Tis crackin'!' When it had cracked to her satisfaction the buttermilk would be drained off, and there followed a great slapping of wooden spades and then two-pound and one-pound slabs of yellow butter would be laid out on the slate shelves and decorated with designs that were a power against evil spirits.

Visitors to Mount Callan were few, except for people from the mountainside coming to look for medicines if they or their children were unwell, for the nearest doctor lived at Milltown-Malbay and it took half a day for anyone to get a message to him. My mother established a cupboard with a selection of syrup of figs, Milk of Magnesia, hydrogen peroxide, Mrs Cullen's Powders, Beecham's pills, Elastoplast and bandages and she said that the rudiments of First Aid she had learned from the two Miss Overends in Sandyford were at last coming in useful.

During the summers we were visited by Killens and Butlers. One Easter – our last, as it turned out – Great-aunt Zane came to stay. Gaay came only once from Dublin, to see us 'settled in' and to get a glimpse of what kind of a place it was that Manners was taking on. When Nick and I made our journeys from school in Bangor, we usually took the train to Monaghan or Dublin – it was a wonderful sensation having the freedom to travel unaccompanied by an adult – staying the night with relatives before my father picked us up in the Ford van, which came with his job. After my Killen grandfather died while on a visit to Aviemore in 1946, my grandmother came to live with us at Mount Callan and took pity on us for all this travelling, contributing to the purchase of a Ford V8 saloon, which made journeys to what she called 'civilization' much easier. I hoped I would be the envy of my contemporaries at Garth House, but we always seemed to arrive at the school before anyone else was present to observe our grandeur. Yet my grandmother aside, whole school terms would pass without my parents being visited at Mount Callan by anyone who might be described as belonging to the same social milieu.

This was hard for my mother, who was gregarious by nature. Though she never said so, it became noticeable that she didn't much enjoy living at Mount Callan. She didn't bother with the garden – it was said that a day had not passed without Mrs Tottenham delving or digging or snipping with Austin Woods in attendance – but spent most of her days reading the detective fiction that arrived each week by post from Switzer's Library in Dublin and which she also found at the well-stocked county library in Ennis. 'Indigestion', of which she had complained at Eldron and Annaghmakerrig and for which she dosed herself with breadsoda in water, turned out to be caused by two duodenal ulcers – brought on, my grandmother confided, 'by worry'. She often had to stay for days in the big four-poster eating only the milk puddings that were supposed to prevent the ulcers becoming aggravated, reading Edmund Crispin and Dorothy Sayers. She spent a week in hospital in Limerick but the doctors decided that a change of diet would be preferable to an operation.

On the day after we returned from Bangor for the Christmas holidays I was sent over to Susan Hinchy's with five shillings in my pocket for the goose that was to be our dinner on Christmas Day. Mrs Hinchy lived in a roadside cottage next to the two-roomed national school where they did not yet have holidays so all her children were out in the playground for their break when I arrived. Her husband John was a farm labourer on the Mount Callan estate and my father said he was one of the best workers he had ever come across and also one of the nicest men – if he lived anywhere else he'd be in a good, responsible job.

Mrs Hinchy took me down to the grassy bank of the Inagh river, where geese were grazing and preening their feathers, and before they had time to take notice of her she had grabbed a big one and twisted its neck so that it could not breathe. I thought it would have been much better to cut off its head with a quick slash of a knife and I would have told her that, had I known what she was going to do, because the goose took a long time to die and must have been thinking all the time of how it had been betrayed after its lovely life of swimming and basking on the riverbank. Mrs Hinchy did not look like a cruel person and I said nothing; in any case, all the scholars were hanging over the wall looking at us so I didn't want to make a show of myself. When she said, 'There's no more breath left in him now,' I gave her the five shillings and said, 'Thank you,' then lifted the goose, which was far heavier than I had expected. It took me a long time to get to the house because I had to put the goose down every few steps, and as it was still warm it felt as if I was carrying the corpse of an old friend who had died unexpectedly by the roadside.

Oranges were in the market again and my mother bought several dozen and also a box of Fry's chocolate bars at Lipton's in Ennis and I helped her to wrap them in red and green crêpe paper. She said we couldn't rise to the kind of Christmas party for the tenants that Mrs G gave at Annaghmakerrig, but we would go round the cottages and give out presents. She had also bought knitting-wool for the women. We packed the parcels into baskets and I set off with her along the lane that joined us to the main road at Hinchy's. Any sense of do-gooding quickly evaporated when I saw the comfortlessness of some of the interiors where barefooted boys and girls, many of them dressed in rags, and some as old as myself, were clustered round hearths where a few sods of turf gave out very little warmth.

Lernahan's was the last house before Hinchy's. The mother had died some years before and the children had only their father and uncle to look after them. It was plain to see that not much looking-after was done. As we walked back in the gathering dusk of Christmas Eve my mother said it reminded her of drawings in old books like *Traits and Stories of the Irish*

*Peasantry*. She said she had not realized the extent of the poverty that still existed.

'They are the lucky ones,' my father said, when we entered the Mount Callan drawing room with its marble chimney-piece and the shaded electric lamps that I had festooned with coloured paper chains. 'Each of those cottages has at least one man earning two or three pounds a week here on the estate. Beyond this estate there are people who are earning nothing at all. When the landlord system was brought to an end the new Irish government failed to replace it with anything better. That's why they emigrate to America as soon as they leave school, if their relatives in Boston and Phila-delphia can afford to send the money for their passage.'

My mother remarked that while she was giving out her paltry presents she didn't see resentment on the faces of the older people.

'That's because the Tottenhams were known as good land-lords. If they weren't, you may be sure this house would have been burned to the ground during the agrarian agitation. Mount Callan is one place where the old system is still surviving, for want of anything better – but for how long God alone knows.'

Margaret Hanrahan got a present from an aunt in Massa-chusetts of a book of five 78 r.p.m. records of the McNulty family singing Irish songs. We carried the gramophone into the kitchen and some of her O'Halloran relatives came down from the mountain to hear them. They made tea and Margaret baked a cake of soda bread, and they played the songs over and over again till they knew the words, then joined in the choruses. The music was nothing like the traditional music we heard on Radio Eireann, for it had a brashness that, my father said, could only have come out of America:

*It's a week ago last Tuesday I left my home in Cork*
*To find my uncle, Martin Kelly, living in New York;*
*I borrowed a di-rectory his office for to find –*
*I found so many Kellys that I nearly lost my mind!*
*I went and told my story to a little German Jew,*
*And the Jew said, 'Please excuse me, for my name is Kelly too!'*
*Oh, there's Kelly from Kerry, Kelly is from Derry,*
*Kelly is a sailorman that came from Donegal,*
*Kelly is from Sligo, Kelly is from Mayo –*
*But the Kelly I was after I couldn't find at all!*

The raucous singing of the McNultys was at the other
end of some musical scale from the quiet voice of Pakky
Scullane when the notion took him – which wasn't often
– after the milking was done and he had boiled the kettle
for Margy to scald the separator in the yard kitchen. A visit
from Mikey Tierney, a farmer from the Hand crossroads,
would sometimes inspire a session round the fire. Mikey
would relate old stories, some containing the names of figures
like Oisín and Setanta whom I'd met in a book by Standish
O'Grady that I'd come across in an old Mount Callan bookcase, others that had to do with long-remembered local
events, but most of them a mixture of the two. The narra-
tive was commented upon by his hearers, with interjections
such as ''Twas true for him!' and 'He did, and why wouldn't
he?' and 'Bad cess to him so!' Then Mikey would call on
Pakky, who was seventeen but looked like a man of twenty,
and he would look into the embers and sing something he
could have learned only recently but which seemed to
come from somewhere much longer ago and further
away:

*As I rambled out one evening, it being in the month of June,*
*I strayed into an old churchyard to view a noble tomb,*
*I overheard an old man say, as the tears rolled from his eyes,*
*'Oh, it is beneath that grass-green sod that Peter Crowley lies'* . . .

Everyone was silent, listening to Pakky, as he continued,

*Oh, Crowley, Peter Crowley, come tell to me the truth,*
*If 'twas you and the dauntless little lad that took the Fenian oath?*
*Who stood beside the brave old oak and fired the signal gun,*
*And fought and died for Ireland's pride? 'Twas Crowley's only son.*

During the spring term of 1947 there was a measles epidemic
at Garth House School. The dormitory named in honour of
General Montgomery was designated a sick-bay. As I did not
seem to be improving as quickly as my fellow patients and was
complaining of a pain in my side, Dr Browne called in a specialist
who evidently advised that I be isolated from the other boys
but preferably sent home because I had pleurisy, and that was
a thing that could turn to something else.

There was no question of my going home because it was
a two-day journey and, anyway, the roads were blocked with
snow and the trains were not running. The occupants of the
smallest dormitory – Mountbatten – were squeezed into
Churchill and Alexander, Mountbatten becoming my sana-
torium. The door was left open, and I could hear Nelly
Swanson exclaiming to herself in her bed-sitting room as
she cut out the coupons from seventy ration-books each
week and at night the creak of her bed and her groans as
she fell into it – she suffered from bunions as well as arthritis,
and I made up a story that she unscrewed her leg upon
retiring and that was what I was hearing. There was another

story that she had formerly been a warder in a women's jail at York. The detail was so plausible it could hardly have been invented and Nelly Swanson certainly had an intensely authoritarian streak. She would parade the grounds during weekends, quite clearly looking for trouble, her bunions peeping out of the shoes she had slit open to accommodate them.

I did not feel ill, but I was bored. One of our teachers, Miss Walker, lent me a gramophone and some Andrews Sisters' records – 'Don't Fence Me In' with Bing Crosby, 'Down In The Valley', 'On The Acheson, Topeka and the Santa Fe' – but I was rationed to the number I was allowed to play because it was felt that the effort of winding the handle would be too great. One Sunday some doctors and a nurse came. I was given a local anaesthetic and a pint and a half of pinkish liquid was drawn off my lung through a long needle; one of the doctors brandished the bottle gleefully in front of my face and I felt quite proud.

It did not occur to me to speculate upon what my parents, away down in County Clare, must be thinking and it only entered my consciousness over the next year or so that because my mother's sister Pauline had died of tuberculosis at the age of twenty-one and the Reverend Alexander's daughter had died of the same thing quite recently – both lay in the Presbyterian churchyard at Smithborough – they would be fearing the worst. My uncle Marcus said that there were many houses in Monaghan where at least one of the children did not survive into adulthood. I stayed at school till the end of term when the other boys went home, and then my father came to collect me. I thought he was quite surprised to see that I was not at all a pale shadow of myself. We stopped for the night at Eldron. Great-aunt Zane was watching for us from the window and she hurried out as the V8 drew up. She told us the bed was ready and a hot jar in it, but on seeing that I wasn't actually carried from the car she said I mightn't want to go to bed yet and there was a nice fire in the sitting room. She had made a green jelly for pudding, and Lizzie fussed about enquiring if I had everything I wanted.

'The war' was blamed for having spread diseases. It was when I got back to Mount Callan and a regime of rest, very mild exercise and a surfeit of egg-flips and buttermilk, as well as my grandmother's fanatical precautions against damp – every garment had to be aired in front of the fire till it was almost smouldering – that I began to feel she must know more than she spoke of; and, of course, she had watched her younger daughter wither away over three years. My father always looked irritated when he came across her reading passages of the Bible in my bedroom, though all he ever said to me was that 'she was always a bit over-religious'.

What with my convalescence, my mother's ulcers, my grandmother's morbid meditations on the topic of neglected colds, the absence of Nick two hundred miles away at school until he returned for the Northern Ireland holidays, which did not start till the end of July, and also that we had no social life in the accepted sense, the summer of 1947 should have been quite dispiriting, and perhaps it was for the adults in the household, but I enjoyed myself with a number of solitary ploys. I took to reading adult novels – the house was full of Edgar Wallaces and Rider Haggards and my mother would occasionally recommend one of her 'thrillers' from the library as 'suitable'. I noticed that a speckled hen was 'clocking', found a quiet nest for her in a disused loft, brought her food every day and watched as she produced egg after egg until there were thirteen. When she heard me coming she would leave the nest, ruffle her feathers, eat her food, do a big poo and then turn the eggs over with her beak before settling on to them again, relaxing into a poultry dream-world for the next twenty-four hours. After three weeks all the eggs hatched, so I put her and her children in a box and carried them down to the hen-run, where they all survived to adulthood, until it was time for the cockerels among them to find their way to the table.

At this time the Guthries were in New York, where Tony was directing *Carmen* for the Metropolitan Opera. Visitors to the United States were forbidden to take their earnings out of the country so he sent food parcels to his relatives in Britain and, to the less deprived such as ourselves in Ireland, subscriptions to *Life* magazine. Every week this treasury of striking images would arrive in the post, its advertisements vying with the photo-reportage for wonderment. I learned that the most prestigious automobiles were the Cadillac and the Lincoln, and that every regular American family aspired to the Chevrolet, the Studebaker and the Dodge. I made tracings of these cars, colouring them with crayons, and decided there and then that I would become a car designer – the outside of cars, for I had no interest in what was under the bonnet. There were also advertisements for chains of hotels, of which none could compare with the Statlers, to be found in every city from Philadelphia to Seattle: all the bedrooms had their own bathrooms! Airlines were also prominently advertised – Pan American, with its blue-liveried fleet of elegant Constellations, and TWA, with its chunkier red-limned Douglases. We were to become familiar with these two airlines, for they were now landing at Rineanna near Ennis – soon to be re-named Shannon Airport – and in the evenings we could see the navigation lights of the enormous aircraft as they climbed the air above the hills to the south of the house, then turned towards the Atlantic. My father predicted that it would not be long before the traditional route for young emigrants from the cottages on the mountainside – the O'Hallorans, the Scullanes and the Lernahans – would cease to be the ocean liners calling to Cóbh and become the sleek airliners rising up from Rineanna.

In spite of my mother's protestations that we had 'no neighbours', a friendly elderly couple lived ten miles away at Spanish Point, the Reverend and Mrs Elliott. Canon Elliott was nominally our clergyman, for he had responsibility for all the Church of Ireland parishes of north-west Clare – it was assumed that there were no Presbyterians living in the county. As it happened, we never went to any service as a matter of religious duty, but if we had some reason to be in the neighbourhood of one of Canon Elliott's churches on a Sunday morning it was natural that we would wish to swell his congregation. He had only two parishioners in Spanish Point, Captain Fitzmaurice, who ran the Strand Hotel, and a Mrs White, who sometimes came to church and sometimes did not, depending upon the disposition of her cairn terrier, Lucy, who was blind; at Ennistymon the only Protestant was the English manager of the Falls Hotel; and Kilfenora had long ago become nothing more than a destination for archaeologists, following the discovery by a Russian *immigrée* of a twelfth-century high cross lying full-length in a bed of nettles. During the summer Canon Elliott could expect to find a few church-goers taking their holidays in Lahinch – for the golf – but he felt they were really only attending through a sense of loyalty.

One weekend in June, Peggy Butler made a foray from Maidenhall with the renting of a holiday home at Spanish Point in view for a combined expedition of Butlers and Perrys in August – she had seen an advertisement for thatched lodges overlooking the strand, owned by the Order of Blue Nuns. I was assigned to guide her to Spanish Point, where we looked at some cottages, one of which Peggy declared to be exactly right because it had a working WC and there were not too many holy pictures. Then we called on the Elliotts, as I had been advised to do. Canon Elliott opened the front door of the lodge, which served as a rectory, and looked at us with his head on one side, his eyes going twinkle-twinkle and his nose sniffle-snuffle, quite like the hedgehog in Beatrix Potter's story. Peggy said we were just 'looking in, *en passant*, so to speak' and that she hoped to see more of him when she returned on her summer holidays.

'You must come crabbing!' said the canon.

'The juveniles will *love* that,' said Peggy. 'I'm sure they'll look forward to it.'

'Oh, but now! Just wait for two minutes while I sort out my tackle!'

He scampered down the passage and was heard opening and closing cupboard doors while explaining excitedly what was going on to an invisible other person. A vast and menacing black lobster, all feelers and tentacles, sat in the hallway under glass; a handwritten label stated that it was the largest ever recorded on the coast of Clare. I mentioned to Peggy that, of course, it was *dead*, and she said, 'I hope so.'

A grey-haired lady in a tweed coat and skirt made a bustling entrance with the words 'Hello there, I must get the kettle – I have a kitchen on the rocks opposite Mutton Island. And I'd better get some brown pepper.'

Surely, we thought, she isn't going to cook crabs in a teakettle and sprinkle them with pepper? But 'pepper' turned out to be her way of saying 'paper' and she returned with sheets of it as well as several baskets, some crockery and an armful of sombre items of clothing. It was as if everything had been arranged in advance. The Elliotts stepped into the Maidenhall car as if it were a taxi thoughtfully ordered earlier, the canon directing Peggy across Stackpoles's bridge and down a long lane on to the promontory where, he told us, no fewer than three vessels of the Spanish Armada had perished in 1588.

'My kitchen's over there,' said Mrs Elliott, indicating a nook in the cliff face where indeed there were the remnants of charred twigs. In no time she had lit a fire of heather and driftwood. Deftly balancing the kettle on three large black stones, she took some striped mugs, a packet of Lipton's tea and a medicine bottle containing milk out of a basket. Meanwhile, the canon had retired modestly into a crevice, presumably to change into his swimming togs. ('"Rock of ages, cleft for me"', said Peggy, under her breath.) When he emerged he was still clad in a clerical suit – but an older one, as he explained: 'I keep it for crabbing.' Barefoot, he padded over the rocks to where the water was deep and dark – not a day to go swimming at all – and we felt slightly ashamed that we were not offering to dive in with him. The canon clambered down the rockface, never wincing when lashed by arrogant waves. Suddenly he disappeared beneath the Atlantic foam.

We waited. Gulls screamed. There was not a sign. Surely he couldn't be holding his breath *this* long? 'I think your husband must be drowning!' observed Peggy, with an exaggerated laugh, but Mrs Elliott, raking the embers of her al-fresco kitchen, smiled and drew our attention to a shiny black figure clambering up the rocks a little to the south. He was festooned with crabs, armfuls of them. Claws were reaching out of his pockets.

'I know all the right places! They hide in the deep fissures where the tide never ebbs,' he explained, dislodging a monster that was clutching his lapel – and with that he was gone again.

Mrs Elliott stowed the crabs in sundry bags and baskets, selecting four for dropping into the bucket that now contained several kettlefuls of boiling water. She buttered a cake of brown bread and cut wedge-shaped slices. It was two o'clock and we were hungry, so we swallowed our distaste at the (mercifully swift) death of the monster crabs and ate her delicious sandwiches.

Mrs Elliott parcelled up a selection of crabs in brown 'pepper': 'For your poor parents – are they surviving? I hope they enjoy them.' The rest would go to Captain Fitzmaurice, where they would no doubt appear on his menu as Atlantic Cocktail Supreme. As Peggy headed the car for Mount Callan she said she'd envisaged a wholesome *baked-beans-on-toast* kind of summer holiday and the additional gastronomic experience supplied by the kind old clergyman would surprise the Perrys no end.

When I returned to Garth House in the autumn it was to find that my classmates had taken their final exams and moved on to other schools and that, due to my seniority, I was now Head Boy. It was a privilege, of course, but one thrust on me by circumstance and for which (I could not help thinking) I was utterly unsuited. I had no sense within myself of being a leader, I was no good at the all-important team games – and, in any case, the doctor had told Matron to make sure I did not get 'wet or overheated', so outdoor sports were out of the question. I did do well in the school play at Christmas and I compèred the concert for parents with what Mr Peyton described as 'aplomb', introducing his piano pupils' scherzos and impromptus as if I knew what the words meant. I was surprised when my school report arrived at Mount Callan at Christmas to read that Captain Hutton said I was 'very helpful as Head Boy' – perhaps I was, but without knowing what I was doing. There were, however, unpleasing comments from other members of the staff drawing attention to my poor performance in all subjects except English and Art. My father took me to task, reminding me of my promise to 'work harder' if I were allowed to stay on at Garth House. I knew that I had failed in my side of the bargain and I also knew that without doubt I would fail the entrance-scholarship examination for St Columba's College in the summer.

There was further cause for discontent. My father announced that he would be taking up the managership of the Annaghmakerrig estate because Tony Guthrie's theatre engagements were keeping him in other corners of the world and Eddie Daley, the farm steward, would be retiring before too long. The thought of leaving Mount Callan, with its wildness and sense of freedom, was a real deadener. The regime of Annaghmakerrig now seemed immensely uninviting. If one of the reasons for the change was the inconvenience and remoteness of Clare, Monaghan was also comparatively isolated and it was certainly less lively.

'But you used to love Annaghmakerrig!' my mother said, in a justifiable tone of bewilderment.

'That was then,' said I, ungraciously, without meaning to hurt.

I thought of how I'd written from school to my mother at Mount Callan a few months previously to say I hoped she wasn't arranging for me to go to Eldron for the half-term holiday. I'd been invited to stay with my friend Capper II in the exhilarating milieu of Belfast's Malone Road. What, I now wondered, had my mother explained to Zane? I felt like a traitor, or, as Capper II would have said, a right bollocks.

★

As my final summer term progressed and my health was seen to be much improved I was allowed to take part in 'easy' sports, such as running and jumping. When my mother came to present the prizes on Sports Day I received from her hands a cup for captaining the Relay Team, a silver trophy for Senior Hurdles and a little tin medal for coming second in the Long Jump. She stood on the front steps and made a speech praising Captain Hutton and Miss Swanson – though she referred to her as 'Miss Swanstone' – and both looked astonishingly pleased. No mention was made on this day that I had failed to win the all-important scholarship to St Columba's, though I had just managed to scrape through the entrance requirements. All that would come out later when my father dilated upon what my education was *costing*. I hadn't liked Garth House, I realized, but then I probably wouldn't have liked any conventional preparatory school and I did not expect to like St Columba's either.

My room-mates in Alexander dormitory and I were looking forward to the 'talk' that Hutty gave to boarders on their last night, hilarious descriptions of which had been passed on by those who had already left the school. 'I know what I have to say will *surprise* you,' he began, as we dug each other in the ribs and tried to avoid catching one another's eyes. After a long preamble, during which his extreme embarrassment was all too evident, he announced, 'You see, the man actually *inserts* his John Thomas between the legs of the woman!' I let out a screech of laughter, not so much at the action described (which was not news) as at the use of the term 'John Thomas'. I guffawed uncontrollably, so much so that the others could not prevent themselves from joining in. 'All right,' said Hutty, 'have a good laugh, all this must come as quite a shock to you – then I'll continue,' and continue he did, warning us of the evils of buggery in a way that made this more novel activity seem quite tantalizing because unexplained. We all knew the word but in the sense of 'bugger off!', or, in moments of acute surprise, 'Well, bugger *me!*', but here there was clearly something mysterious and fascinating and none of us had the bad manners – or the audacity, whichever way you looked at it – to enquire further on that memorable evening.

I was surprised and embarrassed by the uncontrollable tears that flowed the following morning when I said goodbye to companions and teachers and to the ugly orange-brick cluster of buildings. My friend Capper II shed about one tear, but really, I thought, as a token of fellow-feeling rather than any deeper sense of loss. I discovered the cane that Nelly Swanson used on the smaller boys and I broke it into little pieces, remembering how she had cruelly beaten a little chap of only four who had suddenly been wished on the school by parents leaving for Africa. I had been very pleased when this infant had turned and bitten her on the ankle and she had screamed, but this had led only to a further and more frenzied attack. I hadn't at all minded being beaten on the bum by Hutty, because he never did so unless there was fair enough reason and, anyway, it was the normal way punishments were meted out and a beating in this spirit was forgotten after twenty minutes, but Nelly Swanson's bad-tempered canings were something different. If I had been brave and had understood that my position as Head Boy could have been influential I would have denounced her, but I was a coward and said nothing.

With these conflicting emotions revolving in my mind I went into the Boys' Hall and washed the tears from my face. All the towels had been removed so I dried my eyes on a forgotten football jersey that had been left hanging on a hook. Then our parents arrived to take us away.

# Envoi

*The sign that a school term was definitely at an end was the receding view from the window of the Great Northern Railway train of Belfast's fog-swathed streets, the Murray's Mellow Mixture tobacco factory, Linfield football ground, the King's Hall at Balmoral, the linen mills and bleach greens of Lambeg and Lisburn. Then the glittering granite spires of Armagh Cathedral on its green mound announced the return of the familiar landscape. Killylea, Tynan, Glaslough, Monaghan. Lakes with moorhens. Hawthorn brakes. Apple trees. McEntee's farm. And all of a sudden, round the grassy hill, the two-storeyed thatched farmhouse would come into view, Great-aunt Zane leaning on the stile waving to us as the train slowed down. Three minutes later we were in the little yellow-brick station of Smithborough with its fretwork canopy and wooden signal-cabin — everything bright and familiar and welcoming.*

*Often in a recurring dream I am travelling in that train, but it is today and I don't know that this journey is impossible for there is no such thing now as the Great Northern Railway. I am like Alice rowing her boat on a brook which becomes the dividing-line between this memory and the next. I lean out of the window of the train to wave, as once again we approach Eldron Cottage, half hidden in its wreath of beech leaves, horse-chestnut blossom and lilac. Instead of Great-aunt Zane, I see myself standing on the stile, waving back. But this cannot be, for the track is overgrown with blackberries and hazels and the yellow-brick station is no more.*

# Acknowledgements

The author thanks Dr Orla Browne for permission to print the chorus from *The Moonshiner*, collected and published by her mother, the singer Delia Murphy. All efforts to locate the copyright holders of other lyrics quoted have been unsuccessful. Thanks are due to Margret Brittain (*née* Killen) who supplied the snapshot, taken at Dunfanaghy, Co. Donegal, in 1944, and reproduced on the jacket.

Dublin – Apulia – Carrickmore 2006